The Hitmen

Stephen Breen, NewsBrands Ireland's Crime Journalist of the Year 2018, is crime editor of the *Irish Sun* and has been writing about the Irish criminal world for two decades. Owen Conlon is an assistant news editor for the *Irish Sun* and is also a respected commentator on crime stories in the Irish media. Together they are authors of the number-one bestseller, *The Cartel*, the definitive account of the rise of the Kinahan gang. Stephen Breen is also author of *Fat Freddie*, the story of the notorious gangster Freddie Thompson.

The Hitmen

The Shocking True Story of a Family of Killers for Hire

STEPHEN BREEN AND OWEN CONLON

SANDYCOVE

an imprint of

PENGUIN BOOKS

SANDYCOVE

UK | USA | Canada | Ireland | Australia
India | New Zealand | South Africa

Sandycove is part of the Penguin Random House group of companies
whose addresses can be found at global.penguinrandomhouse.com.

First published 2021
001

Copyright © Stephen Breen and Owen Conlon, 2021

The moral right of the authors has been asserted

Set in 13.5/16 pt Garamond MT Std
Typeset by Jouve (UK), Milton Keynes
Printed and bound in Great Britain by Clays Ltd, Elcograf S.p.A.

The authorized representative in the EEA is Penguin Random House Ireland,
Morrison Chambers, 32 Nassau Street, Dublin D02 YH68

A CIP catalogue record for this book is available from the British Library

ISBN: 978–1–844–88558–9

www.greenpenguin.co.uk

Penguin Random House is committed to a
sustainable future for our business, our readers
and our planet. This book is made from Forest
Stewardship Council® certified paper.

Contents

Family Trees   vii

Prologue   1
1 Beginnings   5
2 The Good Samaritan   20
3 Murder Spree   34
4 The Soldier   45
5 First Kill   60
6 Cracks in the Facade   74
7 Luck Runs Out   88
8 Strike Back   101
9 Going Down   119
10 'We found her'   133
11 Feeling the Heat   149
12 Death of a Strongman   165
13 Off the Hook   181
14 Ups and Downs   195
15 Practice Runs   209
16 Target Identified   224

CONTENTS

17 No Christmas Bonus   237

18 Guilty as Charged   255

Epilogue   271

Acknowledgements   279

Family Trees

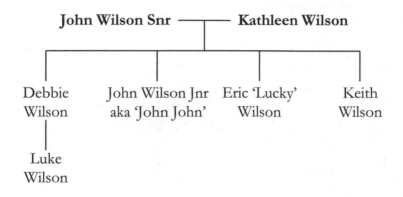

John Wilson Snr ——— Kathleen Wilson

Debbie Wilson — John Wilson Jnr aka 'John John' — Eric 'Lucky' Wilson — Keith Wilson

Luke Wilson

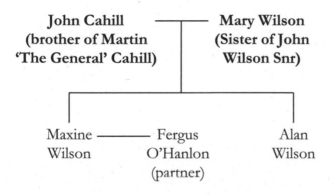

John Cahill (brother of Martin 'The General' Cahill) ——— Mary Wilson (Sister of John Wilson Snr)

Maxine Wilson ——— Fergus O'Hanlon (partner) — Alan Wilson

Prologue

There's gonna be his missus there, there's gonna
be a child there. If they get in the way,
they're gonna be killed . . .

The phrase overheard by the garda surveillance team on 2 November 2017 added yet another chilling dimension to a carefully planned murder that was on the verge of being carried out.

By itself, it might be dismissed as the boastfulness of a young, coked-up hitman desperate to impress his getaway driver. But when the threat was repeated by Luke Wilson's cousin Alan and then by another fellow gang member, investigators realized they were racing to avoid the contract killing of not just a criminal rival, but also potentially that of his toddler son.

Gardaí had been watching the assassination team for two months. They knew the identity of the target and where the attempt on his life was most likely to be made. They knew who was putting forward more than €100,000 to have him eliminated. They also knew that Luke Wilson was only acting in accordance with how he had been tutored by his cousin and uncles.

Between them, the five Wilsons had been responsible for more than a dozen deaths stretching right across Europe. Some victims were gunned down before they knew what was happening, others coldly dispatched even as they begged for their lives.

There was no room for sentiment in the business of paid murder. Paradoxically, John, Eric, Keith, Alan and now Luke had always combined cautious and careful planning with a reckless regard for the lives of innocent bystanders. They had access to military-grade sub-machine guns and explosives and had trained themselves in their use.

And if someone 'got in the way', it was their own bad luck. One target's sister had been shot and wounded along with her sibling; a man had been murdered in full view of his young children; and innocent customers and a bouncer had been gunned down outside a pub. Former criminal acquaintances had been ambushed and tortured or set up to be riddled with bullets by those they considered friends. Someone who had come looking for protection was executed in case he turned state's witness. And an innocent young girl had been abducted from the street, held captive and slaughtered, her body hidden in a cold mountain grave, though the man accused of the crime was exonerated by a jury.

The investigators listening in were aware of all this, but still had to bide their time. Move in too soon and charges could not be made to stick. Too late and the country might see its first-ever gangland murder of a baby.

There was another factor to consider: without the right intervention, those looking to intercept a shooting might end up dead themselves. Informants had previously warned gardaí that Eric Wilson would not be taken alive. Now, his nephew Luke Wilson could be heard vowing to 'start fuckin' shootin' the police as well' if any member of the force turned up to interfere. It was a life-or-death judgement call and the consequences of making it incorrectly were enormous.

For more than twelve years the Wilsons had relied on blood connections to enforce their own particular form of *omertà* – the gangland code of silence. Threats of extreme violence against potential witnesses and members of An Garda Síochána were common, and active efforts were made to carry them out. The clan's homicidal reputation had been enough to see off powerful enemies in the past, including the might of the Kinahan cartel.

But the Wilsons' reign of terror across Europe was coming to a close. Eric, Keith and John had already been taken out of the picture. One was the architect of his own spectacular downfall, another nailed by patient and clever police work. A third had fallen victim to his own kind. Now there remained just two.

Like the others, Alan and Luke had no intention of ever stopping.

Just like the others, they would have to be stopped instead.

1. Beginnings

That fella's off the smokes

— Eric Wilson

The assassin's unusual choice of ammunition meant Martin Kenny had never stood a chance. The first shotgun blast that hit him in the neck was a Brenneke round, a solid steel slug known as a 'rad buster' by police in the US, who use them to disable the engines of speeding cars. They are also routinely carried by cops in Alaska, who say they are the only ammo capable of stopping a grizzly bear if necessary.

On 14 May 2005 Martin Kenny had been staying at the Ballyfermot home of his girlfriend, who had been disturbed at around 5 a.m. by the sound of glass breaking downstairs at the front door. There had been a similar attack on the front of the house the previous week and she woke Kenny to investigate. He was getting out of bed when the killer, wearing a balaclava and a bomber jacket, burst into their upstairs room.

The first shot disabled the victim, who fell to the floor. The killer then walked over and fired the second round into his head, before he turned and fled. Garda intelligence would later indicate that Kenny had been allocated the blame when a stash of drugs went missing. The murder was a relatively run-of-the-mill gangland murder except for one thing: it marked Eric Wilson's debut as a contract killer. Up until that point, Wilson, still three months shy of his twenty-second birthday, had been just another up-and-coming young drug dealer in west Dublin.

Eric Wilson was born on 25 August 1983 to John and Kathleen Wilson. The third of four children, his older sister, Debbie, had been born on 12 December 1975, followed by a brother, John, on 27 March 1977. After Eric youngest brother Keith completed the family on 6 June 1988. The children's father died while they were young and his eldest son John – known within the family as 'John John', to distinguish him from his dad – became something of a replacement father figure to his brothers. Unfortunately, he did not set much of an example. Despite being a talented boxer who was viewed as a real prospect if he applied himself, 'John John' instead became sucked into the petty crime scene which plagued Ballyfermot during much of the 1990s. A few days after his seventeenth birthday in April 1994, he was sentenced to twelve months for car theft. Gardaí who know the family say both Eric and Keith looked up to John and sought to emulate him: but both would soon come under a much more malign family influence.

Alan Wilson was a cousin of the boys on their father's side. He was born on 24 February 1979 in Ballyfermot to John Cahill and Mary Wilson, a sister of John Wilson Snr. Alan Wilson's father was an older brother of the infamous Dublin criminal Martin 'The General' Cahill. But after he was sentenced to sixteen years for robbing a labour exchange, John Cahill and Mary became estranged and she reverted to using her maiden name. Though he had no convictions and was not on the garda radar, Alan Wilson was involved in varying degrees of criminality. At that point a clean-living teetotaller who did not touch drugs, he was nevertheless dealing himself. And as he spent more and more time hanging around his cousins' family home in Ballyfermot, Eric in particular began to notice that Alan was never short of cash.

'Eric was a fairly normal lad,' one underworld source told the authors. 'He was a nice enough young fella, there was no badness in him. But when Alan started whispering in his ear about the money to be made, he wanted a slice of the action himself for the drug business.'

Never much of a scholar, as he grew up Eric followed his older brother John into petty crime. By the time he reached his late teens, he and his neighbour Martin Kenny had become targets for the local garda drug unit.

The pair had been pals since childhood and lived just two minutes' walk from each other. 'They would have been close buddies, they would have been involved in boxing and football all the way along,' one investigator familiar with the pair said. 'They were tight not only with each other but with each other's families as well.'

But once money entered the equation, things soon went sour. A few months before the murder, Eric Wilson had moved to Naas, where he was continuing to sell to local addicts, and it was not long before he came to the attention of the local drugs squad down there too. That April 2005 gardaí had come across him and an associate parked under the motorway bridge at Oberstown near Naas. A search of the vehicle revealed a night scope and weighing scales, but though both items were obviously suspicious, neither was illegal. They were handed back and both men were free to go.

Wilson returned to drug dealing and gardaí continued trying to catch him in the act. However, in his absence, trouble was brewing. A stash of drugs went missing – and Eric Wilson felt Kenny was responsible.

Gardaí learned that a number of threats had been issued and a week before the murder there had been the failed attempt to kick in the door of Kenny's girlfriend's house. But then things appeared to simmer down a little. Wilson had called round to the Kenny family home on O'Hogan Road a few days later for a chat with his pal and all seemed well. According to gardaí, Martin Kenny would have had no reason to suspect he was in serious danger.

Within hours of the killing though, Eric Wilson had been nominated as the chief suspect. The murder probe soon began to back that up. There was no CCTV at the murder house on Ballyfermot Parade, but one property nearby did have a security camera. That showed a Volvo estate car cruise up the road towards the crime scene shortly before the murder took place and then speed back the same way soon afterwards. Inquiries revealed that Eric Wilson had access to such a vehicle.

Further inquiries were made and it emerged that in the hours after the killing, Wilson had phoned an associate and told him, 'That fella's off the smokes' – considered by gardaí to be a reference to the shooting. He was pulled in and questioned, but gave nothing away.

With no reason to hold him, gardaí were forced to release him. However, that was not the only grilling Eric Wilson would face. Gardaí later learned that a delegation of criminals, led by the violent Ballyfermot drug dealer Derek 'Dee Dee' O'Driscoll, called up to Wilson's home to have a word. As well as having a number of other heavy-duty friends, Martin Kenny was related to another serious criminal, Mark 'The Guinea Pig' Desmond. (Desmond had gained his ludicrous nickname after taking part in paid clinical drug tests as a younger man.)

But there was nothing funny about his behaviour. He had shot two junior gang members dead in 2000 and had a reputation for sexually assaulting addicts who owed him money.

The same year, Desmond had been questioned by gardaí over the rape of a fifteen-year-old boy.

Gardaí never discovered how Eric Wilson had talked his way out of the bind, but he returned to the midlands. Herbert Kilcline, a solicitor Alan Wilson knew, was asked to provide a reference so Eric could rent a house there.

'I was told that he wanted a house down the country, he wanted to get out of Dublin so that he wouldn't get involved in drugs and stay out of trouble,' Kilcline told the authors. 'So I was asked for a reference to say I knew the family and they were okay. I had no reason to believe he wasn't.'

Duly vouched for, Wilson secured a house for himself in Portarlington, Co. Laois, where he continued to deal and also began to branch out into armed robberies. Together with his crony from Naas and another individual, Wilson was the chief suspect for a series of hold-ups across Laois and the surrounding counties, including one raid on a Hackett's Bookmakers with a knife in August 2005.

Though Eric Wilson had moved down the country to escape garda attention after the murder, he kept popping back up on their radar. On Saturday 27 August 2005, a local man named David Thompson and one of his friends were out socializing in Portarlington. At the end of the evening, they got into a row with 'a couple of Dubs' outside a takeaway in the town centre. The scuffle was broken up and those involved went their separate ways. But as Thompson was walking home with a neighbour, a silver Golf pulled up and two men jumped out. One was wearing a balaclava and both of them set about Thompson with hurleys and beat him unconscious. The victim spent five days in hospital with a fractured skull.

When he was able to be interviewed, David Thompson reported the assault to the gardaí, who soon tracked down

Wilson and his associate to their Portarlington hideout. A car similar to the one used in the attack was found and balaclavas were also recovered inside the property, which had been set up with an extensive security system.

Eric was arrested and charged, but skipped town. In keeping with his established behaviour, he rented another low-level rural hideout, this time in the tiny village of Killerig, halfway between Carlow town and Tullow.

The house was in the Killerig Golf Lodges, some of which were rented out to those visiting the nearby Des Smyth-designed golf and country club. Eric was not there to work on his putting game, however. By now, he and Alan were heavily involved in drug dealing, hold-ups and other assorted criminality and had access to a wide range of arms. The house in Killerig was being used as a location to store the weaponry.

In late November 2005 Alan and two Dublin criminals named David 'Babyface' Lindsay and Alan Napper paid Eric a visit. He had recently received a delivery and the visitors were there to check it out. Included in the haul were Heckler & Koch MP5 sub-machine guns and Sig Sauer P226 handguns, both equipped with silencers. There was also a variety of sawn-off and automatic shotguns in the house, plus a replica AK-47. This was some serious firepower.

The MP5s are used by military and police units in more than a hundred different countries, including the Irish Defence Forces' elite Army Ranger Wing, the London Metropolitan Police's Specialist Firearms Command and the FBI's Hostage Rescue Team. The Sigs, meanwhile, have been the favoured handgun of the US Navy SEALs since the late 1980s and are also used by the SAS and ECTLO, the French navy's counter-terrorism and hostage rescue squad. Satisfied that all was in order, Alan Wilson, Lindsay and Napper returned to Dublin.

But gardaí were continuing to look for Eric and a few days

later, they received a tip-off about where he was staying. Detectives travelled from Dublin to carry out surveillance on the property and confirmed he was there. They obtained a warrant to search the property on 2 December and burst in. Garda intelligence had already indicated that Eric Wilson was extremely volatile and had access to several weapons. Those taking part in the raid had been warned that he was liable to shoot at them in order to escape, so they entered with weapons drawn, shouting, 'Armed gardaí!'

True to form, Eric Wilson did not go quietly. He kicked the first garda through the door and punched him in the chest, knocking him to the ground, but was quickly over-powered by the officer's colleagues and positively identified. He was then cuffed and held at the scene while a search was carried out.

Fortunately for Eric, most of the haul that had been at the house had been removed. All that remained were two sawn-off shotguns and the AK-47. The latter was quickly discovered to be a replica but the shotguns were very real and, more importantly, had been stolen during a burglary in Cork the previous month.

Unfortunately for Eric, gardaí found several pictures of him posing with the weapons on his mobile phone – they believed he was offering them out for hire to other criminals. As well as being a favourite of armed robbers, sawn-offs leave little ballistic signature. The only real way to identify them is via the firing pin, so unless a criminal is dumb enough to eject the shells at the scene, the same weapon can be used over and over without being traced.

Eric Wilson was charged with assaulting gardaí and was remanded in custody to Cloverhill prison. But even though he had been caught red-handed in a house with hidden guns, sources close to the investigation say the DPP was slow to issue directions on how to proceed. After two weeks, he appeared again before Cloverhill District Court and was granted bail on the assault charge. It was not until much later that a decision to charge him over the guns would be made. Eric's good fortune aroused the suspicions of his cousin Alan.

Herbert Kilcline had originally been introduced to Alan via Kilcline's neighbour Fergus O'Hanlon, who was in a relationship with Alan's sister Maxine. An armed robber with a record stretching back to the age of fourteen, O'Hanlon was at that point Alan Wilson's right-hand man.

'Fergus and Alan were in a car together when Alan got a call to say he [Eric] had been released from custody,' Kilcline said. 'Alan went ballistic. He said, "You must have done a deal, there's no other way they'd let you out with all those guns." And Eric was saying, "No, there was no deal. I just got out."

'Alan was shouting and roaring, "I'll fucking kill you." At that time, had Eric been in front of Alan, he might have killed him.' For gardaí though, Eric's release meant they were once more forced to play catch-up.

They discovered that he was staying in a house up in Lucan and a raid was organized again. This time, no chances were being taken and the elite Emergency Response Unit (ERU) was sent in. However, the target had abandoned the property just three days beforehand and, once again, they were out of luck.

By this stage Eric Wilson was taking large amounts of cocaine and decided that becoming a killer for hire was the best way to feed his habit. His favourite weapon was the .357 Magnum, made famous by Clint Eastwood's *Dirty Harry* movies. Like the Brenneke round, the Magnum had no shortage of stopping power. It was initially used by US police to penetrate bank robbers' cars in the 1930s, a time when much more steel was used in the bodywork of automobiles.

One senior investigator told the authors, 'It became quite apparent that he had gone completely mad. There was intelligence that he had been involved in a number of serious incidents, including murders, and that he was offering himself for hits for hire.

'His fee was a kilo of cocaine at the time. He was taking a kilo as payment and it was for his own personal use, not to sell onwards. He was off his head, he wasn't thinking straight and he was paranoid. Everybody we spoke to told us that if and when you do catch up with him, he won't be taken alive.'

A year after his first murder, Eric would soon carry out his second and third – one because a man had been accused of informing to gardaí and the other because a witness to the first slaying was unable to keep his mouth shut.

In August 2006 gardaí, following a tip-off, raided a small shed outside Athboy, Co. Meath. Inside they found three men standing beside a bench holding weighing scales, money, a razor blade, a coffee blender and what turned out to be a red compressing machine modified to compact cocaine into blocks. Also uncovered was cocaine worth €170,000, which is a sizeable seizure for a rural area like Athboy.

The three men – Adrian Boyle, Sean Fennessy and Paul Reay – were all charged with unlawful possession of cocaine with intent to supply, along with a fourth, Seamus Halpin. Fennessy and Halpin pleaded guilty early on, but Boyle and Reay decided to fight the charges. Only one of the two would live to see trial.

The seized cocaine had belonged to one of the biggest drug barons in Dublin, Finglas-based Martin 'Marlo' Hyland, and the Athboy operation was typical of his modus operandi. Hyland, who was by then one of the top three narcotraffickers in the state, imported drugs from middlemen in Spain. He would move them to isolated rural spots to have them bulked out with various cutting agents, before they were brought back into the towns and cities to be sold.

Hyland was also known for his paranoia. When gardaí raided one of his operations, they would always carry out follow-up searches of the various homes Hyland owned. Sometimes, Hyland would be there, sitting round a table with some of his associates trying to figure out if they had a mole in the camp or not. On this occasion, Hyland became convinced that Reay had tipped off gardaí about the location of the cocaine factory.

Gardaí will never reveal details of who acts as informant for them, though at the time senior officers were quoted by the *Irish Independent* as saying that Reay had not provided them with any information. Moreover, if Reay had been touting, it was unusual that he would be charged in relation to the seizure. But none of this seemed to cut any ice with Hyland. Detectives received intelligence about the threats on Reay's life and visited his home in the Tredagh estate in Drogheda where he lived with his partner Eleanor and his young family. Reay bought himself a bulletproof vest and regularly wore it when he left the house. However, there was one occasion when Hyland felt he would be unlikely to have it on.

Shortly after 9 a.m. on 23 November, Reay was being driven from his home by his sister Emmajean on his way to appear before Kells District Court in relation to the drugs charges against him. There is only one way in and out of the Tredagh estate and as they approached it, a man got out of the passenger side of a white Mazda 323 parked to the right of the exit onto Marley's Lane. Wearing a yellow hi-vis jacket and with a cap pulled down over his face, he walked towards the car with his hand in the air. Believing there were roadworks in operation, Emmajean slowed down.

At that point, the man pulled out a handgun and fired six bullets into the silver Renault Scenic. Four of them hit Paul Reay in the upper body, while a fifth struck his sister in the shoulder and a sixth lodged in the car chassis. The gunman then turned and walked back to the Mazda and its waiting driver and the car took off at speed. Reay was just twenty-five and left three children, then aged eight, two and one month old. One eyewitness told the *Drogheda Independent* that the gunshots sounded 'like firecrackers'. She said, 'When I went out I could see Paul's partner Eleanor at the car saying, "Please wake up Paul, please wake up."'

The murder was the second violent death to hit the family in the space of a few years. Reay's father Ned, a civil servant, had been beaten to death by a local thug named Peter McArdle in January 2000. McArdle had engaged in a street row with Paul Reay, followed him home and kicked in the family's patio door. When Ned Reay came out to investigate, McArdle attacked and killed him with a plank.

Following the shooting, the white Mazda 323, which had false registration plates and had been stolen two weeks beforehand in Clondalkin, was driven to Oldbridge in Co. Meath and set alight. The hit team then transferred to a van which had been left parked there for them and drove off. Further proof of Hyland's involvement in the murder would come from an alert witness out walking her dog, who took down the van's registration and later provided it to gardaí.

The van was registered to two Dublin criminals with links to Hyland who were also close associates of slain brothers Noel and John Roche. The Roche brothers had been murdered the previous year as part of the Crumlin–Drimnagh gang war in the capital. The van owners' Drogheda base was later raided and searched and a glove bearing Eric Wilson's DNA was found in the back of their van. But both criminals refused to cooperate with detectives, while the DPP ruled that the glove, as a 'moveable object', was not sufficient by itself to bring a murder charge against Wilson to court.

Meanwhile, Paul Reay's distraught family issued a statement, declaring, 'Irrespective of the crimes to which Paul had been charged, no one deserves to die in the way Paul did. We would appeal to anyone who may have information regarding the identity or whereabouts of Paul's murderers to contact Drogheda gardaí.'

There was one person who had such information and had witnessed the murder himself, but he had no intention of going to the authorities. Instead, he believed he could turn what he had seen to his advantage. It was a fatal mistake.

Roy Coddington was thirty-six years old and lived on the same street in the Tredagh estate as Paul Reay. They knew each other but did not mix in the same circles. Coddington was much further up the criminal food chain and had, until recently, been one of the biggest drug dealers in Drogheda. However, shortly after Reay's murder, gardaí believe he had taken the decision to move out of the drugs trade. Unfortunately for him, this was not enough to stave off some unwanted attention.

'Taxing' dealers had long been a significant source of income for the Provisional IRA and, since it officially disbanded in 2005, had been continued by former members and other paramilitaries. Some members of the INLA across the border had noticed Coddington's activities and demanded a share of his profits. Coddington is believed to have handed over an initial contribution of €30,000, but this was not enough to satisfy the republican thugs. They wanted more, but, since he was now 'clean', Coddington was unable to provide it. When the cash was not forthcoming, Coddington was abducted, taken across the border and given a severe beating. This was a warning, they said, and if it was not heeded, there would be further consequences. Terrified for his life, Coddington took the wrong decision.

By sheer chance, he had been out walking in the vicinity the morning Paul Reay was murdered and had seen the entire thing happen. Coddington had also recognized Eric Wilson and believed this was something he could use.

Sometime in March 2007 he made contact with the young hitman and told him what he had seen. Garda intelligence indicated that Coddington did not threaten Eric with exposure, but instead tried to point to the fact that he had kept his mouth shut. This, he felt, was proof he could be trusted. All he asked of him in return was that the Dubliner sell him a Glock so he could protect himself from the dissidents. Eric agreed and a meeting was set up for Mornington beach, downstream from Drogheda at the mouth of the Boyne estuary.

At around 4 p.m. on 22 March 2007, Coddington drove his van to Tower Road near the beach and parked. He got out of the van and into a blue Ford Focus in which Eric and his getaway driver from the Reay murder were sitting. The car drove down a track towards the beach before stopping near the sand dunes. There, Coddington was dragged from the vehicle into the dunes by Eric Wilson, who pulled out a gun and shot him in the chest. As his stunned victim lay bleeding on the sand, Eric leaned over him and fired two more bullets into his head. Both men then turned and ran for their car before speeding away.

Mornington is a popular spot in summer, though in chillier March it is primarily left to those out walking their dogs. When the shots were first heard, locals believed someone was out hunting rabbits on the nearby golf course. However, one German woman and her four children were just a few metres away on the other side of the dunes. The woman came upon the scene and tried to comfort Coddington in his last moments, but his injuries were too great and he died on the spot.

A local woman told the *Irish Times*, 'A few people who spoke to the German girl said she was very traumatised. Other people in the area heard the shots. It's incredible to think that somebody could be taken out of a car and just shot like that.'

Gardaí were initially baffled by the murder and it was later assumed to be part of Coddington's drug-dealing past. A number of his former criminal associates thought likewise and immediately went into hiding, but it was only sometime later that the real reason emerged.

At the time of the murder, Eric Wilson was living in Omeath and had formed a relationship with a woman from Clogherhead. Unable to flush him out, gardaí decided to try and sweat his girlfriend instead. The woman was arrested and questioned on suspicion of withholding information about a crime. She did not provide anything of use, but Wilson's paranoia antennae were up and, after the woman was released, Eric Wilson never contacted her again.

The Coddington slaying also provoked another dispute between Alan and Eric. The younger cousin was supposed to have taken away the Ford Focus used to flee the scene and burnt it out to destroy any forensic traces inside. Instead, Eric hid the vehicle and changed its plates, planning to eventually use it in another hit. This broke every rule in the criminal handbook, but it would not be the last time Eric took serious risks for the sake of convenience.

Eric Wilson had now killed at least three people in little over a year, but these would not be the only murders linked to the Wilson clan in 2007. Two months after Roy Coddington was lured to his death, a drug dealer named David 'Boogie' Brett met a similar fate on a dark and lonely road outside a school in Cork.

Brett was an established dealer from Cork city who had several drug-related convictions. Following his release from a two-year term in jail, he had moved with his partner and their three young children to the village of Liscarroll in north Cork. Gardaí who were keeping an eye on him believed he was making an effort to keep his nose clean, but he was being pressured to pay back a debt of up to €100,000. The night he died, the thirty-four-year-old drove 40 kilometres from Liscarroll to tiny Ballydesmond, right beside the border with Kerry. Intelligence later indicated that though Brett had cleared some of his debt, those he owed were demanding more and more from him.

Finally, his debtors decided to make an example of him. At 10.20 p.m. on 21 May 2007, Brett's body was found beside his car outside Foilogohig national school, not far from Ballydesmond. He had been shot in the head and neck and had died instantly.

The investigation remains active, though the Wilsons have been ruled out as the hitmen in the murder. However, ballistics would later reveal that Brett had been shot with a .357 Magnum and the murder weapon would subsequently be definitively linked to the Dublin cousins. This time it was Alan, so fond of berating his cousin, who had taken a silly and unnecessary risk.

2. The Good Samaritan

There was nobody there when I came back
— Dumitru Rostas

'Help me' were the first words Marioara Rostas said to her older brother Alexandru in Romania as he picked up the phone on 7 January 2008. A cousin passed him the mobile device – to be used by the extended Rostas family only in the case of emergencies – at 2.42 p.m. that day, explaining that Alexandru's younger sister was on the line from Ireland.

Frantic with worry, struggling to breathe, eighteen-year-old Marioara told him she had been violated, was being held against her will some 200 kilometres outside of Dublin and was desperate for her father Dumitru to find her. Alexandru listened in horror, then pleaded with his sister to tell him where she was as she struggled – she had no English – to read a street sign identifying her location.

Then the line went dead. It was the last time anyone would ever speak to Marioara. The call was made just twenty-four hours after an attempt to report the teenager missing by her family, who had moved to Ireland four months previously.

Dumitru, his wife (also called Marioara) and their thirteen-year-old son Dumitru Jnr had flown into Dublin from Bucharest on 12 October 2007 in search of employment opportunities in the land of the Celtic Tiger. That night they made their way to Gardiner Street, where they spent the next two weeks in a hostel at a cost of €12 per night.

With money low, they left the hostel and spent three nights on the streets before joining Dumitru's brothers, Alexandru and Doni, along with their children, in Portmarnock, north Co. Dublin. Unable to find accommodation due to lack of cash and huge housing waiting lists, for the next three weeks the families slept in tents just 50 metres from Portmarnock train station.

Despite receiving nightly checks from the gardaí, the families were forced to move after three local men threatened to tear down the tents with mechanical diggers. From there, Dumitru's family moved to Lusk, also in north Co. Dublin, and stayed in a friend's four-bedroom house in cramped conditions alongside twenty other Romanians. Dumitru appreciated the kindness of his friend, but knew he couldn't stay long in the house. The family would have to find their own place.

Along with his two brothers and their children, they set up home in a vacant, run-down property in nearby Donabate at the beginning of December 2007. It was not much of an upgrade on the house they had left behind in their native Tileagd: neither had electricity, heating or running water. Despite finding themselves in similar abject poverty, the family still held hope that Dumitru would soon find paid employment.

Persuaded to remain in Ireland by family and friends, Dumitru now asked his daughter, the fifth-oldest in a family of twelve children, to join them in Ireland. At just five feet three inches tall, and weighing only eight stone, Marioara looked a lot younger than her eighteen years.

'I asked her to come here because some friends of ours who were living here for ten years told us that we could get a house, social benefits and a right to work,' Dumitru said. 'We came here looking for work, but I was unable to get any because I don't have English.'

Marioara's uncle Alexandru added, 'Marioara was totally devoted to her family. She would have done anything for them. Her main concern was helping her parents get the money they needed to return to Romania.

'She didn't speak English so the only contact she had was with her family and cousins. This is the way people from the Roma community do things; this is our tradition, history and culture. We could never tell if she was sad because she had no money as she was always smiling.'

Marioara was recovering from a broken leg after an accident in Romania the previous year, but arrived in Ireland on 19 December 2007. She stayed with her family in Donabate, often taking it in turns to sleep on damp mattresses, wearing layers of clothes and lighting fires.

The family decided to hold on to their hopes of a better life, at least until the New Year. The cold winter nights in Ireland may have been bitter although they were nothing compared to the sub-zero temperatures they had endured in Romania. But without paid work, Dumitru was not earning enough money to feed the family he had in Dublin, let alone send funds back to those waiting at home.

In desperation, he decided the best hope for him was to beg for cash on the streets. Begging is seen by many members of the Roma community as a legitimate means of making an income. Dumitru realized the attitudes in Ireland were far from the same, but felt he had no other option. 'I was trying to save money to go home but also to try and buy some gifts for my other children who were in Romania,' he said. 'I didn't get all the things I expected.'

Each day over that festive season of 2007 Dumitru (who had worked in a furniture company in Romania before losing his job), along with his wife Marioara and their two children, would take the train and arrive in the city centre at 9.50 a.m.

There they took up positions at the junction of Lombard Street, Pearse Street and Westland Row.

'My son Dumitru and daughter Marioara stayed together and my wife and I would go to other parts of the junction. We went there because it was close to the Dart station and because there would be plenty of people around,' the family patriarch said. Throughout the Christmas and New Year period, they brought home less than €10 each per day. What they did earn was spent on the family having a small lunch as they sat on a bench overlooking the Liffey.

Though there were fewer people on the streets in the early days of the New Year as most offices were closed, the family still made their daily pilgrimage into the city centre. On 6 January 2008 Marioara, along with her parents and younger brother, boarded the 9.25 a.m. train from Donabate station. Like every other day, Marioara and her family walked to the junction of Lombard Street, Pearse Street and Westland Row. Once outside the Bank of Ireland, they began begging from cars and pedestrians approaching the junction.

One person who saw Marioara begging that day was Trinity College student Pearse Sweeney. 'I was on the way up to the coffee shop and I saw a young Romanian-looking girl begging,' he later told gardaí. 'When all the cars were stopping at the lights, she was going up to the driver's sides looking for money. She could have been between fourteen and eighteen years of age. That was the last time I saw her.'

Mortgage broker David Orr was another who remembered seeing the teenager. 'Over the previous three weeks, I had seen a Romanian female, around early twenties, late teens, denims, hoodie top and padded jacket,' he said. 'She always wore the same clothing. On 6 January I saw this female at the line of cars begging. She had a cup in her hand.'

Just before 2 p.m. that day, Dumitru left his spot at the

junction of Pearse Street and Lombard Street, crossing the road to speak to his two children to ask them if they needed to eat. 'I went to the children and I asked them if they were hungry, and because I knew they were,' he said. 'I went to buy some food on the street beside Connolly station. I bought chips and sandwiches for the children. It took me maximum thirty minutes to get there. But there was nobody there when I came back.'

When Dumitru returned, his daughter had vanished. According to his son, the pair had been approached by a man in a car who greeted them with the term '*Ce faci?*' which means 'How are you?' in their native language. The 'Good Samaritan' then offered the pair €10 before promising to get Marioara a meal from a McDonald's.

Dumitru said, 'My wife told me that my son had run to tell her his sister had gotten into a car with a man. He was around twenty-five years old, a slim guy. I don't know what nationality he was, because he knew a few words in Romanian, like "*Ce faci*". My daughter had gone to my son and told him that the guy with the car was taking her to buy food in McDonald's and he was bringing her back in twenty minutes. This is what my son told my wife. He made a sign to say he would be back.'

With no way of knowing who the stranger was or where he had taken their daughter, all Dumitru and his wife could do was wait. Three hours later the family walked into Pearse Street garda station to report her missing. But once more, Dumitru's lack of English would prove frustrating. The garda on reception was unable to understand him and the disappearance went unreported. He returned to their family and friends in north Dublin and they all waited anxiously for news. Morning arrived and there was still no sign of Marioara. Word soon spread among the Romanian community, with friends combing the city for clues.

The family briefly had their spirits raised when they learned Marioara had contacted her brother back in Romania. 'My family had one mobile phone, which we shared with our cousins,' Dumitru explained. 'The number to this phone was known especially by the children and we would also write it on a piece of paper.

'It was organized that every member of our family would carry this number on them at all times. So, everyone always had this number on them and knew if they got into trouble, they would be able to ring it and some member of my family would always have this phone on them and it would always be answered. This is the number Marioara rang after she was taken and she rang it from an Irish number.'

But the sense of relief soon turned to despair when Dumitru discovered the content of the harrowing call. The teenager's family spent the next twenty-four hours waiting for another call that never came.

Feeling helpless, they returned to the city centre on 9 January and made their way to Bridewell garda station. At 11.30 a.m. that day, Sergeant Larry Brady rang Detective Inspector Michael Cryan at Pearse Street garda station to inform him a Romanian girl had been reported missing by her family. Detective Inspector Cryan, now a detective superintendent with the Garda National Economic Crime Bureau (GNECB), immediately arranged for the family to be brought to Pearse Street. At the same time, an interpreter named Oleg Bocancea was summoned to assist with taking statements from the missing girl's relatives.

Gardaí were shocked as Dumitru's statement was translated to them. 'Alexandru told me he [the abductor] had sex with her and abandoned her two hundred kilometres from Dublin,' he told investigators. 'He threw her out of the car and she told my son for me to collect her, because she didn't have any money. My daughter tried to explain to Alexandru where she was, but I don't know where this is. We came to the police because we still don't know where my daughter is.'

The following day gardaí made contact with Romanian police, who spoke to Alexandru. In his statement, he said his sister had mentioned the letters 'BRU' and 'ID' while trying to explain where she was.

Marioara's mother was desperately worried about her young daughter, who she described as socially naive. 'She is eighteen years old but she is like a thirteen- or fourteen-year-old,' she told gardaí. 'This is the first time she ever went away. It was in my mind the police had taken her, because my son told me the police had arrested somebody the day before, so we thought that maybe she was at the garda station. Even back home in Romania, she would never go out on her own like this. She would always stay close to home. She is not allowed to talk to strangers and I cannot understand why she would do something like this. She doesn't know any boys from here and she didn't have any boyfriends in Romania. I don't know anything else to tell you that will help find my daughter. If I knew anything, I would tell you to get this stress out of my head.'

Dumitru Jnr, who had been with his sister as the stranger's car approached, also made a statement to gardaí. 'This man called me over by waving his hand, so I went. When I got there he pointed to my sister and said, "Food, McDonald's," and said two times ten with his fingers. My sister walked around and got into the front seat of the car. Since we arrived in Ireland, we have always been together.

'The only reason I can think of for her to go in a strange car with somebody that she doesn't know is because she is inspired by the fact that she can get from McDonald's and €10, which is more than she would normally get from begging for a whole day. She didn't have much cash, maybe two or three euro. She didn't have any English because she is only here three weeks. She has nobody else to go to because she doesn't know anybody.'

Crucially for gardaí, Dumitru Jnr was able to provide a description of the car. 'The car, grey in colour, Ford Mondeo,' he recalled. 'I saw the registration number, 01 LH. I can't remember the rest. This man in the car spoke in broken Romanian. He was skinny with white skin. He had small black eyes – that's all I can remember of him and the car.'

On 9 January 2008 an investigation into the teenager's disappearance was launched under Senior Investigating Officer Cryan, Detective Sergeant John Doyle and Superintendent Joseph Gannon. Marioara's parents insisted their daughter had no boyfriend, Romanian or Irish, and had never left their side. But one angle detectives had to check out was whether she had been abducted as part of an arranged Roma marriage, which had not been sanctioned by her family. In September 2007 gardaí in Pearse Street had investigated a similar incident in which two Romanian girls were dragged into a car. They suspected that one of the girls, who was later found in a room in north inner-city Dublin, had been raped by her unwanted groom.

The practice of arranged marriages among members of the Roma community across Europe is still common. During extensive interviews with Roma people living in Ireland, gardaí established how Marioara's father had been approached by his cousin, Baron Rostas, a father of six, for his daughter's hand in marriage. In Roma culture it is not uncommon for cousins to wed, provided they have the blessings from their families. However, Baron Rostas confirmed to gardaí that the offer of marriage was rejected, with Dumitru insisting his daughter was too young. Another theory explored by detectives was that she had been kidnapped and forced to work in a brothel as a prostitute. At that time, the idea that

Irish criminals might have been behind the abduction was not on the garda radar.

Without any further contact from Marioara, investigators decided to launch a public appeal for information. Her photograph was sent to the garda press office, placed on the Missing Persons section of the force's official website and added to a website on missing children shared by police agencies around the world. Gardaí also conveyed their concerns to their colleagues in the PSNI [Police Service of Northern Ireland] in the North and on mainland Britain. Interpol were placed on alert to ensure gardaí would be notified if Marioara was spotted travelling across different borders. A general press release, providing information on her last-known whereabouts, was circulated to every newsroom in the country. The image was also sent to the Romanian media in the hope that she had returned home as a 'runaway'.

Meanwhile, statements were taken on 10 January from thirteen Romanian nationals who had been staying at the Donabate property. All of those interviewed had their fingerprints and photographs taken but could offer no information on the disappearance. The following day a site in Lusk, north Co. Dublin, was also searched. It would be the first of twenty-two separate searches over the following weeks.

Investigators sought to identify the registered owners of every 01 LH four-digit car in Ireland to establish if they were linked to any Romanian nationals. This confirmed that a Mr Alan Wilson, who lived with his former street-trader mother Mary at New Street Gardens in the south inner city, was the registered owner of a silver Ford Mondeo, registration 01 LH 3884. With only one previous conviction at district-court level for possession of a screwdriver, he was not considered an immediate priority.

*

On 21 January 2008 Garda John Paul Holland from the Divisional Crime Task Force at Kilmainham garda station attempted to contact Alan Wilson about the vehicle. He repeatedly called to the family home, but Wilson was never present. 'Mr Wilson was never there when I called,' Garda Holland later said. 'I spoke with his mother, Mrs Mary Wilson, and I gave her my contact details.

'I also asked her for a number for Alan Wilson but she said she didn't have one and provided me with her own mobile number, which was 085 1120052. Mrs Wilson was unable to provide me with any information in relation to the silver Ford Mondeo. Mr Alan Wilson never made contact with me. I spoke with Mrs Mary Wilson on a number of occasions both in person and by contacting her on the telephone number she had provided for me. On 29 February 2008 I once again called to the home in relation to another matter. During this meeting I informed her that Alan Wilson still hadn't contacted me and she had no explanation for this.'

But Wilson would soon have dealings with gardaí he could not avoid. On 27 March he, his sister Maxine and Maxine's boyfriend Fergus O'Hanlon were arrested over a suspected aggravated burglary at Highfield Road in the upmarket area of Rathgar in south Dublin the previous 19 August 2007.

During the raid, four masked men armed with knives and bats had stormed into the home and placed the terrified owners in handcuffs before attacking them and fleeing with a collection of valuable stamps in a stolen BMW fitted with false plates. The stamps were later found in O'Hanlon's home in Raheen Close in Tallaght. Sometime after this the trio would be charged with unauthorized taking of a car from a house in Terenure on 2 August 2007 – the car subsequently used for the burglary on 19 August. Wilson would also be charged with handling stolen property and intimidating a witness.

However, over the next two months – and despite their best efforts – gardaí had made no progress in their investigation. They had no clear suspects, no motive or any idea if Marioara was alive or dead. Investigators had exhausted every avenue. Gardaí also explored the possibility that she was murdered in a so-called 'honour killing' – in which women from certain minorities are lynched to avenge perceived insults to their family or other men – but this was quickly discounted.

With no fresh leads emerging or information coming into the incident room, the decision was made towards the end of April to hold a fresh media appeal. This time it would have a higher profile on RTÉ's *Crimecall* programme on 20 May 2008. Marioara's mother, with the help of a translator, would appear on the show alongside Detective Sergeant John Doyle. This turned out to be a crucial move. Clutching a picture of her daughter, Marioara's mother made a heartfelt plea for her daughter's safe return. Finally, four months after her disappearance, the teenager's image was displayed on television screens across the country.

Crimecall also provided gardaí with the opportunity to reconstruct events leading up to the disappearance and give a description of the car used by the man who approached her in January. Unknown to investigators at the time, a family in Tallaght was also watching the programme. As the appeal was broadcast, they were shocked to discover one of their relatives vomiting in the back garden of their home. That man was Fergus O'Hanlon. O'Hanlon's family had no idea his sudden bout of sickness had anything to do with the programme, but in time they would make the connection.

In the immediate days after *Crimecall* was aired, the telephone lines at Pearse Street station remained silent. Along with the television appeal, investigators had laboriously trawled through CCTV footage from businesses around the Pearse Street area, but all to no avail. They still had no sightings of the teenager, or of the car in which she had been driven away. It was hugely frustrating.

After five months no evidence had emerged to suggest the abduction had been organized by anyone living in Romania and there were no solid leads from Ireland either. Although the possibility that she had been coerced into an arranged marriage or had been the victim of a paedophile remained in play, gardaí were now fearful they were dealing with something even more serious.

Detectives continued to hope for a breakthrough and the information they had been waiting for finally arrived, altering the course of the investigation for ever. Shortly after lunch on 2 June 2008 Garda Enda Dowling was in the main office of Pearse Street station when the phone rang. The anonymous caller's first words were that he had information relating to the disappearance of the 'missing Romanian girl'.

The man, who to this day has never been identified, was calling from a phone box in Enniscorthy, Co. Wexford. He told Garda Dowling that he had been enjoying a drink on his own in the now closed Lamplighter pub in the Coombe in south inner-city Dublin exactly two weeks earlier when two men walked into the bar.

He explained that the two men had sat at another table close to his before ordering drinks. The caller said he recognized one of the men in the pub as being a nephew of either Martin 'The General' Cahill or Martin 'The Viper' Foley, two of Ireland's most notorious criminals. Sitting quietly on his own, he found himself listening in on a conversation that left him shocked and sickened.

The man told Garda Dowling that he had overheard the

conversation start with the mention of the name of the missing teenager. He was horrified when he heard one of the men then say that he had shot the girl three times in the head before burying her. The informant outlined how the same man told his friend he had murdered the girl because he was high on cocaine. More crucially still for gardaí, the mystery caller also revealed that this same man said the car he had used in the murder was now up for sale.

A number of those who would have fitted the brief given by the caller were either in prison or had few convictions. None had ever been connected to the abduction – or attempted abduction – of other teenage girls either. The crime did not match the behavioural pattern of the hardened gangster, whose only real love in life was cash.

Retired Detective Superintendent Gabriel O'Gara, who would go on to play a significant part in the investigation, explained, 'Criminals associated with the gangland culture were rarely involved in crimes of this nature. The call certainly gave a new impetus to the investigation. It was great to receive the new information at that time, but it wasn't enough, the team just needed that little bit extra. The main priority for SIO Cryan and his team all along was to find [Marioara].'

Shortly before the anonymous phone call was made in June 2008, Marioara's family had decided to return to their homeland. They had been in Dublin for eight months and spent the last five of those months fearful they would never see their daughter again. 'It was too painful for us to stay in Ireland,' her father said.

'We came to Ireland for a better life but the whole experience turned into a nightmare. We had great support from the gardaí, from family and friends, but we just wanted to be in our own home. I was very keen to be kept informed of any developments and I told everyone I would be back in Ireland at a moment's notice. We had an assurance from the gardaí that they would do everything in their power to find her. We left Ireland with heavy hearts but we knew deep down some day we would return to bring my daughter home.'

After months of nothing, it was a relief for the investigation team to now have an alternative and more substantive theory on which to concentrate their investigation. But they little imagined that the game-changing phone call would soon be followed up with a second anonymous tip-off. This time, the caller named the alleged killer and identified a potential crime scene. The killer, she claimed, was Martin 'The General' Cahill's nephew, Alan Wilson.

3. Murder Spree

His exact words to me were, 'See that job? Eric did that'
                              – Fergus O'Hanlon

On 4 February 2008, just under a month after Marioara Rostas vanished off the streets of Dublin, three men were driving back to an apartment on the Costa del Sol after a session at the gym. An established gangland criminal named Gary Hutch was at the wheel, with another, Paddy Doyle, beside him and a third, 'Fat' Freddie Thompson, in the back. The trio were in Spain because of trouble at home: they had all begun working with the nascent Kinahan cartel, headed by Christy Kinahan and his veteran sidekick, John 'The Colonel' Cunningham.

Hutch had fled to escape the heat from the drug-related murder of Derek Duffy, who he had shot dead outside a house in Finglas in September 2007: gardaí believe he was the gunman who fired five bullets into the small-time dealer before setting alight his car with the remains inside. Meanwhile, Thompson and Doyle were up to their necks in the vicious Crumlin–Drimnagh gang war, which had claimed twelve lives up to that point. The feud had begun after a seizure of cocaine and ecstasy at a city-centre hotel exploded into violence amid allegations of informing to gardaí. Thompson was the leader of one faction and Doyle, a hulking 6 foot 4 inch plus, was his chief enforcer.

That sunny afternoon, all three men were on their way

back to the place Doyle and Hutch were renting in the Bel Air estate outside the town of Estepona, where the Kinahans had made their base in Spain. The black BMW X5 was a regular sight on the roads through the estate, where villas are expensive and have large gardens. It always took the same route when returning from the town: left off the A-7 motorway, then up through two roundabouts and right into Calle Hinojo. Despite its name, this was little more than an alleyway, barely wide enough to accommodate the large SUV. Anyone emerging from Hinojo would have to stop and edge out slowly at the crossroads with Calle Yerbabuena and look right and left for any oncoming traffic – it was, in other words, the perfect place for an ambush.

An assassin was waiting for Hutch to exit the junction. As the SUV emerged, another BMW, a green 3 Series saloon, pulled forward to block its way. A gunman, who gardaí later learned was Eric Wilson, leaned out of the passenger side. The left side of the SUV's windscreen was sprayed with bullets, three going through the glass and one penetrating the metal stanchion on the left-hand side. Two more went into the passenger door.

Hutch floored the accelerator and drove the vehicle beyond the crossroads and into a lamp post on the far side. All three men got out and ran for their lives in separate directions, but the killer was only interested in one of them.

Paddy Doyle opted to sprint straight back down the narrow Hinojo lane and the assassin followed, firing as he ran. Doyle made it about halfway down before the number of shots he received in the back proved too much even for his strapping frame as he fell to his knees and forward against the wall of a neighbouring house. Having reached him, the hitman shot him twice further in the back of the head and then ran back towards the junction where his getaway driver was waiting. The 3 Series then sped off in the direction of the A-7 motorway.

The shooting was over in a matter of seconds. It had taken place at 2 p.m., a time when most local families were either eating or engaging in the traditional siesta, which is particularly common down in Spain's baking southern provinces. As a result, there were few eyewitnesses around to see what happened, though neighbours quickly emerged at the sound of gunfire. A hired gardener in one of the villas was able to provide the make of the getaway car, but little more.

Eight shells were recovered beside Doyle's body, but the autopsy later revealed he had been hit a total of eleven times before the 'double tap' was applied to the back of his skull. It was a miracle he had made it as far as he did. Intelligence later indicated that both Hutch and Thompson were aware of what was coming, though perhaps not exactly where and when. They had driven the man who thought he was among friends to his death.

Nonetheless, Hutch gave a convincing performance of innocence. He reappeared at the murder scene around an hour later looking badly shaken and gave police a statement. By mid-afternoon, reports of Doyle's demise were making their way back to Dublin, where gardaí showed no surprise. The victim was no stranger to them and was chief suspect in at least three murders himself.

Despite hailing from Portland Row in the north inner city, Paddy Doyle had aligned himself with Thompson's faction in the southside Crumlin–Drimnagh feud and had been in the thick of it from the beginning. The feud had begun when an ally of Thompson's named Declan Gavin was stabbed to death by another gang member, Brian 'King Ratt' Rattigan, who accused him of being a garda informant following a drugs seizure. The mob splintered and seven months afterwards, Doyle and Thompson burst into Rattigan's home on St Patrick's night 2002 and shot him in the chest.

Remarkably, Rattigan survived, but others to cross Doyle's path were not so lucky. They included Darren Geoghegan and Gavin Byrne, murdered by two unmasked gunmen as they sat in a car after being lured to a meeting in Firhouse on 13 November 2005. The pair were allies of Freddie Thompson in the feud but investigators believe they were set up and killed by him in a double-cross. Gardaí are certain one of the gunmen was Doyle.

Two nights later, Doyle was dispatched to kill Rattigan acolyte Noel Roche. Roche had been spotted at a Phil Collins concert and tried to flee, but was caught and gunned down following a high-speed chase along the Clontarf Road. Though Doyle and his sidekick, Craig White, fulfilled their task, they failed to properly set their getaway vehicle alight afterwards, leaving it full of DNA evidence. White would later be jailed for life, while Doyle fled to Spain. There, he became involved in trafficking drug shipments back home and hired himself out as muscle to whoever was paying. For almost two and a half years, he led the high life.

Several theories emerged following Doyle's murder as to who was responsible. Some said Doyle had been throwing his weight around on the Costa del Sol and had given the son of a Russian mobster a serious beating in a nightclub. Others claimed both Doyle and Thompson had refused to pay a group of Turkish drug traffickers for a haul of heroin seized in Dublin and that Doyle had personally laughed and given them two fingers when they pressed him for payment. His murder was also linked to the seizure of 115 kilogrammes of cocaine bound for Ireland and the UK by Spanish police the following day.

But, as revealed by the authors in their book *The Cartel*, the real orchestrators of the hit were the Kinahans themselves. Spanish investigators later uncovered that Doyle had been working as an enforcer for on-the-run British drug dealer Simon 'Slapper' Cowmeadow during the previous year. Cowmeadow had fled the UK for Holland in 2002 after being caught red-handed unloading 100,000 ecstasy tablets hidden inside a load of frozen chips. In November 2007 Cowmeadow was discovered shot through the eye on a deserted Amsterdam street. No weapon was found nearby and the body had suffered a broken leg post-mortem, leading cops to suspect it had been pushed from a moving car. The Spanish police file compiled for Operation Shovel, the two-year probe into the Kinahans, which ended in May 2010, was definitive on why both men died. It read, 'In November 2007, the killing in Holland of Simon John Cowmeadow coincided with the disappearance of €400,000 or €500,000. It appears Patrick Doyle and Cowmeadow were responsible for the disappearance of this money, which belonged to the Kinahan organization.'

The information would not have come as a shock to those who knew the organization well. The cartel at that stage was still wholly under the control of Kinahan Snr and Cunningham, both of whom disliked flashy young criminals such as Doyle. The numerous other stories circulating following Doyle's murder may very well have been put out by the cartel, both as a smokescreen and as a means of flushing out any informants within their organization passing on information to gardaí.

Once it had been established that the Kinahans were responsible, Wilson's name began to circulate as the gunman. It was a considerable step up in gravity for the then twenty-four-year-old.

Up until that point, Wilson's victims were all small-time or individual criminals whose removal had posed little risk of retribution. Now, he had taken out a leading light in one of Dublin's most powerful and violent criminal gangs. The murder had also given a sizeable boost to the Rattigan faction, which was definitely beginning to lose the battle back on the city's southside. Even though Doyle faced arrest on sight, it was still possible for him to slip back into the country via the North to carry out more killings.

The hit would not be the last time Eric Wilson intervened to level up the scores in the Crumlin–Drimnagh feud, though next time round, his involvement would deal a death blow to Rattigan's ailing regime. Doyle's murder was significant for reasons far beyond that, however.

Gardaí were by now aware of the full extent of the Kinahan cartel's activities and seized €3.5 million worth of their cannabis just two days after he was killed. There had been two other seizures of the cartel's drugs in Newcastle-upon-Tyne, and a haul of weaponry linked to Christy Kinahan's oldest son and heir apparent Daniel impounded in London a month later. There was also Cowmeadow's killing in Amsterdam and the ongoing investigation into Christy Kinahan's money-laundering activities in Antwerp. The shooting of Doyle and the very public, violent way in which Wilson carried it out proved to be the straw that broke the camel's back.

Five months later in July 2008, gardaí, Spanish police and those from Belgium and Holland met in The Hague and agreed to launch Operation Shovel. Things would never be the same for the cartel again.

If the killing of Paddy Doyle was Eric Wilson's step into the big time of gangland hits, he was not prepared to rest on his laurels. His next commission would be less high-profile, but a lot more gruesome. It also came straight from the same playbook as the slaying of Roy Coddington.

By the middle of 2008 Wilson had set up a permanent base for himself in Spain, far from the reach of the warrants out for him over the Portarlington attack and the Carlow gun seizures. Gardaí also wanted to question him over the Kenny, Reay and Coddington murders and he would almost certainly have been arrested on sight if spotted back home. Eric had initially been aided out on the Costa del Sol by a Baldoyle criminal and associate of another drug trafficker, Micka 'The Panda' Kelly. The Baldoyle criminal helped Eric find a luxury apartment in Mijas Costa. But preferring to stay out of sight, Wilson later found himself an isolated farmhouse, the Hacienda Sambargo, near the mountain village of Coín, itself about 20 kilometres inland from the coast. However, he still needed to return to Ireland periodically.

At the time, the criminal fraternity had gained control over a public servant who worked within the passport-issuing process in Dublin and who had a problematic cocaine habit. Unable to pay for his drugs, the man was being pressured into handing over genuine documents in false names. Eric Wilson secured several of these IDs and was using them to fly in and out of Belfast with the aid of disguises. To taunt gardaí, he occasionally bought tickets for flights from Spain to Dublin, which he never boarded, knowing that officers would be wasting their time at the airport waiting for him.

On some of these visits back to Ireland he would meet up with his cousin Alan Wilson and they would go up the Dublin mountains to try out some of the latest weaponry Alan had managed to get his hands on. On one occasion they went up with a pair of Mossberg pump-action shotguns and some old televisions – they were less interested in gauging the accuracy of the guns than using the TVs to check out the devastation they would cause at close range.

That summer 2008, yet another vicious dispute between two

drug traffickers had broken out in Dublin. David 'Babyface' Lindsay, who had visited Eric to check his arms cache back in late 2005, was at war with his former subordinate Kelly. Lindsay claimed Kelly owed him seven figures for a drugs shipment, but there was no sign of the money being handed over.

Lindsay, who was thirty-eight years old at the time, had been heavily involved in drug dealing for almost two decades. When he was just twenty-three he was a passenger in a car which was stopped on the M50 following a high-speed chase on 28 November 1994. The driver pleaded guilty over the 50 kilogrammes of hashish on the back seat, but Lindsay denied both possession and possession with intent to supply. Remarkably, he was set free when the DPP dropped charges on the day of his trial. He continued to be heavily involved in gangland activity, however, and in 2002, he was arrested and questioned by gardaí over the kidnapping of a woman named Helen Judge: Mrs Judge was the ex-wife of Liam Judge, a money-launderer for gangster John Gilligan.

Gardaí found it difficult to get to the bottom of exactly why Mrs Judge had been abducted, but her estranged husband told the *Daily Express* following her release that he had received a ransom demand for €250,000. He insisted, though, that 'not a penny was handed over' and that 'each and every one of them will regret it'. Whether or not that came to pass, Lindsay remained free to continue drug dealing and, while his initial business relationship with The Panda was solid, tempers began to fray over the money owed.

To up the ante, Lindsay decided to teach The Panda – whose bizarre nickname originated with the dark circles around his eyes – a lesson. One of The Panda's closest associates was another convicted drug dealer, named Anthony Foster.

Shortly before 2 p.m. on 18 July 2008 Foster left his apartment in Cromcastle Court in Coolock to meet his partner

Joanne and collect their children from crèche. He was coming down the steps of the stairwell when he was confronted by what gardaí believe was a lone assassin with a shotgun who opened fire, hitting him directly in the face. There were no witnesses, but neighbours saw a man in a top with the hood up cycling away from the apartment complex. Foster, a father of four, was found lying against the wall on the top-floor landing with massive head injuries. He was still clutching a baby's bottle in his right hand.

Gardaí believe the killer's escape from the scene was aided by a drug addict named Christy Gilroy – of whom more later. Foster's murder was a major blow to The Panda. The dead man had been one of his few allies in the row against Lindsay and the shooting sent an unmistakeable message that Kelly could be next if he did not pay up.

Meanwhile, Lindsay continued about his business. On 23 July, five days after Foster's murder, he and Alan Napper – who had also been at Eric Wilson's house in Carlow to check out the arms shipment back in 2005 – left their home area in Dublin's Baldoyle and drove to Clane in Co. Kildare. There they were spotted drinking in a pub: they subsequently borrowed a Volkswagen Golf from a friend of Lindsay's living locally after their car developed engine trouble.

The pair then set off on the two-hour drive to Northern Ireland, where The Panda was now hiding out. Kelly was feuding with other Dublin criminals as well as Lindsay and had managed to convince him that he was finally prepared to pay up to get Lindsay off his back.

A meeting was set for the village of Rathfriland in the middle of rural Co. Down. Until now, Rathfriland's primary claim to fame had been as the birthplace of the father of the literary Brontë sisters. It was about to become known for something a lot worse.

Neither gardaí nor the PSNI have been able to definitively establish what happened to the two men after that, but Lindsay and Napper were never seen again. Underworld sources claim that both men were lured to an isolated bungalow on the Drumdreenagh Road outside the village, the interior of which had been covered in plastic sheeting. It is said that upon their arrival, Napper was shot dead on the spot, while Lindsay was taken inside and tortured before being murdered.

The house in Rathfriland belonged to a man from Warrenpoint who had rented it to a Southerner. He was described as a good and respectful tenant, but did not mix with neighbours, who noted a number of Southern-registered cars visiting the property. Gardaí believe that tenant was Eric Wilson.

A year after Lindsay and Napper vanished, the PSNI carried out an extensive search of the bungalow. The entirely innocent owner had by now got married and was living there himself. After moving in, he had renovated the property and dumped a number of items left behind by his former tenant. The PSNI asked him to move out for a week while the place was searched from top to bottom. Traces of blood were discovered on a wall and, when a newly fitted carpet was lifted, more spots were found underneath. Tests revealed the blood belonged to David Lindsay. There was no trace of any DNA from Alan Napper, however; nor was there any sign of the two men's bodies, despite an extensive search of neighbouring lands.

Various stories floated around gangland about the pair's remains having been brought out to sea and fed through a woodchipper. Cops also received reports that The Panda had been overheard boasting that both men had been chopped up with chainsaws and their bodies disposed of. Other informants indicated that their corpses had been dismembered, shoved into large plastic barrels with screw-on tops and dumped into pre-dug holes, which were then filled in under cover of darkness.

However, the only on-the-record indication of what really happened subsequently came from Alan Wilson via Fergus O'Hanlon, to whom Wilson had opened up over the double murder. 'He trusted me with many things over the years and one of them was the killings of Napper and Lindsay,' O'Hanlon later told gardaí. 'We were in a car in the North on one occasion and it came on the radio about the two murders. His exact words to me were, "See that job? Eric did that." He then went on to explain that Eric had been hired to do the job by The Panda because they were involved in some feud or something. Alan pointed to a field about where the bodies were buried and then that was the end of it . . . the conversation just ended and he never brought it up again.'

Despite telling gardaí what had happened, O'Hanlon was unable to recall exactly where they had been driving at the time, so they could not instruct their PSNI colleagues on where to search.

One person who definitely was not happy at the way things had turned out was The Panda. Terrified of retaliation from Lindsay's associates, he fled to Spain immediately after the gruesome double murder.

Before he left he ordered Eric Wilson to torch the house in Rathfriland to destroy any forensic traces, but for some reason Wilson did not comply. Instead, he decided to clean up the property to remove any evidence that way. Gardaí can only speculate as to why he undertook that extensive task, but think it may be because he was worried about being traced as the tenant. Like the incident with the Ford Focus used in Roy Coddington's murder, it was another unnecessary risk, and one which came close to having fatal consequences down the line for Eric Wilson.

4. The Soldier

I know my son — he's not what you're making him out to be
                                                    — Mary Wilson

Throughout August 2008, with no new telephone tip-offs or fresh information to go on over the disappearance of Marioara Rostas, detectives turned to their informants in the underworld. Often rumours sweep through these communities after a violent crime has been committed, with the perpetrator's name an open secret.

But in the missing girl's case, there was an unnerving wall of silence. Nobody seemed to know anything. Details of the first call in June were definitely interesting, but detectives were also conscious that it might be a deliberate attempt to send them off on a wild goose chase.

By September the confidential line had gone quiet and the trail once again went cold. Despite the lack of intelligence, investigators tried to remain hopeful that someone who knew where Marioara was would come forward. On 23 September that faith was rewarded. At 5.33 p.m. that day, the phone rang in the Garda Communications Centre Command and Control in Harcourt Square, which receives and records 999 calls. Garda Karen Whelan found herself talking to a woman with a thick Dublin accent who asked to pass on information regarding a missing teenager.

When pressed by Garda Whelan, the woman said she had

information relating to a 'foreign girl' who had been missing since January. The girl, she claimed, had been 'murdered' in a house in the Meath Street area of south inner-city Dublin and the building had subsequently been destroyed in a fire.

The caller refused to reveal her identity and said she did not know the missing girl's name, though she knew the case had been highlighted on RTÉ. But far more importantly, she insisted she 'saw the girl in Alan Wilson's company before and on previous occasions going in and out of the house that was burnt'.

Even more crucially for detectives, the caller claimed Wilson's mother Mary, his sister Maxine and another relative were aware of what had happened. Once recorded, the information was passed to Kevin Street station, which had responsibility for policing the area where the fire was located.

On 15 October 2008 Detective Garda Garvan Ware passed the information to the incident room at Pearse Street, informing his colleagues that Alan Wilson was the registered owner of an 01 LH 3884 silver Ford Mondeo in January 2008. By this stage the investigation team had established that 2 Brabazon Street, located in the same area as described by the mystery caller, had been badly damaged in a fire on 29 February.

They also discovered the house had once been listed as the home address of Wilson's sister Maxine. During this pivotal period, officers also established that Wilson's father was John Cahill, brother of Martin 'The General' Cahill, confirming the first caller's report that a nephew of his had been linked to the Romanian girl's abduction. For the first time, gardaí now had a potential chief suspect, his associates, a vehicle and a possible crime scene. SIO Michael Cryan ordered a fresh technical examination of 2 Brabazon Street.

The house had already been checked out as part of the

routine investigation into the blaze. Then, Detective D. J. McCarthy and Garda Niall Guinan from the Garda Technical Bureau had discovered traces of 'hydrocarbon' fire accelerants – petrol and white spirit vapour – inside the property. Like any probe into a suspicious fire, part of the gardaí's role was to establish a motive, along with a suspect. With no traces of DNA, footprints or fingerprints, and the owner having a clear record, the only plausible explanation was that the house had been targeted by vandals.

However, when gardaí moved in on the property for a second time, on 30 October 2008, they were looking for other evidence. This second examination was conducted over ten days by the Divisional Scenes of Crime Unit for the area along with the Garda Technical Bureau. The three-storey property had a living room, small hallway and kitchen on the ground floor. On the first floor there was a bedroom, another living room and a bathroom.

The lower halves of the walls in the first-floor living room were painted red, and it was on one of these on the left-hand side of the room that a startling discovery was made. Five feet up from the floor, forensic experts discovered two .22-calibre bullets embedded in the crumbling plaster. Initial indications were that the bullets had struck the wall at high velocity from close range. Once the search of the house had been completed, gardaí were satisfied a total of seven shots had been fired into the wall.

The bullet holes were not the only major discovery. On the top floor, officers found the bedroom door had been fitted with a large sliding bolt latch, enabling it to be locked from the outside. House-to-house inquiries were carried out, but nothing of any evidential value was gleaned.

The Garda Technical Bureau returned to 2 Brabazon Street on 6 November 2008 after a detective received a tip that Alan Wilson's sister Maxine, her partner Fergus O'Hanlon and the couple's two children had been living there at the time of Marioara's disappearance. It would not be the last time the officer would receive confidential information linked to the teenager's disappearance.

The informant said O'Hanlon had been living in fear of Alan Wilson and that Maxine had confided in close friends about the murder. Gardaí also received intelligence that Wilson had beaten his sister when he was told she had been 'talking about' the murder and how 'Maxine had been very upset when she saw the girl's photograph.'

They were also told how Maxine Wilson is 'absolutely terrified for her own and her family's safety' and how Mary Wilson had been issuing threats to people she suspected had provided gardaí with information. As part of their case file when compiling profiles of the suspects, gardaí concluded Alan Wilson was 'closely associated with his cousin Eric Wilson' and involved in the illegal selling of firearms, while O'Hanlon and Maxine were 'drug addicts committing a lot of crime, usually burglaries, in order to feed their habit. At the moment she is drinking a lot also. He is violent and aggressive.'

A close relative told the authors, 'I remember hearing that she told people she heard one or two shots and when she went upstairs she found the young one's body. She was telling people she was rubbing the young girl's hair and telling her everything was going to be okay. There's no doubt in my mind that both she and Fergus later fell apart because of what they knew about that innocent young girl.' Just as in June and September, the third piece of intelligence again had Alan Wilson in the spotlight.

The new search of the house wasn't the only operation launched on the morning of 30 October 2008. Gardaí also searched a house in Drumcairn Avenue in Tallaght, where they seized a silver Ford Mondeo, registration 01 LH 3884.

Dinah O'Hanlon, Fergus O'Hanlon's older sister, was the registered owner of the vehicle. Although Ms O'Hanlon was not involved in crime or in any way linked to the disappearance of Marioara, the Mondeo was seized because of its previous owner. Detectives established that Alan Wilson had been the owner between 26 September 2007 and May 2008, when the car passed to Fergus O'Hanlon, who later sold it to his sister. The car was examined for clues but no evidence was discovered. Trawling through hours of CCTV, detectives unearthed an image of Alan Wilson getting into the same car on 1 January 2008. This was vital, as it established beyond doubt that he was still using it five days before Marioara disappeared.

Meanwhile, the missing girl's parents and younger brother returned to Ireland from Romania to assist the investigation. On 15 November 2008 Dumitru Rostas Jnr was brought to the garda vehicle pound in Santry. 'When I got out of the car, I noticed and recognized the car, a silver Ford Mondeo 01 LH,' he said in a statement. 'This is the car that I saw my sister get into. This is the last time I seen her. It was the same car because it was a Ford Mondeo and on the driver's handle, there was some plastic missing compared to the other side of the car.'

Alan Wilson became the target of the search in Brabazon Street and, after the seizure of his old car, he knew it was only a matter of time before the law came calling.

At 6.42 a.m. on 28 November 2008, ten months after the Romanian teenager was reported missing, gardaí swooped on the Wilson family home in New Street Gardens. Wilson was arrested under Section 30 of the Offences Against the

State Act. He was questioned on suspicion of unlawful possession of firearms with intent to endanger life at 2 Brabazon Street, Dublin, between 2 January and 29 February 2008.

During the course of the search, gardaí recovered a bulletproof vest, a knife and a scanner, which could be tuned into garda frequencies, beside his bed. Also seized was a notebook containing car registrations along with a log of number plates, the pictures of which were on his mobile phone. At the same time investigators also arrested Wilson's mother Mary and sister Maxine. Maxine's partner, Fergus O'Hanlon, was detained the following day at his home in Tallaght, during which a 9 mm Luger round of ammunition was recovered.

Following the arrests, Pearse Street Superintendent Joseph Gannon sought permission from the District Court to extend the periods of detention for Wilson and his sister. He told the court, 'It is our belief that Marioara Rostas got into 01 LH 3884 driven by Alan Wilson. We also believe she was kept in a locked room in 2 Brabazon Street for a number of days before for some reason or another she was murdered.

'It is our belief that Marioara Rostas was shot dead by Alan Wilson sometime between 6 January and 29 February and that Maxine Wilson witnessed the murder. I am also not satisfied that Fergus O'Hanlon is cooperating with this inquiry. We are satisfied the investigation is being conducted diligently and expeditiously and that an extension was required for the proper investigation.

'I am morally and legally obliged to make every effort to find Marioara's body. She was just eighteen years of age, in a strange country for a very short time. She was from a desperately poor family and had a neglected childhood and young adulthood. While she and her family survived by begging, it was not a lifestyle choice by any of them.

'Neither she nor her parents were involved in any type of crime and had no criminal convictions. She was hungry and cold and took up the offer of food from what she thought was a Good Samaritan. Unfortunately, she is now dead; buried in an unmarked grave. Her family cannot begin any grieving process without a body.'

Prior to his arrest, gardaí had information that Alan Wilson was always on the move, despite being registered, and receiving state payments as his elderly mother's carer. Gardaí had also received intelligence that due to his family ties to Eric Wilson – by now a suspect in a number of gangland murders – Alan slept wearing a bulletproof vest and may have had access to firearms. However, at the time of his arrest, he offered no resistance and went quietly.

For detectives at Kevin Street, Crumlin and Pearse Street stations, all heavily involved in investigations into organized crime and gangland activities, Alan Wilson was not a known criminal 'face'. Their only interaction with him had been in 2006, when he was arrested for drink-driving and possession of a screwdriver. But unbeknownst to officers at the time, within Alan Wilson's inner circle were some of the most feared gangsters in Ireland, including Brian 'King Ratt' Rattigan. Rattigan had, it seemed, nicknamed Alan 'The Mad Man' because of his apparent willingness to 'do anything'.

Unlike some of his associates in the south inner city such as 'Fat' Freddie Thompson, Wilson did not crave publicity. Whenever he was stopped by gardaí, he was friendly and affable. One garda report on him read, 'Alan Wilson has a plausible attitude to gardaí when stopped and spoken to. He appears to keep a low profile and cooperates with gardaí when stopped. Gardaí believe him to be astute and intelligent.' On another occasion, however, officers gained an insight into his macabre interest in violence when they found videos on his mobile phone that depicted the beheadings of hostages and American soldiers in Iraq.

Although considered a loner during his school years, a child who very rarely left his mother's or sister's side, Alan Wilson was feared because of his close family connection to Martin 'The General' Cahill. Wilson had been a shy child with little interest in formal education, who idolized his late uncle. 'I got to know Alan when he was a bit older but I remember Fergus telling me that he was always very shy when he was younger,' his former friend Herbert Kilcline said.

'Others said he was a strange lad who never really had any interests or engaged in conversations with his peers. He never said too much and his inner circle included his mother and sister Maxine, Fergus, and his cousins Eric, Keith and John in Ballyfermot. I sometimes think he only let me into his inner sanctum so he could manipulate, control and threaten me with violence.'

One associate who did not want to be named also remembers Wilson as a young man. 'When I came out of prison in 2000 Alan Wilson didn't even have a charge for stealing a bar of chocolate,' he said. 'He was still very shy and hardly spoke. He would have sold some cigarettes now and again but that was the extent of his criminal career. As he got older he just progressed into more serious forms of organized crimes.'

Kilcline also recalled how he had helped Wilson with his applications for housing as he got older. 'Alan was very bad with paperwork,' he said. 'He was almost illiterate. He'd get me to fill in forms for a medical card or car insurance or things like that. When I look back, I know Alan was just using me.'

Wilson was brought to Kevin Street garda station at 6.50 a.m. and questioned in fifteen separate interviews about Marioara's disappearance. He sat through all of them with his head bowed or stared at the wall in the station's upstairs interview room and he made no comment when asked if he had abducted the Romanian teenager.

He also refused to answer when it was put to him that he had shot her in the head and when asked to account for his movements on 6 January 2008. At the same time as O'Hanlon's arrest, gardaí made an application to extend Maxine Wilson's detention period.

In his submissions to the court, Superintendent Gannon said, 'It is our belief that Marioara Rostas got into 01 LH 3884, driven by Alan Wilson. We also believe she was kept in a locked room in 2 Brabazon Street for a number of days before for some reason or another she was murdered. It is our belief that Marioara Rostas was shot dead by Alan Wilson sometime between 6 January and 29 February and that Maxine Wilson witnessed the murder.' In their application, gardaí also told the court that it was their belief Wilson's mother also had knowledge of the murder.

Even when confronted with the evidence that the Ford Mondeo seized by gardaí had been registered to him and details of when he had been stopped at garda checkpoints, Alan Wilson remained unfazed.

Hours after his arrest, at 2.39 p.m., Wilson agreed to participate in a formal identification parade. But the plan was abandoned after gardaí were unable to locate Marioara's brother Dumitru. They searched the length and breadth of the capital but could not find him. Without anything further to tie Alan Wilson to Marioara, they had no choice but to inform him that the ID process had been cancelled and to release him without charge. When Wilson was told this at 10.32 p.m. on 30 November, he gave a slight, smug smile and returned to his family home. By the time he got there, his mother Mary had also just been released.

Little concrete had come from the detentions, but gardaí

were confident they were on the right track. On the morning of her arrest Mary Wilson was told by Detective Garda Rebecca Deveney that she was being detained for withholding information. As she left her home, she asked how long she would be held before saying, 'He said if I tell, he'll kill me.' But when she was asked to repeat those words by a member of the garda search team, she replied, 'I said nothing.'

At one point she was brought to St James's hospital after complaining of chest pains but was later deemed fit for interview. The first question put to her was, 'Who owns the bulletproof vest in your house?' Mary Wilson replied that her son had it for 'protection' from 'the guards'. When asked why her son needed protection, she replied, 'They raided my house one time and I seen them put a gun to his head and saying they would blow his head off. You think I'm bad . . . I can't even work.'

Mrs Wilson was then asked if her son had the body armour or had access to firearms and replied 'no' on both occasions. She was questioned as to whether Alan 'ever hit Maxine'. 'No,' she insisted. 'Why would he hit her? He's not a violent person. They were close. They were brother and sister. He's never lost his temper or been violent towards his girlfriend. He probably only went to Brabazon Street to see Maxine. To my knowledge he didn't have anyone else with him.'

Gardaí next queried whether Alan, as his mother's registered carer, should not have some medical training in case something happened to her. 'He would ask me where the pain was and phone the doctor,' Mary said. She told detectives her son was hoping to get work as a taxi driver – if gardaí would leave him alone. 'Hopefully, he'll get his taxi if the detectives stop taking his pen off him outside where he goes to do his lessons for his taxi,' she said. 'I don't know of any reason why the gardaí would watch him – he's being harassed.' Questioned on whether she thought gardaí were 'annoying' her family for 'no good reason', she replied, 'Yes, for what I'm in for.'

Despite being told of the evidence, gathered by detectives, which had sent them in the direction of her family, Mary resolutely stuck to her story. 'It's ridiculous,' she said. Detectives asked if she believed anonymous calls pointing to her son's alleged involvement in a teenage girl's murder were also crazy. Her answer was, 'Well, they would have to be, wouldn't they?'

During one of the ten interviews during her detention period, she fielded some tough questions over the discovery of bullet holes in her daughter's home, but adopted a similarly vague approach. She claimed she 'knew nothing' about the bullet holes and, referring to Marioara, said she had 'no information other in that she was similar to my niece Debbie who passed away from a drugs overdose'. There had never been any suggestion that Marioara took drugs.

The garda interviewer accused Mary of 'being evasive in answering the simplest questions in an attempt to withhold information in relation to what happened to Marioara'. She was asked if her son had known the missing teenager. Her reply was, 'I know my son – he's not what you're making him out to be.'

At the same time as her mother and brother were being questioned, Maxine Wilson, who was a year older than her brother, repeatedly denied any knowledge of the Romanian girl's disappearance. However, in her third interview before her release, she finally admitted she had seen Marioara at the door of 2 Brabazon Street.

Maxine was asked in another interview to provide an explanation for the bullet holes found, but said only that they had been caused 'by accident'. Between 8.17 p.m. and 9.17 p.m. Maxine Wilson went with gardaí to Sally's Bridge on the Grand Canal, close to Donore Avenue, where she insisted the firearm used in the incident had been discarded. But despite an extensive search by the Garda Water Unit, detectives were unable to find the gun. Although nothing of evidential value was found during the search of the Wilson family home, a mobile phone taken from Maxine Wilson's home would later prove crucial. A SIM card previously used in the phone had been in contact with Alan Wilson's number and the phone had been given to her by O'Hanlon. Along with her mother and brother, Maxine was also released without charge on 30 November.

Fergus O'Hanlon, however, remained in custody after his period of detention was extended over the seizure of ammunition. As it drew to a close on 2 December and after sixteen long recorded interviews, the suspect asked to speak to Detective Sergeant Doyle in private. O'Hanlon had consented to previous interviews being recorded, in both audio and video format, but on this occasion insisted on speaking to the senior detective away from any official recording devices.

Detective Sergeant Doyle brought the prisoner to the doctor's room in the station. Once behind closed doors, O'Hanlon stunned him by announcing he wished to 'clear his name' and that he would ask 'the right people' to find the missing girl. Pressed to reveal his knowledge on her whereabouts, O'Hanlon refused to acknowledge whether or not he was involved in the suspected murder.

His only insistence was that the garda forensic team would prove his innocence. During the conversation, O'Hanlon made repeated assurances that he did not want any reward for any information he supplied. He did not provide any information at that stage, but the moment was another huge step forward in what was increasingly heading towards a murder investigation.

Coinciding with the arrests was a fresh appeal by Superintendent Gannon, who gave an interview to RTÉ's crime correspondent Paul Reynolds aimed at encouraging others with information to come forward. This did not generate any new leads and a second appeal was made by gardaí on 9 January, the first anniversary of Marioara's disappearance.

A number of weeks afterwards, two detectives called to the Wilson family home. Invited in by Mary Wilson, the pair were directed to Alan's bedroom. The perception of him had changed considerably as a result of the Marioara inquiry, and both gardaí had their hands by their holsters as they entered the room, just in case he was inside with a weapon.

Instead, Wilson was in his bed, surrounded by lit candles. He greeted the detectives and struck up a sinister conversation about the issue of torture, saying people who had been tortured must feel relief knowing that their demise is within sight.

The detectives asked him why he had brought the subject up, but he refused to expand any further. Gardaí believed Wilson was talking about personal experiences, but the issue would never have stood up in a prosecution. The tactic of talking about oneself in the third person is regularly used by gangland players to taunt gardaí or supply information to them in a way that cannot be used in evidence. Kinahan cartel member 'Fat' Freddie Thompson had previously used it to convey his fears about cooperating when he said in off-the-record conversations with investigators, 'Deccy can't get out because they will kill his family.' The 'Deccy' he was talking about was Declan Gavin, whose name Thompson had tattooed on his arm.

One senior security source said of Alan Wilson, 'He was a strange character and it could never be proven if he was talking from personal experience about torture because he wasn't being interviewed under caution.

'He was becoming increasingly paranoid then and had a new, fortified front door installed at his home. He also spoke to the two officers of how people who do bad things in the world often atone for it by doing something good for their families. The whole encounter was rather bizarre but could never be used in a court of law.'

Following the one-year anniversary appeal, the investigation team were desperately hoping that the anonymous callers who had provided crucial information in June and September the previous year would sense the case building against Wilson and would pluck up the courage to contact them again.

But in the weeks and months afterwards, the phones in the incident room at Pearse Street station remained silent. Gardaí suspected the individuals who had made the original calls were still in the country, but were afraid of revealing their identities. Meanwhile, Wilson's name was increasingly being linked to other, more serious crimes. On 12 May 2009 he was identified by gardaí as the main suspect in an incident where shots were fired at a house in Wellview Avenue, Mulhuddart, in west Dublin.

Investigations revealed that the incident was over a squabble between Alan Wilson's kids and those of the owner of the house, Paul Campbell. Wilson twice had words with Campbell before returning a third time and attempting to kick in the kitchen door while firing two shots from a handgun at the property.

In June the investigation team received a welcome boost when experienced officer Detective Superintendent Gabriel

O'Gara was appointed to the South Central Division of the gardaí's Dublin Metropolitan Region. O'Gara, who was involved in the investigation into the murder of journalist Veronica Guerin on 26 June 1996, among other major probes, had also served as a detective in Ballyfermot and was well aware of the Wilson name.

'They ruled through fear and surrounded themselves with people who were much weaker than them,' he said. 'In reality, the Wilsons were . . . extremely dangerous criminals with a propensity for violence.'

Just a few weeks into his new role, Superintendent Gannon visited him in his office where the pair chatted about crime trends in their division. Gannon got up to leave, paused, and said, 'There's one thing I would like you to do for me, Gabriel. Can you find Marioara Rostas?'

O'Gara's reply was instant and unequivocal. 'We will get her,' he vowed.

Detective Superintendent O'Gara retired from the force in 2013, after thirty-five years of service. 'I was early enough into my new role and I will never forget Superintendent Gannon saying that to me,' he told the authors. 'It wasn't just me – everyone involved in that investigation was determined to find her, and we would keep plugging away.'

5. First Kill

The lure was from Eric to get Cannon into that area
                   – senior garda investigator

By the middle of 2009 Eric Wilson was well established in southern Spain, where he was just as willing to carry out hits as at home. He had already made his bones there with the execution of Paddy Doyle on behalf of the Kinahans. Soon the cartel called on him again to do a favour on behalf of one of its leading customers in Dublin.

Finglas gangster Eamon Dunne had taken control of the city's drugs market by eliminating his old boss, Martin 'Marlo' Hyland in December 2006. Hyland, who had contracted Eric to murder Paul Reay, was infamous for not trusting any of his associates and never spent two consecutive nights in the one place. Even so he was no match for the scheming of Dunne, who eventually found out where he was sleeping and had him shot – along with an innocent plumber's apprentice, Anthony Campbell, who happened to be working in the same house at the time and saw the gunman's face.

In January 2009 Dunne was at the beginning of a paranoid blitz against any and all rivals – real or imagined. One figure who did represent a genuine threat to him, though, was another northside heroin dealer named Michael 'Roly' Cronin.

Cronin was a veteran drug trafficker who had been jailed for thirteen years after being caught with a stash at his north inner-city corporation flat in 1996. (In an ironic twist showing how regularly the same Irish gangland figures run up against one another, he had once been given an unmerciful hiding in Amsterdam by Paddy Doyle.) Upon Cronin's release from prison he had begun vying with Dunne for control of Hyland's old turf and over the course of 2008 had dodged three attempts on his life. This had made him extremely wary, but Dunne had an ace in the hole.

Christy Gilroy – who David Lindsay had ordered to assist the killer of Anthony Foster – was still knocking around Dublin. Gilroy was also still heavily addicted to heroin and continued to be manipulated into carrying out serious criminal acts in order to fund his habit, including a spate of armed robberies. However, he would not have been considered dangerous by those further up the chain. Dunne was aware Cronin was selling heroin directly to Gilroy and decided to take full advantage.

On 7 January 2009 Cronin and his pal James Moloney drove into town from Finglas, where both had been topping up their colour at a tanning salon. Cronin had arranged to meet Gilroy and picked him up as they made their way through Summerhill in the north inner city. But minutes after getting into the back seat of the black Northern-registered Volvo, Gilroy shot the pair in the back of the head. The car then rolled down a side street and out into the middle of the thoroughfare, where it crashed into the railings that divide the two carriageways.

Gilroy, hardly the cold-blooded hitman, panicked. He opened the rear driver-side door, got out and ran off, leaving behind the gun, a mobile phone and his jacket, all plastered with his fingerprints and DNA. The hit was so botched that gardaí who arrived on the scene initially thought they were dealing with a traffic accident. It was only when a witness told them they had seen a man carrying a gun get out of the car and they noticed the smoke still rising from the hole in Moloney's neck that it became clear they were looking at something far more serious.

It would not be long before gardaí caught up with Gilroy, which of course would put Dunne at risk, so the gangster ordered him to fly to Spain. There, he was placed in a rehabilitation clinic in San Pedro de Alcántara, near Marbella, under a false name. Gilroy was promised he would be weaned off heroin and spent several weeks at the facility. But Dunne was not inclined to leave loose ends.

Gardaí believe he contacted Christy Kinahan, who in turn called in one of his chief lieutenants, Gary Hutch. (At that time the Hutches and the Kinahans were part of the same gang. This all changed later when Gary Hutch was shot dead in September 2015, and the two families are now sworn enemies.) Hutch had shown his willingness to betray his friends by assisting in the murder of Paddy Doyle. He had no problem doing so again with Gilroy, who he knew from mixing in the same criminal circles back in north inner-city Dublin. It was Hutch who was paying Gilroy's bills at the drug clinic – in cash, to avoid being traced – and who was Gilroy's only visitor. Gilroy considered him a friend.

The blundering hitman was progressing well through his treatment, which was being closely monitored, at a distance, by Eamon Dunne. Hearing that Gilroy was on the verge of kicking the habit, Dunne ordered him to be murdered to prevent him coming back to Ireland and spilling the beans if arrested.

Hutch called to the clinic and took Gilroy for a drive up into the mountains. Waiting for him there was Eric Wilson, who a year beforehand had fired several shots at an SUV Hutch was driving. Christy Gilroy was never seen again. He is thought to have been shot and buried in an unmarked grave; garda intelligence indicated he was dumped in a lime-lined pit, which Eric Wilson kept ready for such occasions.

And the remains have never been found, despite repeated calls by Gilroy's family for information on their whereabouts. His sister Glenda told the media in one appeal, 'I accept that Christopher did very bad things but he was threatened into those murders because he was soft, like a child trapped in a man's body, but justice has been done for that. He's been murdered so let us have him home to bury him.

'Me and my mum and Christopher's partner and daughter did nothing wrong, so why are we the victims now? Why have we been left in this nightmare with no closure? What-ever he did he's gone now, so let us bury him with his daddy.'

Meanwhile, back in Dublin, Alan Wilson was continuing to spiral out of control. On 3 June 2009 he was arrested along with his cousin David Crowley after a man was attacked with a shotgun and meat cleaver at a house in Blanchardstown following an alleged row over a woman.

David Lindsay had previously given Alan Wilson two bullet-proof vests. The afternoon of the incident in Blanchardstown, Wilson and Crowley picked up Fergus O'Hanlon and another man, Noel Cahill. The four drove to a house on Dromheath Drive, Blanchardstown, where Wilson and Crowley went into the kitchen and a struggle began with a man named David O'Brien. Both shells in the gun went off harmlessly into the air before Wilson and Crowley fled the property.

Gardaí were alerted that shots had been fired in the area and given a description of a car involved. A silver Toyota Corolla with a Wexford registration fitting the description was spotted at the junction of Church Road and the Old Navan Road in Mulhuddart. It initially failed to stop, but pulled over 500 metres later with all four men inside. Wilson and O'Hanlon were both wearing bulletproof vests. The four were arrested and taken to Blanchardstown garda station. There was no sign of any gun.

That evening, gardaí interviewed O'Brien's girlfriend, a woman named Lisa Murray. In her statement, she said she had witnessed O'Brien being struck on the head with a meat cleaver by Crowley. Ms Murray told Detective Garda Kieran Mullally, 'My name is Lisa Murray and I live at the above address with my two kids, who are two years old and six years old. This evening I was at my house with David O'Brien and Jacko – I don't know his real name [. . .] I think he is from Blanch, but I don't know where he is from. He dropped David over in his car. I don't know the type of car, but it is a big red one. David is my boyfriend on and off for the last five years.

'At about 7.40 p.m. this evening I was in the sitting room with the baby and I went to get his soother in the hall. I saw two people walking into my kitchen. I recognized Alan Wilson straight away. I know him 'cause my sister is going out with his cousin and I have seen him around the estate. I think he lives in Wellview now.

'I didn't see the second fella's face straight away. After they went into the kitchen I heard a scuffle. I heard the chairs in the kitchen falling around the place and the bin being knocked over. I ran to the door of the kitchen and saw David Crowley hitting my boyfriend David O'Brien.

'He was hitting him in the head with a handle of a knife. It wasn't a knife from my house. It was about 6 to 8 inches long and 4 inches wide. It was a meat cleaver. I grabbed David O'Brien and pulled him out of the kitchen into the hall.

'David Crowley turned around with the knife in the air towards me. I thought he was going to hit me with the knife. I was so scared I ran out of the house. I ran to Drumheath

Grove and got my dad. As I was running around to his house I heard two gunshots. I got my dad, and me, him and my brother ran back to the house.

'As I got to the house I saw three people getting into a silver car. I saw David Crowley roaring at my dad before he got into the car. The car went off down the road and I came into the house to see if someone was shot. David was in the sitting room. There was blood on his head.

'At the moment there is trouble with our family and Vera Cahill. She is going out with David Crowley. My brother Martin used to go out with her. That ended about five years ago, then they were on and off for a while and for the last three years they haven't been with each other.

'They have a child with each other. She lives in Parlickstown Court. I think for the last three years there has been trouble with her. I cannot remember the clothes the two fellas in the house were wearing. I remember Alan Wilson had a pair of black gloves on. I got a good look at Alan Wilson and David Crowley. I was 100 per cent sure it was the two of them that were in my kitchen. I didn't see who the third fella was. I didn't give any of the three of them permission to come into my house today or to damage my property.'

Lisa Murray's father, Noel Murray, also gave a statement to Detective Garda Tom Cooney that evening. It read:

'I remember Wednesday 3rd June 2009 I was at home in my own house. I was out the front, sweeping up my driveway. It was still very bright and sunny out. It was around 7.30 p.m. to 7.45 p.m. I know this because my daughter had just dropped my wife to her bingo. I put my tools back in the shed when I was finished and I came back into the sitting room of my house which is at the front of the house and the windows are wide open in the sitting room. I heard two loud bangs, like two loud bangers. They were within a couple of seconds of each other. I lifted a net curtain to see if I could see anything, but I couldn't. Then I heard screams, "Da, Da." I didn't realize who it was at first.

'I opened the porch door and I saw my daughter Lisa Murray standing at the kerb outside my house. She was hysterical. She said, "Somebody is after shooting at my house." I immediately thought of the kids. I ran around and my son Martin followed me.

'When I got around to the house, I saw a silver-coloured car parked up around 10 to 15 yards from Lisa's house. It was facing me. It was a silver-coloured saloon. There were three lads walking away from the house. I roared at them, "You big hard man, shooting up where there is kids."

'I think there was one sitting in the car. The other three were walking towards the car. When I roared at them Davy Crowley turned around. None of them were wearing balaclavas or anything. I know Davy Crowley over ten years, even fifteen years. My daughter Lorraine is living with Davy Crowley's brother Denis. Davy Crowley's mother lives in town. Davy is from there. I didn't recognise the others, but it was definitely Davy Crowley. Davy Crowley was holding a shotgun. It was a sawn-off shotgun. Somebody roared at him, "Come on get into the car, get into the car." I am nearly sure Davy got into the passenger side. The car spun around then to head out of the scheme. When the car was turning I away [sic] some of the reg. I am nearly positive that WX was the county on it. I walked into the house, then I saw blood all over the floor.

'I was trying to calm my daughter down because my two-year-old grandson was here. I ran out the front again and I seen the blood on David O'Brien's head and hand. I shouted to get an ambulance. I seen a tall lad with tight hair with Davy O'Brien. I think his name was Jacko. I didn't see them leave. I went back in and mopped up blood. My daughter showed me a plastic bag. I lifted it up and looked in. It was some sort of grubby T-shirt.

'This is all over my son Martin, breaking up with Vera Cahill who is a relation of Davy Crowley. He broke up with her after eleven years and she didn't take it too well. I couldn't describe the other three because they kept their back to me. I was angry and frightened when I saw the gun. I feared for my grandchildren's safety.'

David O'Brien himself declined to talk to gardaí. All four men were released without charge after questioning pending instructions from the DPP. But for someone who had previously been under the radar, Alan Wilson's links to serious crime were certainly on the rise.

Eamon Dunne's rampage across Dublin's gangland scene was only one killing spree affecting the capital. On the south-side, the Crumlin–Drimnagh feud between gangs led by 'Fat' Freddie Thompson and Brian 'King Ratt' Rattigan had been ongoing for eight years now.

By 2009 the Thompson faction had definitely gained the upper hand, despite the enforced elimination of his right-hand man, Paddy Doyle. The next murder connected to Eric Wilson would ensure the tubby, bald gangster remained in the ascendancy. But to do that, Eric would have to introduce his younger brother Keith to the family trade.

Anthony Cannon would be a lot more difficult to murder than a trusting dupe like Christy Gilroy. As Brian Rattigan's chief enforcer, Cannon was well aware of the various threats against his life. Cannon's main role for Rattigan was to collect drug debts and he was known for dishing out serious hidings to addicts who owed the gang small sums of money. (*Cocaine Wars*, Mick McCaffrey's book on the Crumlin–Drimnagh feud, outlined how the sight of Cannon approaching in his van had on occasion made drug users soil themselves in fright.)

However, Cannon also had a lucrative sideline as a middle-man in drug deliveries. Gardaí received information that his method was to ring a gilly and direct him to a location where a couple of kilos of heroin and another mobile had been left in a holdall. The courier would receive further instructions via the second phone on how to break down the gear into smaller amounts and drop it to another spot, where €2,000 in cash would be waiting for him. Cannon would then pick up the bag of smaller packages and deliver them a short distance onwards to street dealers.

The twenty-six-year-old had a lucky escape the previous summer after letting himself into a house in Crumlin with his own key minutes after gardaí had burst in on a raid and found €1 million worth of heroin inside. The DPP later decided charges would not stand up in court as Cannon had not been there during the raid and he was freed to go on his way. However, if there was one way to coax him to a place where he was vulnerable, it was via a drug pickup.

At around 3.30 p.m. on 17 July 2009 Anthony Cannon was sitting in the driver's seat of a car near Ruby Finnegan's pub in Ballyfermot. The bar lies near a small housing estate known locally as The Ranch. Cannon had no business behind the wheel of a vehicle at all, given that he had been handed a ten-year driving ban just eighteen months beforehand, but such things did not matter to a criminal of his calibre.

As he waited for his contact to appear, a motorcycle drew up alongside him, with a pillion passenger wearing a ski mask and carrying a pistol. The gunman was supposed to unload the magazine into the car as his target sat stationary inside. Instead, underworld sources told the authors how he inexplic-ably pulled up his mask to show Cannon his face – giving the startled gangster the chance to bolt out the passenger side and take off down Phoenix Street, a small residential thoroughfare leading towards the Liffey Gaels GAA club on the other side of the estate.

The bike roared after him and caught up with him as Cannon frantically attempted to climb over railings around the perimeter of the GAA club on St Mary's Avenue West. Cannon habitually wore a bulletproof vest and had one on that afternoon, but the force of being hit will still floor anyone, especially someone out of breath.

A shot from the gunman hit him in the back and knocked him to the ground. The killer walked up to where Cannon was lying, bent over him and shot him twice between the eyes. He then walked back towards the motorbike, got on, and the pair sped off.

The murder was witnessed by several locals, including children who were out playing in the street. Any of them could also have been killed by the eleven shots the assassin had fired while chasing Cannon down. A female witness described how several neighbours went to where Cannon was lying prone in a pool of blood. When one man tried to turn the injured gangster onto his side, she said, 'The back of his head fell away.'

As investigating officer Detective Inspector Colm O'Malley later told the inquest into Cannon's death, 'It would appear he was lured to the scene by someone he knew and may have dropped his guard.'

Phone evidence pointed convincingly towards Eric Wilson's involvement, but the why was less clear: Thompson in particular was desperate to get revenge following Cannon's involvement in a number of attacks the previous year.

In March 2008 Cannon and another Rattigan heavy named Neil 'The Highlander' Fitzgerald had gone to Thompson's family home armed with machetes and iron bars and broken several windows, demanding the gangster come out. After those inside managed to convince them Thompson was not there, they travelled to another house on Bride Street where they believed he might be and smashed that up too. Cannon then shot up the home of Thompson's innocent grandfather three months later.

Cannon's father Patrick would sadly tell the same inquest, 'I wasn't surprised to hear that Anthony had gotten shot. There's been too many threats. What I knew, there had to have been four or five. They're the ones I knew of. I didn't know where the threats were coming from. He wouldn't tell me. I always told him to be careful every day.'

However, a familiar face later emerged as the chief suspect. Three years previously, Mark 'The Guinea Pig' Desmond had been driving along the Old Bawn Road in Tallaght when a motorbike had pulled up alongside his car at traffic lights. The pillion passenger had opened fire, grazing Desmond in the arm and his passenger, Martin Kenny's older brother Kevin, in the backside. Desmond had driven his cousin to nearby Tallaght hospital, where he needed emergency surgery to remove the bullet. Desmond himself refused treatment and drove off. The shooting was later attributed to an attempt by Cannon to murder The Guinea Pig rather than pay him an outstanding drug debt.

In yet another illustration of how fickle gangland allegiances can be, Desmond enlisted Eric Wilson to help in killing Cannon – even though Wilson had murdered his own relative Martin Kenny just four years earlier.

In true Wilson style, Eric made it a family affair. His younger brother Keith was selected as the gunman in what is believed to have been his first gangland hit, a month after his twenty-first birthday. The driver of the motorbike was John Wilson.

Cannon was extremely cautious about his safety, but would have figured he was not at risk from Eric Wilson, simply because Wilson was thousands of miles away in Spain.

One investigator told the authors, 'The information was that the lure was from Eric to get Cannon into that area. Cannon would have trusted him. The arrangement was for the exchange of a substantial amount of drugs. That was the lure. Cannon was buying. Eric Wilson was supposed to be selling. Keith was the shooter and the bike had been readied for use by Keith and John not long beforehand. That was really the first time that Keith was seriously on the guards' radar.'

Herbert Kilcline, who had first met Keith during a visit to the Wilson family home when he was around seventeen, said he would never have expected him to follow in his older brothers' footsteps.

'He [Keith] was a bit of a big softie,' he said. 'He wouldn't have come across as a gangster type at all. I was out in the house in Cremona Road and Keith had some kind of injury that had happened to him in a chipper in Drimnagh. They were inquiring from me about making a claim, but it never came to anything. He was like a normal lad, there was no badness in him. You'd imagine he was the last person ever who'd become a gangster.'

Gardaí who had dealings with Keith said that was a common misconception about the youngest Wilson brother. One told the authors, 'That's the impression a lot of people got, but John took him under his wing. Eric had made his name as a hitman and the young fella thought it was easy money. He would have been trained up to a certain extent by Eric, but Eric was unstable, so John took him and groomed him to be something similar to what he was himself. He might strike you as a little clueless when he was younger; but, as he was growing up, he got a lot cuter. There was a more sinister side to him, something sly going on behind the eyes.'

There had never been any of the same doubts about John Wilson's criminal pedigree.

Though just thirty-two years old at that point, 'John John' had already racked up a string of serious convictions around his native Ballyfermot, where he was known as a violent thug and a gun for hire.

In 2001 gardaí believe he had been the driver of the motorbike used in the murder of Simon Doyle, a young drug dealer shot while getting out of his car outside his mother's home on Christmas Eve. The gunman, John Berney, would himself be shot dead some years later. Since then John Wilson had picked up a string of convictions for firearms possession, possession of an offensive weapon, burglary and road-traffic offences.

Like his brothers, John could be extremely reckless. The eleven-month sentence he received for possession of a sawn-off shotgun in April 2004 came after he sought and was given the gun for his own protection – and then test-fired it in his back garden.

John Wilson was also continually involved in feuds with other criminals, but always seemed to come out the other side. On 5 March 2009, four months before he drove his younger brother to carry out his first murder, Wilson had another narrow escape. Emerging from his home on Cloverhill Road in Ballyfermot, he checked under his van as usual and noticed a pipe bomb. The army was called out and spent several hours examining the device before taking it away without the need for a controlled explosion. The bomb was viable and certainly powerful enough to kill Wilson had it not been noticed, but had been fitted with a faulty detonator.

However, the most important role he would ultimately

play was in convincing his brothers and nephew to follow in his footsteps. Gardaí learned that Eric, Keith and later Luke all looked up hugely to John and idolized him. Garda intelligence compiled on Eric declared, 'It is thought Eric is attempting to follow the lead of his brother.'

One senior investigator familiar with the clan agrees. He told the authors, 'As far as I was concerned from watching that family, John groomed Eric, then Keith and then Luke.'

John Wilson was a thorn in the side of gardaí in west Dublin, who were regularly forced to call to his home to give him security advice because of the number of arguments he was in with other criminals. A tall, well-built man, he was not afraid to use his strength and could be aggressive with gardaí if stopped and questioned about his activities.

He would be called upon to use that heft in the months to come on behalf of another man who was about to become a pivotal figure in the lives of all the Wilsons – a veteran smuggler named Sean Hunt.

6. Cracks in the Facade

Maxine said she heard shots and then found
the girl lying up against the wall
— Fergus O'Hanlon

At 4 a.m. on 4 August 2009 two security guards, one from Pakistan and the other from India, were starting their shift at St James's hospital in Dublin's south inner city. The two men were just fifteen minutes into their shift when a green van pulled up in front of them. The stunned pair scrambled for cover as two masked figures inside fired a volley of shots in their direction. One of the security guards was hit in the leg, the other wounded in the arm.

Staff who had heard the shots raced outside before helping them inside to the emergency ward. By the time they underwent surgery, the gunmen had made their escape in the van, which turned out to be stolen and was later found burnt out on Aughavannagh Road in Crumlin.

Leading trade union SIPTU led the chorus of condemnation against the early-morning gun attack. It said, 'While it is unusual for our members to be shot in such circumstances, security work at hospitals has become very demanding and dangerous in recent years.'

Detectives were baffled by the attack and had no idea why anyone would shoot at two innocent security guards with absolutely no links to criminality. Weeks later they received intelligence that the gunmen had targeted the hospital after being ejected for abusing staff and patients on previous occasions. The following month gardaí identified Alan Wilson, Fergus O'Hanlon and his brother Patrick, who had a lengthy criminal record, as potential suspects.

Around the same time, Patrick O'Hanlon was pinpointed as someone who might have knowledge of the Rostas disappearance. Garda suspicion also coincided with another public appeal for information on the missing teenager – this time it was directed towards the two anonymous callers from June and September 2008.

In his address, Detective Superintendent O'Gara said, 'Somebody knows what happened to Marioara and I'm appealing directly to those people who contacted gardaí last June and September to do so again. It's not too late for them to get in touch again. They can contact the gardaí or Crimestoppers. These people could have vital clues on what happened to Marioara, who has not been seen for eighteen months. We have a lot of missing people in Ireland and the trauma for the family, who have now gone home to Romania, is great.'

By now detectives had drawn up a detailed list of people who were close to Alan Wilson and Fergus O'Hanlon. From the previous arrests, it was clear Wilson's mother and sister had nothing to add, so gardaí turned back to O'Hanlon. He had remained quiet despite indicating the previous year that he would do all he could to help find the missing girl. At the same time gardaí learned that both O'Hanlon and his partner, Alan's sister Maxine, were drinking heavily and slipping into frequent bouts of depression. Others identified as possible candidates to assist the garda investigation were Patrick O'Hanlon and Herbert Kilcline.

At 7.55 a.m. on 6 October 2009 Patrick O'Hanlon was arrested by Detective Sergeant Michael O'Brien over the hospital shooting and taken to Kilmainham garda station. Detectives from Pearse Street station informed their colleagues they had 'reasonable grounds' to request the continued detention of O'Hanlon on suspicion of withholding information over the abduction of Marioara Rostas and this was granted.

The suspect was interviewed ten further times about the disappearance but did not provide any answers before he was released without charge at 11.57 p.m. on 8 October. Undeterred, investigators resolved to continue to focus on Fergus O'Hanlon's circle.

Herbert Kilcline was arrested and pulled in for questioning. Kilcline said, 'At the time, I was living in fear of Alan because I knew just how dangerous he was but I still wanted to do my bit to keep the pressure on Fergus. Fergus was Alan's sidekick and because of the threat posed by Alan's cousins Eric, John and Keith, I knew I was putting my life on the line. I suffer from a mild form of obsessive compulsive disorder and finding that poor girl became an obsession for me despite the huge risks.

'I was told that there was a bigger chance I could be killed than find the girl but I had to keep going. Fergus was obviously thinking about his own family time and there was the obvious conclusion that he may have sided with Alan. I had no specific knowledge of the events surrounding Marioara's disappearance and from that moment on I agreed to work with the gardaí in trying to get Fergus to come forward. From that day on, I would remain in contact with Detective Sergeant Doyle and would provide him with whatever information I could.'

Throughout the course of his six recorded interviews with detectives, Kilcline also informed gardaí that Maxine had information on the case and had been 'drinking heavily'. He said that on one occasion she told him that she could 'see the teenager's face when she went to sleep and screamed when she saw her face on *Crimecall*'.

In another series of exchanges with gardaí, Kilcline revealed various threats Alan Wilson had made to him over the years: 'He always wanted his own way and when I was trying to help him with forms for housing he would often lose patience. He was very poor at communicating with people. I've also no doubt that he was behind attacks on my car so I could pay him extortion to get the attacks to stop.'

Kilcline outlined how another female associate of O'Hanlon's also had information on the missing girl. He recalled, 'She was a law-abiding citizen who was a mother and was just trying to do the right thing. She just told the gardaí what Maxine had told her.' In her statement to gardaí, the woman claimed she had been watching *Crimecall* in April 2008 with Fergus and his partner Maxine when Marioara's image was shown.

As the teenager's photo filled the screen, O'Hanlon got up, saying he needed to 'take a phone call' outside. When she went looking for him later, she found him 'vomiting his guts up'. At the same time, Maxine had also been visibly upset at the image.

The woman informed gardaí that Maxine said Alan had come back to the house with a Romanian girl before going upstairs. She said Maxine had claimed that she and Fergus had found the girl lying dead wearing only her underwear. In her statement, she said, 'Maxine said Alan brought this girl home and asked to mind her and that one day, Alan and the girl came in from being out and Alan said they were going upstairs. Maxine said she heard shots and then found the girl lying up against the wall, that the girl was shot. Maxine was crying when she was telling me. She told me Alan thought the girl was the devil.

'I asked Maxine, "What did you do?' and she said, "I just went over and was rubbing her hair."' Also interviewed during that period was a young associate of Fergus O'Hanlon's. Gardaí knew the young man had no involvement in crime but he was interviewed because he had been seen in Wilson's car and also in the hope that Maxine might have shared information with him. He was questioned five times before he was released without charge on 9 October having said 'little of consequence'.

A deeply rattled Alan Wilson soon demanded a meeting with his sister's partner and Kilcline. 'He was like a madman pacing up and down the room demanding to know every specific question that was asked by the gardaí,' the solicitor recalled. 'I was afraid of him then and, at the time, I believed I had convinced him that I wasn't cooperating with the gardaí. It was only afterwards that I learnt that he said to Fergus that he thought both Dinah [O'Hanlon's sister] and I were working for the gardaí. He was paranoid and clever but I remember we somehow managed to convince him that if I was working with the guards I would have been in protective custody.'

On 27 November 2009 Wilson, his sister Maxine and O'Hanlon were at Dublin District Court to hear that charges over the burglary in Rathgar, in which the valuable stamps had been stolen, were being dropped because the victims had refused to make a statement or give evidence.

At the beginning of 2010 those who knew Fergus O'Hanlon had no doubt he was close to a nervous breakdown. He was increasingly turning to drink and struggling to cope with his knowledge of the circumstances surrounding the disappearance of Marioara Rostas.

O'Hanlon's behaviour was also made known to gardaí

through Kilcline as they prepared to launch a fresh public appeal for information on the second anniversary of her disappearance that January. 'We were once again appealing to the two anonymous callers to come forward,' ex-Detective Superintendent O'Gara told the authors. 'But the media strategy was another way for us to remind the perpetrator, along with those close to him and especially Fergus O'Hanlon, that our efforts were still ongoing and we would never give up. Our objective all along was to find her for her family.'

The missing girl's picture, taken from her identity card, was once again in the headlines.

Although there were no new calls, the investigation received a boost when Fergus O'Hanlon asked to meet gardaí on 21 February 2010. O'Hanlon refused to elaborate why over the phone and was then secretly brought to Pearse Street station. Once there, following a brief conversation about the teenager, he asked Detective Sergeant John Doyle and Detective Garda Sara Berry to drive with him to Newry, Co. Down.

An hour later O'Hanlon brought the officers to fields on the outskirts of the border town. He informed them this was the general area where Marioara was buried, before getting back into the car. However, O'Hanlon had actually led them to an area where he believed the criminals Alan Napper and David Lindsay had been buried.

Sitting in the vehicle, O'Hanlon became agitated and started talking about the dangers to his family before refusing to pinpoint the exact location of Marioara's body. In a statement to gardaí, he explained, 'I wanted to assist John Doyle to recover the body of the Romanian girl and I went down and when we got moving in the car I lost my nerve. I lost my nerve. I wanted to bring them to the spot. I thought of my family, my brothers and sisters and the repercussions of me doing it. And if the body was recovered, what would happen? Members of my family would have been killed.' Although the trip was unsuccessful, it proved to gardaí that O'Hanlon was their best chance of recovering the missing teenager's remains. O'Hanlon's information had been passed to the PSNI on 23 February during a meeting between them and SIO Cryan and Detective Sergeant Doyle. Although the PSNI carried out an assessment of the area, there was no dig.

As Alan Wilson continued to enjoy his freedom, he also emerged as a suspect in a violent aggravated burglary at a property in Templeogue, south Dublin. On the morning of 3 February 2010 James Mountaine was on the phone and his wife Sally was preparing to go to Mass when the doorbell rang. Answering the door, Mrs Mountaine was confronted by four masked men before she was knocked to the ground and repeatedly kicked. Her husband dropped the phone he was holding and rushed to intervene, but he too was punched, kicked and pushed to the ground, before being told he would be 'put in a wheelchair' if he didn't cooperate. The intruders were unaware that Mr Mountaine's phone call had not ended. Hearing the screams on the other end of the line, his friend realized the couple had been attacked and immediately hung up and rang gardaí.

In the meantime, the gang – armed with hammers and hatchets – threatened to kill the couple if they did not hand over cash that they believed Mr Mountaine had brought home from the golf club where he worked. During the raid on the property, which lasted between ten and fifteen minutes, the gang managed to steal US $4,000 in cash and two necklaces worth €900. As the friend waited for gardaí to arrive, he went to the house and interrupted the burglary by ringing the doorbell.

The gang then fled in different directions, leaving their victims screaming on the floor. One of the intruders, Michael Delaney, was caught by Garda Emma Jane Redmond a short distance away and would later receive an eighteen-year sentence, with the last six suspended, on 11 March 2011, after he pleaded guilty to false imprisonment and aggravated burglary.

Another of Wilson's friends, Paddy Ryan, a drug addict from the south inner city, later received a five-year sentence for his role in the raid. In a victim impact statement presented to Dublin Circuit Criminal Court, Mrs Mountaine said, 'I too feel lucky to be alive. I felt our family home had been violated. I was bound, threatened with being set on fire and had hair pulled out.'

Before sentencing Delaney, Judge Tony Hunt (who would go on to officiate at the Special Criminal Court during the Kinahan and Hutch feud) said the couple had suffered a terrifying experience meted out by an organized gang of 'depraved barbarians'.

Six days after the raid on the Mountaines' home, Alan Wilson was arrested after he was identified as a potential suspect but later released without charge. A file was sent to the Director of Public Prosecutions (DPP). Over the course of the next few months, Wilson kept a low profile, rarely leaving his mother's home as he remained at the centre of three major garda investigations.

While Alan Wilson was desperately trying to stay out of garda hands, the sands of Irish gangland were shifting yet again.

Eamon Dunne had by now ordered or committed the murders of at least seventeen people, including the hapless Christy Gilroy, when his own luck ran out on 23 April 2010. Attending the birthday party of a taxi-driver pal, Dunne was cornered by a hitman in the Fassaugh House pub in Cabra. Dunne's desperate attempts to hide behind a lounge boy out collecting glasses could not save him and he was assassinated where he sat.

His murder was quickly followed by the Operation Shovel raids on the Kinahan cartel in Spain in May 2010. This left a power vacuum at the top of Dublin's criminal scene but no dominant figure to seize power; it also meant the myriad up-and-coming criminals competing to gain control of the chaos would be vulnerable to extortion.

Ireland's paramilitaries had long had a symbiotic relation-ship with the country's criminal fraternity. The largest and strongest organization, the Provisional IRA, had regularly 'taxed' Dublin's criminals in order to raise funds for their campaign in the North. However, following the Good Friday Agreement in April 1998, the Provos' control waned. A number of splinter groups emerged, the largest of which was the so-called Real IRA. Following the Omagh bombing in August 1998, the dissident organization was largely put out of action by determined law enforcement on both sides of the border. But it did not disappear altogether and began to rebuild quietly and steadily.

One of the Real IRA's biggest problems was that it lacked the Provisionals' money-making apparatus to fund the pur-chase of weapons and explosives, but one man was determined to change that. Alan Ryan was just eighteen when a garda raid on his home in September 1998 uncovered a revolver and five bullets. He was on bail for that offence when he was caught again at a Real IRA training camp in Stamullen, Co. Meath, in October the following year.

Ryan, who came from a staunchly republican family in Donaghmede on Dublin's northside, was given a total of seven years for both offences. Upon his release from jail,

Ryan decided to dedicate himself to extortion. His first targets were busy pubs across north and west Dublin. Ryan gained control of a network of doormen, an area traditionally run by the IRA, and owners were approached and told they were taking on new door staff. If they resisted, they and their employees were attacked and threatened and elaborate hoax bombs were placed in the toilets of their premises.

Other extortion attempts by Ryan were no less subtle. He and his cronies would approach business people at their offices and identify themselves as members of the Real IRA. They would ask for up to 25 per cent of the firm's profits in return for 'protection'. If this was refused, Ryan would begin making pointed remarks about the owner's family and where his children attended school. Gardaí learned of eight such incidents across the city, but none of those targeted felt brave enough to make the statement of complaint required to begin an investigation. The dissident-controlled bouncers were also instructed to begin charging drug dealers for the right to operate in certain nightspots. Those who could not or would not pay would find themselves refused entry.

Slowly but surely, criminals across the city began to give in to Alan Ryan's demands. All would have been aware of the fate of Martin 'The General' Cahill, the last major gangster to defy the IRA back in the 1990s. Ryan represented a new, flashy breed of paramilitary, far from the shadowy days of the IRA of old. He and his gang regularly worked out in gyms and liked to wear tight muscle-top T-shirts.

They always appeared perfectly groomed and tanned and in one raid on a dissident stronghold, gardaí found melatonin tablets – illegal tanning pills, which give a long-lasting orange skin tone. Ryan himself had been nicknamed 'The Model' and had a string of female conquests on the go at any one time. None of this impressed the strongest of Dublin's crime figures though, and he and his cohorts had to endure taunts that they 'hadn't the balls' to go up against the biggest drug dealers themselves.

The murder of Eamon Dunne and the Operation Shovel raids changed all that.

By summer 2010 Ryan had collected a large group of followers and built up a list of targets. Several mid-ranking criminals across Dublin were visited and told to pay up or they would be executed. Most did, but some refused. One of those was Sean Hunt.

Hunt was at that point a fifty-year-old father of six who was ostensibly such a successful street trader that he drove a Lexus. His real business, however, was smuggling. Since the late 1980s Hunt had been bringing cigarettes, alcohol and fireworks into the country, which were sold out of black bags on the streets of his native Ballyfermot and elsewhere. This meant he was of lower priority to gardaí than drug dealers, whose trade tends to be more chaotic and violent and has more immediate consequences. But Hunt was still earning a considerable amount of money from his illicit activities.

He had first come to serious garda attention on 15 August 1990 after customs officers in Belfast intercepted and impounded a large consignment of fireworks destined for a Sean Hunt in Dublin. Garda raids on the family home on Ramillies Road in Ballyfermot followed on 6 November 1991 and 23 October 1992, during which quantities of fireworks were seized, though no charges were brought. Hunt's bootlegging talents had not gone unnoticed by paramilitaries and he was soon assisting Provo associates in Ballyfermot with their own smuggling activities, as well as providing a money-laundering service for them.

Hunt had been arrested and questioned over the Ballyfermot murders of two men who had come into conflict with his IRA pals – drug courier Gerry Connolly in August 1995 and petty thief and drug addict Eric Shortall the following November. Connolly was suspected of being a garda informant, while Shortall had been accused of burgling a property belonging to republicans. Hunt was also one of the few criminals to take on and beat the Criminal Assets Bureau (CAB) in court after a marathon five-year legal battle. The CAB had presented him with an IR£1.77 million tax demand, telling the High Court that IR£3 million had passed through the accounts of Hunt and his wife Rosaleen between 1988 and 1998.

Hunt finally won the case in the Supreme Court on a technicality in July 2004, leaving the CAB with a €3 million legal bill instead. Thus, when Alan Ryan came with a cash demand of his own, Hunt was not in a mood to back down.

'The Smuggler' – as he was referred to in the media – was now dividing his time between Dublin and Spain, from where he was still sending back millions of cigarettes a year to be sold out of black bin bags on the Irish capital's streets. He had seven separate properties in the south-eastern region of Murcia and was a regular visitor to the area around Málaga, where he had rented a warehouse in Guadalhorce, just outside the city.

The warehouse was a staging post for the smuggling back to Ireland of tobacco that had ostensibly been imported for sale in Spain. There it was hidden inside cargos of furniture and driven up through France and across via ferry to Rosslare or through the UK to Holyhead and on to Ireland.

On 7 May 2006 Spanish police, who had been watching the gang, moved in on the warehouse and arrested two men in the process of loading a pair of lorries. Almost 500,000 packs of cigarettes – worth €1 million in Spain and at least three times that on the streets in Ireland – were impounded.

Hunt was not there, but was arrested in a follow-up search in the small town of Rojales in Alicante.

Hunt was subsequently sentenced to twenty-two months suspended for his role in the smuggling operation. Ironically, Spanish authorities boasting about their success had erroneously identified him as a leading member of the Real IRA – in whose name Alan Ryan was attempting to extort him.

By 2009 Ryan felt emboldened to act because Hunt had distanced himself considerably from his old Provo pals and was now aligned with local criminals in Ballyfermot instead, particularly Mark 'The Guinea Pig' Desmond. Though not a dealer himself, gardaí believe Hunt was allowing Desmond to import heroin amid his stashes of illicit tobacco, with Desmond then selling it on the streets.

Threats flowed back and forth between the two sides, with Ryan warning Hunt that his oldest son Sean Jnr, who ran the family pigeon-feed business, the Corn Store, with outlets in Ballyfermot and Finglas, would be harmed if he did not pay up. But Hunt had not just been working on his suntan out in Spain following his release from sentence: he had been introduced to Eric Wilson by mutual associates out on the Costa del Sol – and recognized Wilson's potential to ward off Ryan. Hunt had also known John Wilson since the mid-1990s and was aware that he was available as muscle for hire. Ryan and some of the dissidents were known to congregate in a particular pub on Capel Street, so Hunt decided to send 'John John' to deliver a message of his own.

Gardaí later became aware of the incident via informants. One senior investigator told the authors, 'There was a row and John Wilson was well able to take care of himself, he was a well-built fella and well able to handle himself. He upended the table over them and knocked them on their arse in the pub. The Ryans were leaning on Hunt, looking for money to allow his activities to continue. This was his answer. I don't know if Wilson realized who he was dealing with. I'm not sure he would have taken them on the way he did if he had realized what he was getting involved with.'

If that was the case, John Wilson would soon find out. But first, his younger brother Eric was about to get himself taken out of circulation through an act of incredible stupidity.

7. Luck Runs Out

You wait there. I'll be back in a minute
— Eric Wilson

Eric Wilson was living the good life in southern Spain by the summer of 2010 when garda intelligence had him involved in the disappearance of a criminal associate from Raheny on Dublin's northside by the name of Alan Campbell. Detectives received information that Campbell had been murdered and dumped in a separate lime-lined, shallow grave in Spain, just like Christy Gilroy. But information beyond that on exactly what transpired and why was scant. The authorities in Dublin had little to offer their Spanish counterparts to aid in a search for Campbell and to this day it remains just another missing-persons case, which has never been solved and likely never will.

Eric Wilson was a familiar sight to his few neighbours near the Hacienda Sambargo as he arrived and left on his powerful black Yamaha R1 motorbike. He received a steady stream of visitors to the property, including his younger brother Keith, who stayed with him for long periods at a time. However, there was not much in the way of nightlife in the nearby village of Coín, so Eric had taken to spending his nights out in livelier, touristy areas, a forty-minute drive away.

One place he frequented was The Lounge in Mijas Costa, an urban sprawl along the coast populated mainly by expatriate northern Europeans. The pub was a simple square room with seating outside and staff there recalled Wilson, known as 'Eric' or 'Lucky', as a mainly pleasant individual. Occasionally though, flashes of the character that lay beneath emerged.

On 31 January 2010 the pub was showing the Premier League clash between Arsenal and Manchester United, with United desperate to close the gap on leaders Chelsea. At one stage Wilson inadvertently stood in front of the TV behind the bar, prompting someone to call him a 'thick Paddy'. Wilson erupted in fury, warned the man he was going to shoot him and stormed out. Another drinker went after him and calmed him down, and Wilson returned, apologizing for his behaviour.

But he was not the only customer who considered himself a hard man.

'Tall Dan' Smith was another regular with a double life. Smith had been on the run for almost three years from his native Essex, where he was wanted for attempted murder. When he was only twenty-two he had called to the home of local millionaire businessman Doug Turner late at night along with two pals, Jason Steele and Wayne Perrey. Turner's son John had beaten up Steele in a pub the previous day and the trio were looking for revenge. When Doug Turner told them to clear off, Smith produced a double-barrelled shotgun and opened fire, blowing off three of Turner's fingers and part of his hand and wounding him in the stomach.

Steele and Perrey were caught and jailed but their trial heard that Smith had fled to Spain. Essex Police issued a European arrest warrant for him, but with bigger fish to fry, they left it to their Spanish counterparts to bring him in and Smith continued life unmolested in the sun.

The warm climate and constant tourism on the Costa del Sol means bars do a roaring trade during the summer months.

At around 8 p.m. on Saturday 5 June 2010, Smith and Wilson were both among customers drinking at The Lounge when a girl named Georgina Hollywood complained that Wilson was groping her leg. At 6 foot 5 inches, Smith towered over Wilson and the pair quickly squared up and began pushing and shoving. According to witnesses, Smith told him, 'Why don't you just get out of here? Nobody wants you here.'

Bar owner Steve Reynolds tried to make peace between them, but an enraged Wilson would not be mollified. He pointed his finger at Smith and declared, 'You wait there. I'll be back in a minute', before storming out. This time, nobody followed to try to calm him down.

Smith and the others moved outside and continued their evening drinking until about 10 p.m., when a motorbike could be heard making its way up the winding residential road on which the bar sits. The bike cruised by slowly and Smith told the others to get inside; there was about to be trouble. The motorcyclist parked in a laneway beside the bar and re-emerged. He shouted something at Smith, which was muffled by the helmet he was wearing although the visor was up. Again Smith told the others to get inside, but remained in his seat as the other man approached.

When the motorcyclist produced a pistol, Smith got up and tried to run. The gunman fired at him once from around twelve metres away, knocking Smith back into his chair. The Englishman tried to get up again, but another bullet sent him to the ground. By now, the killer was standing over him and shooting at will. One round hit Smith in the jaw, knocking out his teeth, while others were pumped into his head and upper body. At one point, the assassin bent and deliberately put a bullet through each testicle. A post-mortem showed the victim had been blasted a total of eight times.

His task complete, the biker strode back to his vehicle, got on and roared away. Steve Reynolds ran outside and attempted to staunch the blood from Smith's wounds as someone called an ambulance. By the time members of the paramilitary Guardia Civil arrived, the pandemonium was such that one of them had to blow loudly on his whistle to get Smith's female companions to move away from his body.

When things calmed down, they began to interview witnesses. The Lounge owner Steve Reynolds told them that an Irishman he knew as Eric, who also went by the nickname 'Lucky', had arrived at the bar at around 8 p.m. Reynolds said he had first met Eric around six or seven months previously, when Smith introduced him to the Irishman along with another man he identified as Eric's brother. He was told that the siblings lived on a farm in Coín along with some horses.

Reynolds said he was into motorbikes himself, and recognized Eric's vehicle as a Yamaha R1. He said that earlier that evening, before the shooting, Eric had come inside and asked him for his backpack, which he often stored behind the bar for safekeeping. Reynolds said the Irishman appeared to be 'very angry'. The next thing he knew was that at around 10 p.m. several customers, who had been on the terrace, rushed inside. He heard several shots, went outside and found Smith lying on the ground with multiple wounds to his head. One of the other customers told him that Smith had been shot by the man he knew as Eric or 'Lucky'.

From the information given, police tracked down the suspect to the Hacienda Sambargo near Coín and the estate was put under discreet surveillance to establish who was living there. The interviewing of witnesses went on long into the night and started afresh the next morning.

At 11.15 p.m. on 6 June, the day after the murder, Spanish police got hold of a man named Antonio Cárdenas Pabon, who told them his job was to take care of the horses at the

Hacienda Sambargo. He confirmed that two Irishmen lived there and that they went about on a powerful black Yamaha R1 motorbike.

At 9.25 the following morning, officers took a statement from the owner of the property, Miguel Rios Cuevas. He said he had rented it to an Irishman who had shown him a passport in the name of Stephen Wall and who resided there with his brother Keith. Rios Cuevas said the two brothers had horses and used a black motorbike.

Another witness to be interviewed that day was a man named Kenneth Ruine. He told police that he had not witnessed the shooting, but had arrived in the aftermath. Ruine said one of those who had seen what happened told him that 'Lucky' had carried it out. He said the man told him 'Lucky' had previously lived in the apartment he was now renting on Calle Jacaranda in the Riviera del Sol estate in Mijas Costa, a short drive from the bar. Checks by police showed the property had formerly been rented to an Irishman who had presented a passport in the name of Stephen Callery.

Having pinpointed the three separate identities, Spanish police got on to gardaí and learned that 'Callery' could be an alias of Eric Wilson. They were given a photograph of Wilson to identify him. At 2 p.m. on 7 June 2010 Karen Wetherell identified the remains of her son Dan Smith at the morgue in Málaga.

Four hours later bar owner Steve Reynolds said he recognized the photo given to Spanish authorities by gardaí as the Eric or 'Lucky' he knew as a customer. The Guardia Civil gathered all the evidence they had collected and went to a judge to obtain a search warrant for the Hacienda Sambargo.

While all this was happening, surveillance on the farm continued. At 7 p.m., an hour after Steve Reynolds had been shown Eric Wilson's photo, two officers watched as a grey

Opel Omega with a Spanish registration emerged out of the gates and onto the main road. The vehicle was now on a public highway, so they drew their weapons, moved in and stopped it. There were two men in the front and a little girl in the back. The driver presented a photocopy of an Irish passport in the name of Anthony Brennan and identified the child as his daughter.

His passenger handed over a genuine Irish passport issued to a Gerard Memery. However, when the Spanish cops checked the gardaí-issued photo of Eric Wilson they could see that he was the man in the passenger seat. Wilson would later claim he had handed over the bogus ID because police had told him they were investigating a bank robbery. Once he realized the game was up, though, he began to resist violently, so that cops had to subdue and cuff him.

He was searched. Along with the Gerard Memery passport he was carrying €325.25 in cash, a pair of Prada sunglasses and a grey Nokia mobile. Wilson was taken into custody and read his rights, but refused to sign a document confirming he understood them.

Spanish law requires serious police probes to be overseen by an investigating magistrate and the judge arrived at the Hacienda Sambargo at 8.45 p.m. Given the brutal nature of Smith's murder, no chances were being taken. Several members of the Guardia Civil bomb squad, known by the acronym GEDEX, were brought out to assist, along with sniffer dogs. But what they found inside stunned even experienced members of the force.

In a locker beside Eric Wilson's bed were two electric detonators and four cylinders containing explosive material. Outside, in a shed on some shelving, officers found two half-kilo slabs of plastic explosives wrapped in waxed paper, nine magazines containing 180 rounds of 7.9 mm × 32 mm

Kalashnikov ammunition and three grenades. The Guardia Civil report noted that two of these were the standard M75 'pineapple' type, while the third was an M79 anti-tank device, at that time a favourite weapon of Islamic militants to attack US military Humvees in Iraq.

The pineapple grenades were packed with over three thousand 3 mm ball bearings and had a kill radius of up to eighteen metres. Meanwhile, the shrapnel from a more powerful, armour-piercing M79 will kill anyone inside two metres of its detonation and seriously wound anyone within twenty metres. All of the explosive material had originated in the former Yugoslavia. The GEDEX report subsequently declared, 'Each and every item seized was in perfect condition and ready for use at any moment.'

There were also two cylindrical smoke bombs of Czech origin and two English-language manuals, one on bullets and the other on explosives and demolition. Another passport for a Stephen Wall but bearing Eric Wilson's photo was found, plus an international driver's licence in the same name. There was a rental contract for the property in the name of Stephen Wall containing the number of what was evidently yet another false passport.

Police further recovered Nike trainers, Zara jeans, a green Crosshatch jacket and a blue Dolce & Gabbana cotton T-shirt, which they took away for forensic examination. Outside was a black Yamaha R1 and grey Ti-Tech helmet. The motorbike and the T-shirt both tested positive for gunpowder residue, but the lateness of the hour meant no comprehensive external searches could be carried out, so the Guardia Civil obtained another search warrant for the following day. This one covered the entire adjoining lands of the property and more police were brought in to assist.

At 12.35 the following afternoon Wilson was returned to

the hacienda in handcuffs to watch the warrant being executed. Not much more was uncovered, except two photographs of Eric Wilson posing with firearms, more documents on the use of plastic explosives, a variety of different notes and a receipt from a supermarket. It was time-stamped at 9.21 p.m. on the night of the murder, indicating that Wilson might have stopped off at the store in the Pino Golf estate in Elviria, about halfway between the murder scene and Marbella, around forty minutes before Dan Smith was shot to death.

The search of the hacienda was concluded at 2.40 p.m. and Wilson was taken away again for questioning, which began at 10.00 the next morning. Meanwhile, several more witnesses were shown the photograph from gardaí, one of whom was a woman who had seen the row between Wilson and Smith over the girl. However, none could actually identify the helmeted man who had shot Smith, except one: at 4.30 p.m. on 9 June, Protected Witness 1/2003/10 said he recognized the shooter as Eric 'Lucky' Wilson. Other inquiries via the British police liaison office in Madrid found that the black Yamaha R1 discovered at Hacienda Sambargo had originally been registered in the UK with the number plate NK65 LOF. It had been certified as the property of a man there named Paul Lildea in October 2001, but when contacted, he told authorities he no longer owned it. Further inquiries revealed it had also been registered in Spain to another man named Victor Conejo Torres, but had not been reported stolen.

Eric Wilson spent a number of days in police custody where he point-blank denied anything to do with the shooting and claimed the explosives were not his either. He gave the same performance when he declared before an investigating judge in nearby Fuengirola a few days later still clad in shorts, T-shirt and flip-flops.

Unlike under Irish law, police in Spain do not have to bring enough evidence for a charge in order for a suspect to be remanded in custody. Instead, he or she will appear behind closed doors before a magistrate who will ask a series of questions. Depending on the answers given, the suspect will either be freed or sent to prison while officially placed under investigation for certain offences, allowing police to further build a case against him. In essence, the suspect has to talk his way out of custody.

Whatever answers Eric Wilson gave, they did not cut the mustard.

After four hours of interrogation, he was remanded in custody and placed under official investigation for murder and illegal arms possession. The hitman had never had his picture in the papers before and tried his best to avoid giving the press waiting outside a shot, bending over and twisting his head away from the cameras as he was led inside. However, photographers can be equally inventive with their angles, and pictures of Eric Wilson's grimacing face caused shock when they appeared across the front pages of Irish newspapers the following day.

Sean Hunt was said to be stunned at what he saw as Wilson's 'highly stupid' behaviour, which could not have come at a worse time: back in Dublin, things were getting even more strained between himself and the Real IRA, not helped by the bar-room brawl instigated by John Wilson. Smarting from the humiliation, Alan Ryan decided to up the ante.

At the time, one of the main employees in the northside branch of Hunt's Corn Store pigeon-feed business was a man named Collie Owens. Though he was from a respectable family and had no criminal convictions himself, Owens was a known associate of Hunt, Eamon Dunne, Alan Wilson and Mark 'The Guinea Pig' Desmond, for whom gardaí believe Owens acted as a courier.

The thirty-four-year-old father of one would not have had any reason to believe his life was in danger. But shortly after midday on 9 July 2010 a man dressed all in black and wearing a ski mask walked into the outlet in the Grove Industrial Estate in Finglas. A customer named Tommy Kane was in the shop at the time and Owens had gone out the back to make a cup of tea for them both. Mr Kane would subsequently tell the inquest into Collie Owens's death, 'He walked past me and in behind the counter and, as he passed, he took a handgun, black in colour, from his left pocket. This guy went into the room where Collie was. Then I heard four bangs which I knew were shots. I panicked and ran out the front door and turned left toward the end of the factory.'

As he ran outside, Mr Kane saw a man in a silver car parked outside, facing toward the exit 'ready to go'. He turned and watched the gunman walk out of the Corn Store, get into the car and speed off. Two men who worked nearby then went into the shop to see what had happened.

'The chaps came out and one said, "They blew his head off,"' Mr Kane said. A post-mortem later revealed that Owens had been shot six times in the head, neck and heart and would have died instantly.

Within minutes of the alarm being raised, garda patrol cars began to pour into the area and the getaway driver panicked as they sped along Tolka Valley Road, crashing into a number of other vehicles. The 08-reg Audi A4 was eventually abandoned on Carrigallen Road in Finglas. The murder weapon was not recovered, but ballistic evidence would later link it to the IRA shooting of a man named Jason Egan the previous October.

However, neither Hunt, Wilson nor The Guinea Pig needed forensics to figure this one out. If they were to keep face in the macho world of gangland, they would have to respond in kind. The Real IRA had taken an easy option by going for Owens, who would not have had any reason to consider himself a target. The Ballyfermot mob decided to go for the jugular instead.

Though John Wilson had confronted Ryan and his cronies in a pub on Capel Street, their favourite hangout was The Players' Lounge, a pub on Dublin's Fairview Strand. The pub was owned and run by John Stokes, the father of Celtic and Ireland striker Anthony Stokes. John Stokes was himself a diehard republican. (Two years later he was threatened with objections to the renewal of his pub licence after he hung a 40-foot-long banner as a publicity stunt outside his pub during Queen Elizabeth's visit to Dublin, announcing that she was barred from entering.) Alan Ryan was personally directing the majority of extortion attempts against the criminals, and Hunt and his cohorts felt that taking him out would solve most of their problems. John Wilson was selected for the job.

Shortly after midnight on 25 July 2010 quite a few drinkers still congregated in and around The Players' Lounge. It had been a warm summer's day and Tipperary had earlier narrowly beaten Galway in the All-Ireland hurling quarter-final just up the road in Croke Park. As always, a doorman was posted outside the pub to screen any undesirables attempting to make their way in. Four or five customers were standing nearby, smoking and chatting.

None of them noticed the man wearing a balaclava and with a pistol in each hand until he was almost directly across the road and running towards them. The gunman opened fire, Wild West-style, with both weapons. Bouncer Wayne Barrett was hit in the head and fell to the ground but the bullets continued to fly. Customer Austin Purcell was hit six times in the legs and chest and collapsed, while his friend

Brian Masterson was also hit in the back. None of the trio were involved in the feud and they were entirely innocent bystanders. Both Barrett and Purcell were rushed to hospital in critical condition, while Masterson miraculously suffered only minor injuries and was later released.

A couple of days later, he told RTÉ's *Liveline* how he had been sure he was going to die: 'I heard a loud pop and Ozzie [Austin Purcell] went down. Then I felt the pain hit me and I was on the deck as well.

'I remember just being outside with Ozzie, watching the screens showing the replays of the games, and then I heard the loud pop behind me. It was surreal . . . it's like a burning pain shooting through you. I couldn't move. I was lying there and I just realized we had been shot.

'I was screaming at Ozzie. I could only see his feet and I didn't know how he was. Then I heard him screaming. At least I knew he was alive then. I heard more popping but I didn't know anything about the other lad [Wayne Barrett] being hit. I was waiting to hear the footsteps and be finished off.'

Meanwhile, John Wilson had fled around the corner onto Philipsburgh Avenue, where his getaway driver was waiting for him in a gold-coloured Volkswagen Golf fitted with false plates. From there, they drove into the south city centre and burnt it out at Verschoyle Court, an apartment complex off Mount Street.

As an attack, it was a complete and utter failure. Sean Hunt was enraged. The incident marked the end of his dealings with John Wilson. One source who would have known the Wilson clan well said John was 'not a hitter'.

The source, who asked not to be identified, told the authors, 'He hadn't got the nerve. I could never understand how some of them could sit down and take a load of coke and then go off and do something. If you're stoned, your wits are not fully about you. John didn't take as much as the others, but he'd have to do a line or two. Eric couldn't do anything without it. Keith was the same.'

Herbert Kilcline agreed. 'I was told that John hadn't it in him to be a killer,' he said. 'If he was sent to kill people, he'd shoot them in the legs. He was a little bit more mature than the other two, Eric and Keith, who were cokeheads. I think John would have seen what he was doing as a way to support his wife and kids and his mother.'

The attempt to take out Alan Ryan had failed, but Sean Hunt was still determined to issue retribution for Collie Owens's murder and Alan Wilson and Mark 'The Guinea Pig' Desmond agreed. Gardaí received word that the killing 'would not be let go'. Owens was so 'tight' to Hunt, sources said, that his murder 'could not be allowed to stand'.

Their informants were right.

8. Strike Back

I just seen a hand on a gun in the corner of my eye
— Sarah Treacy

By the beginning of August 2010 Sean Hunt, The Guinea Pig and the Wilsons had ascertained who had carried out the shooting of Collie Owens.

Daniel Gaynor was a nasty individual with a string of drug, firearms and intimidation-related convictions who was already the chief suspect in three murders. Gaynor did not have any political leanings himself, but was used by republicans as a gun for hire in cases where they wanted to have deniability if it all went wrong.

One such instance was the shooting of innocent postman Robert Delaney, who was blasted with a shotgun and left in a vegetative state after intervening in a pub row involving an IRA figure. The Ballyfermot mob was already facing retaliation from the dissidents over the attempt at The Players' Lounge. But they could kill a lone wolf like Gaynor without any serious consequences. The only problem was, who to do it?

Ordinarily, Hunt and the others would have been able to call on Eric Wilson to fly home from Spain and carry it out, but he was now on remand for the murder of Dan Smith. Alan Wilson was available, but for some reason Hunt did not engage him. Following his successful elimination of Anthony Cannon, Keith Wilson was the obvious other choice.

No longer a 'softie', Keith was now twenty-two years old

and already had nine convictions to his name for driving offences, damaging property, and threatening and abusive behaviour. His transformation into a serious criminal was complete and it was he who was tasked with the hit on Gaynor.

The target was placed under surveillance in the estate in Finglas where he lived. Gaynor, who was then still just twenty-five years old, was an extremely violent man and would have to be approached with caution.

His first conviction, at eighteen, was for firing a shotgun into the home of a teenager who owed him €100 because Gaynor wanted the money to buy his girlfriend a Valentine's Day present. Five years later, on 12 June 2009, he followed his ex-girlfriend back to the property they used to share. The woman had been out in a city-centre nightclub and was going back to her home with a man Gaynor did not know called Maurice Martin. Gaynor and another man burst into the house and stabbed the innocent carpenter's apprentice to death as he tried to flee for his life down a nearby road.

Gaynor's DNA was found all over the murder scene, but could not be used to prosecute him because he had previously lived at the property. Gardaí had learned to take a cautious approach when dealing with him: when Gaynor was just seven years old, his father Robert McGrath was shot dead for pointing a sawn-off shotgun at armed responders during a post-office raid in Tara, Co. Meath, in 1992. Gardaí noted that his son 'appears to have a coloured view of the world after his father's shooting. He has a violent disposition and is aggressive when dealing with gardaí.'

Just three months before the planned hit on him, Gaynor was charged with threatening and abusive behaviour and failing to follow the directions of a garda at Barnamore Grove, Finglas, on 7 May. Blanchardstown District Court subsequently heard that he had told officers present, 'Look at you all. You think you're hard in your uniform and with all your back-up. Take off your uniform and let's see how hard you are.'

It was perhaps because of his confidence in his own physical abilities due to his hulking 6-foot-plus frame that Gaynor chose to ignore an official garda warning that his life was in danger when they called to his home three weeks after the shooting of Collie Owens.

That choice would cost him his life. Shortly after 6.30 p.m. on 14 August 2010 Gaynor and his partner Sarah Treacy left his family home with his two young sons from a previous relationship, who were aged six and seven. It was the couple's two-year anniversary and they were walking along St Helena's Road on their way to Sarah's aunt's home to drop off the kids. They made their way past the main entrance to the Barnamore estate and were crossing the road towards a gap in the railings leading to Barnamore Crescent when a figure wearing a hoodie, a black peaked cap and white gloves came up from behind them and appeared to one side.

The couple were taken completely by surprise. Sarah Treacy later told gardaí in her statement, 'I just seen a hand on a gun in the corner of my eye. I turned and looked at him and could see his hand kinda shaking. I thought, the way he is is as if he shit himself or as if the gun jammed.

'I think it was more like the gun jamming. I got a fright and kinda thought it was a joke. I screamed "Oh" and as I did this, Daniel was turning around to his left to look at me and behind him. He knew something was happening and it was as Daniel was turning, the gun started to go off. He didn't even get a chance to turn around fully, it all happened so quick.

'I don't know how many shots were fired, the gun was close to me, right in me ear and the first shot deafened me. When I looked at the gunman, he was about five foot eight, ten. He was slim build, normal. He was wearing a dark cap with writing. I don't know what it read. He had white gloves, mad-looking gloves, like magician gloves.'

A ten-year-old girl from the area also witnessed the killing. 'I remember the man walking up as normal [. . .] and then he took the gun out and started shooting the other man,' she told gardaí. 'The hood was up over his head. I couldn't see his face. I think the man took the gun from his pocket but I didn't see what pocket. It was definitely a gun – it was black and half silver. It was a small gun and he shot the man then. I heard three bangs.'

Keith had indeed fired three times and Gaynor was hit once in the neck and once in the chest. 'Suddenly I heard three loud bangs . . . more of a pop,' another local said in a witness statement. 'I heard the first pop, there was a gap and then two more. I saw a girl screaming and I saw people coming from their houses. I think she was shouting, "He's only after being shot. He's dead." She was hunched over the fella. I could see the gunman carrying a gun. He was limping as he ran. He wasn't sprinting, it was more of a jog. I remember thinking that this fella looked unhealthy, like a junkie-type.'

The gunman ran off to an overgrown green area known locally as The Den. 'When the gunman got to the railing, he grabbed the top of the rail with both hands and pulled himself up,' another eyewitness told investigators. 'I remember thinking he must be agile.'

A local woman told the *Irish Independent* her mother and siblings were just yards away when the shots rang out. She said, 'They were only after going round the back when they heard three shots going off and they ran around and my ma saw the blood coming out of his mouth. His kids were there with his girlfriend and the kids froze – they didn't cry or anything but the girlfriend was saying, "Don't leave me, don't leave me."'

As he ran off, Wilson threw away the Sturm Ruger SP101 revolver. This is common practice in gangland murders, as to be caught with a murder weapon virtually guarantees a life sentence. However, he then followed this up by dumping the cap, the gloves and finally the hoodie as he ran. These were gratefully scooped up by gardaí examining the scene long into the evening, before dusk finally fell. The cap and gloves were recovered near railings at Gortmore Road, while a McKenzie tracksuit top was found hanging from a bush.

Meanwhile, job done, Keith Wilson was whisked away and put on a plane to Spain, where he was sheltered by Sean Hunt. Sources close to the Wilson clan confirmed he had been extremely nervous both before and after the shooting, after which he had vomited as he recalled the 'yellow stuff' that had come out of Gaynor's neck as the bullet struck.

Needless to say, the shooting did little to settle matters. It was only a matter of time before there was another killing. With Hunt out of reach in Spain, Alan Wilson difficult to track down and The Guinea Pig hiding out in the North, the dissidents went for another fringe member of the mob.

Forty-year-old Sean Winters was a former member of David Lindsay's gang who had sunk into a deep depression following the disappearance of his old boss. He had developed a drug habit and had tried to kill himself, slashing his wrists as he sat in the bath, before he was discovered and saved.

Winters had moved out to Portmarnock to put some distance between himself and those he considered a danger to him, but he was still prepared to issue threats of his own. Gardaí learned he had vowed to kill The Panda over Lindsay's death, though there was little chance of him actually carrying it out.

Alan Ryan believed Winters had money stashed away, and

when it was not forthcoming, he ordered his murder. At 10 p.m. on 12 September 2010 Winters received a call on his mobile at his apartment in Portmarnock and told a number of visitors there he was 'going outside to meet someone'. When he did, he was approached and shot twice in the head. Philomena Deans, who was one of those at the apartment, later told the inquest into his death that Winters was 'quite depressed and anxious. All his friends were dead and I think he had given up on life.' When Winters did not return, she was not immediately suspicious. She recalled, 'I thought he was meeting a girl, he'd been seeing someone for a few weeks.'

Gardaí could see the feud had the potential to spiral even further out of control, but could not have predicted the next step Hunt and his associates would take.

In the 1980s Martin 'The General' Cahill had attempted to fend off IRA extortion attempts via the republican-controlled Concerned Parents Against Drugs group by forming his own ad-hoc organization, the Concerned Criminals Action Committee. Now, with the Real IRA again attempting to gain the high moral ground by claiming it was putting dealers out of business, Alan Wilson and The Guinea Pig took a leaf from Wilson's uncle's book and formed their own grouping, the Criminal Action Force (CAF).

In its first 'press release' to the *Irish Daily Star* newspaper, the CAF claimed it was behind the attack on The Players' Lounge and Daniel Gaynor's murder and said it had decided to act because the Real IRA had extorted over €400,000 from criminals across Dublin. The statement said, 'We are a big group and have lots of guns and men. All crime gangs are with us. We want to state categorically we'll execute any criminals big or small as collaborators who act with this gang.

'It is our duty to reply in the language that brings these

vultures to their senses. The leadership of the extortionist gang will be held responsible for any retaliation, the consequences of such would see a reply of merciless reprisals implemented with a ruthlessness that would do justice to Joseph Stalin.

'We have warned all criminals who work with the Dublin Real IRA that they will be executed. None of our members will be extorted or take threats.' The article was accompanied by a photo of a motley collection of men wearing balaclavas and anoraks in front of a black background with the letters CAF printed on white A4 sheets of paper.

Initially, it was difficult to know how solid this supposed paramilitary organization actually was and how much of it merely existed in the minds of Alan Wilson and The Guinea Pig. The *Sunday Tribune* reported that its garda sources believed the whole thing was 'a joke'. 'The Criminal Action Force does not exist as far as we're concerned. It is a publicity stunt, plain and simple,' one source told the paper. However, the dissident leadership in the North was taking things seriously enough to send two senior figures to Dublin to investigate. A number of criminals were pulled in and asked what they knew, though it appeared not many of them knew anything.

In the meantime, John Wilson had another very narrow escape. On the morning of 27 September 2010 a blue BMW 3 Series parked across the street from his home on Cloverhill Road in Ballyfermot. Witnesses saw two men wearing balaclavas get out and cross the road towards Wilson's house.

As they approached the gate, one of the men drew a long-barrelled pistol from under his jacket. Just then, however, the front door opened and Wilson's two young children came out in their school uniforms. The pair of assassins then turned and ran back towards their car before taking off at speed. The vehicle was followed by one witness, who tracked it as far as the Kylemore Road before losing sight of it. Despite alerting gardaí to the incident, nobody was prepared to make a formal statement about what they had seen and the identity of the men remained a mystery. Elsewhere, the Real IRA had decided to respond in kind to the CAF 'statement'.

At the beginning of November, Ryan and his cohorts issued a statement through its political wing, the 32 County Sovereignty Movement. In it, the group boasted it had shot five 'drug dealers' in the previous thirteen months, including Collie Owens and Sean Winters. In a reference to the CAF, it said, 'Anyone caught up in the world of criminality, drug dealing, or issuing threats to republicans should come forward and admit their involvement now.

'Anyone who does not avail of this opportunity will face the inevitable consequences. Those who wish to take on the republican movement should realize this. These parasites are members of a gang, the IRA are members of a disciplined army with experience of war.'

Things then got worse for the Wilsons with the arrest of Keith upon his return from his exile in the sun. Gardaí probing the Gaynor hit had been busy and had received information from a confidential informant just a day later that Keith was responsible. The tip was classed as 'very accurate'.

Investigators concluded, 'It is believed the murder was a revenge killing. It is believed Sean Hunt, who employed Collie Owens and who was a good friend of Collie Owens, believed that Gaynor was responsible for the murder and that he instructed Keith Wilson to carry it out.'

A check of flight records revealed that Keith Wilson had arrived into Dublin from Málaga five days before the shooting on 9 August, his ticket on Aer Lingus flight EI585 costing €250. He had returned to Spain via Ryanair on 18 August, this

time paying €88.47 for the seat. Both flights had been paid for
with a Visa card in the name of Nicolas Johnston. As is normal when someone has been identified as a suspect in a
criminal investigation, Wilson's passport had been flagged
and, unlike his cautious older brother Eric, he had travelled
under his real identity.

Apparently oblivious to the file built up on him, the youngest Wilson sibling decided to take another trip home. On 7
November he was arrested as he disembarked from a plane
from Málaga at Dublin airport at 11.35 p.m. The only apparent precaution he took was to leave the plane last.

But gardaí were confident of their intelligence and were
certain they had their man. Different DNA samples had
been recovered from the baseball cap and the hoodie, meaning more than one individual had been in contact with them.
However, there was biological material from only one person in the white cotton glove, which appeared to have been
on the hand holding the weapon when the shots were fired.

The only obstacle that remained was to take a sample from
Keith to compare against that glove. On the way to Finglas
garda station following his detention at the airport, he had
complained that his expensive Bulgari watch was too tight
on his wrist. The watch was removed and sent off to be
checked for DNA. Arrest on suspicion of murder with a
firearm allows a suspect to be held for up to seven days.
Upon his arrival at the station at 12.12 a.m., Wilson was asked
if he would permit the taking of a mouth swab for evidence
purposes. His reply was, 'Not a chance.'

In the days before the arrest, gardaí had discussed at length
how to address the issue of obtaining a DNA sample if
Keith – as expected – refused to provide one voluntarily. In
doing so, they had to be conscious of the inevitable legal
challenges that would be brought against such evidence

should a conviction arise from it. The Criminal Justice (Forensic Evidence) Act 1990 requires gardaí to obtain consent to collect a sample of blood, pubic hair, urine or swabs from a bodily orifice, but makes no mention of consent for mouth swabs. However, cops could not be sure that a superior court would not determine down the line that the law also applied in spirit to saliva and thus throw out any conviction if they held Keith down and took it forcibly.

Then there were the finer points of how such a sample might otherwise be collected. A Court of Criminal Appeal ruling three years earlier had declared that no evidence should be gathered within a garda station by 'stratagem, trickery or deception'. It recognized that, while in custody, suspects depended on gardaí for 'necessary' items, such as food, cutlery or medical devices like asthma inhalers.

Detainees have a constitutional right to such material while in custody and the subsequent analysis of them might also have consequences for the infringement of such rights in the eyes of an appeals court. Whether a sample from the Bulgari watch might come a cropper under the 'trickery or deception' rule down the line was open to debate too. But there is no 'constitutional right' to cigarettes – and Keith Wilson was a smoker.

Those in custody for long stretches are entitled to periods of exercise in the fresh air, which usually takes place in an enclosed yard within the station. Head of the investigation Detective Inspector Colm Fox ordered the yard where Wilson was to stretch his legs to be swept clean, photographed and videoed before he was allowed in there. Three Marlboro cigarette butts were recovered after Wilson had taken his exercise and sent off to the lab to be analysed. All three matched the major DNA profile on the gun, cotton glove, cap and hoodie.

In the meantime, Wilson underwent ten separate interviews. In the first, he denied any involvement in the murder and said he worked for a removal company based in the Costa del Sol town of Benalmádena called Blue Vista. He said he had been out in Spain for the past four months, during which he had been residing at the El Oceano Beach Hotel in Mijas. The luxurious, four-star beachfront property was an unusual lodgings for someone describing themselves as a removal-firm employee.

While in custody Wilson received a visit from his older brother John warning him to keep his mouth shut. In his second interview he clammed up altogether and gave the standard gangland 'no comment' to each question.

In the third, he once more refused to provide a saliva sample and spent interviews four, five and six repeating the same mantra. During interview seven, he was shown the items recovered from the murder scene and informed they were full of DNA.

Next he was quizzed on what phone numbers he had for Sean Hunt and whether he worked for him. In the ninth grilling, Wilson was shown CCTV footage of him smoking a cigarette outside. He was presented with a toothbrush and a towel he had used in custody and informed they had been sent to the forensic lab.

Lastly, during interview number ten, he was warned that inferences could be drawn in court from his refusal to provide a sample. It was all designed to convince Wilson that the evidence against him was overwhelming and it would be in his own interests to cooperate.

Still, he refused to budge. The evidence was all packaged up and sent off to the DPP by Sergeant John O'Hehir and a direction to charge was received. Three days after he was arrested at Dublin airport, Keith Wilson appeared in court accused of Daniel Gaynor's murder.

He spent Christmas behind bars and an attempt to have him released for his grandfather's funeral in January also came to naught thanks to his bumbling performance during a bail hearing.

Wilson's family had offered to put up a €5,000 surety to allow him to attend the service, but gardaí objected at the High Court. Cross-examined by prosecutor Gráinne O'Neill, Keith Wilson claimed he had been very close to his granddad and used to clean his house. However, he was unable to give the late pensioner's address and when Ms O'Neill pointed out that the deceased had been in a care home since the previous February, said he must have visited him the month before that. Unsurprisingly, Judge Patrick McCarthy refused to grant bail and Keith Wilson was carted back to prison.

With Eric and Keith now locked up and Sean Hunt still furious at him over The Players' Lounge fiasco, John Wilson was seriously isolated. Gardaí were doing their best to hamper the activities of the Real IRA and a raid on The Players' Lounge had uncovered three stun guns and some cocaine.

Pub owner John Stokes was subsequently charged with possession of the items, though the case against him eventually collapsed. Meanwhile, Alan Ryan, along with Stokes and two other men, were charged with demanding that two rival publicans, brothers Stephen and Shane Simpson, close down their bar, The Castle Inn, on Dublin's Summerhill. Those charges would eventually be withdrawn by the state too, but it kept the pressure on Ryan.

In the meantime, John Wilson was involved in an odd incident. John was continuing to engage in feuds with various parties across Ballyfermot, one of whom was a figure in the INLA. Desperate to get the man off his back, he decided to make use of his nephew, Luke.

Luke Wilson was still four months shy of his seventeenth birthday. He was the son of Debbie – the sister of John, Eric and Keith – who had died of a drug overdose in February 2008. He had been brought up in the family home on Cremona Road and had become obsessed with following his uncles into crime. John decided to take advantage of his wholly inexperienced nephew's enthusiasm and send Luke after the INLA man.

As a ploy it seemed doomed to failure and so it proved. A source with knowledge of the incident told the authors, 'Luke cycled up beside where yer man was walking and fired a shot at him. But he wasn't counting on the recoil, which sent him flying off the mountain bike.

'Yer man went over and took the gun off him and clattered him across the side of his head. He knew Luke to see, of course, so John John was in big trouble after that happened. Yer man got in touch with him and told him, you're going to be kneecapped for this.'

Searching for a way out of his predicament, John Wilson turned to his cousin Alan, who suggested an unusual tactic first dreamed up by his uncle Martin 'The General' Cahill. Back in the 1990s Cahill had shot an underling named Jo Jo Kavanagh in the legs to convince gardaí that Kavanagh was not involved in the kidnapping of a bank official. It did not work, and Kavanagh was later given twelve years. However, Alan told John that he had shot Fergus O'Hanlon so he could avoid prosecution over an armed robbery a few years earlier – and that this time, the rather painful ruse had succeeded.

Shortly after 10 p.m. on 6 May 2011 gardaí received a call that a man had suffered gunshot wounds to the leg at Raheen Drive in Ballyfermot. When they arrived, they found the injured party was John Wilson. He had been shot outside No. 6 and walked across to knock on the door of No. 13, whose occupants rang 999.

A gunman, dressed all in black and described as between 5 foot 6 inches and 5 foot 7 inches was seen running away in the direction of Le Fanu Park, but was not found in follow-up searches of the area. An investigation began but was later halted after gardaí uncovered the truth about what had happened. They believed Alan Wilson had carried out the shooting. When Sean Hunt heard about it, it convinced him even further to sever his links with John Wilson.

John was not the only one going off the rails, though. Alan was becoming increasingly paranoid, and reinforced the security at his mother's home. He slept in a bulletproof vest and only left the property to cash his weekly €200 carer's allowance.

Given his state of mind, it was only a matter of time before he emerged as a suspect in another violent incident. On two separate occasions in mid-September 2010 he was investigated after shots were fired from a shotgun into a house in the Bride Street area of Dublin. Gardaí received intelligence that he had threatened to kill an ex-lover in St Teresa's Gardens when he learned she was in a relationship, but were unable to bring any charges because no complaint was made. A few days following the shooting, gardaí in Pearse Street received further insight into his volatile personality from a female associate who was speaking to gardaí on another matter. She told them, 'He would always watch DVDs and use coke. When he was on coke, he would talk crazy. He was always trying to control his anger.'

Over the next few months and into 2011 Alan Wilson continued to maintain a low profile, doing his best to avoid any interaction with gardaí as the investigation into the murder of Marioara Rostas continued. According to senior security sources, Wilson had been left like a 'wounded animal' after the arrests of his cousins Eric and Keith, and was turning to his cousin Richard Cawley – a well-known burglar – and impressionable teenagers, all from the south inner city, for support.

One source said, 'The arrests of his cousins was a big blow to him because they were family and the only real people he could trust. He still had Fergus O'Hanlon in his life but he wasn't family.'

The setbacks for Wilson continued to mount. On 3 February 2011 he appeared before Dublin District Court charged with aggravated burglary and false imprisonment over the terrifying raid on the Mountaine family home the previous year. Initially remanded in custody, Wilson received bail at the High Court after an independent surety of €20,000 was paid. Part of his bail conditions included signing on at Kevin Street garda station each day and adherence to a nightly curfew.

Alan Wilson was free once more but now set his sights on his former friend Herbert Kilcline. Convinced that Kilcline was a 'weak link' and the most likely candidate to cooperate with the gardaí, he dispatched Maxine to shoot the solicitor at his home in Rathmines.

Kilcline said, 'Alan kept telling Fergus, "Herbie is the weak link – he has to go." But Fergus told Alan that if he killed a solicitor, it would be like the murder of Veronica Guerin. Maxine came into my house and pointed a gun at me, fired and thankfully missed.

'Fergus was with me and he had a lucky escape too. He took the gun off Maxine and later told Alan if he wanted me dead he would have to do it himself. I know Fergus was very angry about this and overall about the way Alan was treating me.

'I was under serious pressure at the time and I just had to keep my head down and keep away from Alan as much as possible.' Lucky to survive, Kilcline knew there would be other attempts on his life.

Detectives in Kilmainham had also identified Alan Wilson as a suspect in the murder of innocent teenager Darren Cogan on 25 June 2011. The nineteen-year-old, who was not involved in crime or linked to any drugs gangs, had been drinking in the Blackhorse Inn pub in Inchicore when a gunman, wearing a mask and surgical gloves, entered and opened fire inside the packed bar. Darren was hit once in the chest, but the real target had been Gerard Eglington, a close friend of convicted killer Brian 'King Ratt' Rattigan and a bitter enemy of senior Kinahan cartel member 'Fat' Freddie Thompson.

Gardaí later received intelligence that Eglington, who would lose his life in a gangland shooting the following year, had been spotted in the same area on the evening of the attack. His murder was supposed to be the latest killing as part of the Crumlin–Drimnagh feud. Eglington was wearing a similar polo shirt to the one worn by Darren Cogan, but had gone by the time the gunman had arrived. The blundering hitman shot Cogan by mistake instead.

Following the shooting, the murder victim's mother Rose spoke of her pain. 'I cry in the morning and I cry at night because I just miss my son so much,' she said. 'My Darren was harmless and the only thing he ever did was carry shopping for old people.'

Wilson emerged as a suspect because of his close relationship to Liam Brannigan, a first cousin of Thompson, who had placed a bounty on Eglington's head. Both men were questioned by gardaí about the murder but were later released without charge. It would not be the last time the pair would be identified as suspects in a major garda inquiry.

For the past six months Wilson had been regularly breaking his bail conditions. Gardaí had received information that he was ignoring his curfew and driving to the Phoenix Park and to a beach in Donabate, north Co. Dublin. Herbert Kilcline also claimed Wilson made two attempts to have Fergus O'Hanlon killed during this period: 'There was one incident when shots were fired at Fergus in Rathmines on 18 June 2011, but he managed to escape because he was wearing a bulletproof vest.

'Another incident was when Fergus was checking up on Maxine and they decided to take a trip to the seafront in Dun Laoghaire. It was a sunny day and Fergus noticed a man in a mask and fully covered coming towards him and decided to run over the tracks to get away.

'I had to collect him and then Alan rang me from a mobile phone and said I was getting in the way of business. Fergus was obviously very worried but then he went to prison. Alan and Fergus were a double act for many years. They also had a pact that if they had ever fell out, they wouldn't kill each other.

'Fergus was Alan's right-hand man but Fergus started to pull back a bit in the first six months of 2011 because he was toying with the idea of giving up the body of the missing girl. I think the first moment he realized he had to keep away from Alan was when they were having dinner one night with Alan's mother Mary and she turned round to her son while pointing at Fergus and said something like, "He knows too much, son, he has to go."

'Alan then slapped his mother in the face before laughing at her. Fergus kept his nerve and told Alan there was no problem but deep down he knew he had to get away from him. The attempts on Fergus's life proved to him that Alan was trying to get him. But despite the attempts on his life, Fergus still wasn't ready to come forward.'

On 15 July gardaí applied to the High Court to have Wilson's bail revoked after he was stopped on suspicion of drink-driving during his curfew hours. Wilson had already received repeated warnings over his failure to sign his bail bond at Kevin Street station and was remanded back in custody. Concerned for his psychological state, warders at Dublin's Cloverhill prison placed him in an isolation unit where they could keep him under constant observation.

It was a considerable relief for gardaí to have him off the streets, particularly those officers investigating the murder of Marioara Rostas.

9. Going Down

You could feel the evil off him, you could see it in his eyes
— senior garda investigator

Thirteen months after Dan Smith was shot dead outside The Lounge bar, Eric Wilson was about to go on trial for the crime. It was July 2011. Before that, though, gardaí wanted to have a word with him about the killings on Irish soil for which he was the chief suspect and so, on 28 June, a delegation from Drogheda garda station and the National Bureau of Criminal Investigation travelled to Málaga to hear what he had to say.

If Eric Wilson had been asked to see the delegation in the remand prison where he was being held, he doubtless would have refused. However, the questions about the murders of Martin Kenny, Paul Reay and Roy Coddington would be put to him not by gardaí, but by a Spanish investigating magistrate, who compelled him to appear in court behind closed doors.

A year in custody had not softened Wilson's cough, however. A source close to the investigation told the authors, 'When he came into the court first, he gave a cut-throat sign to all the gardaí that had come over, as if to say, "Fuck you."

'He was brought in with two prison guards and the judge was looking at him. The judge called one of the guards up and they brought him off away again. The judge got up then and said, "Not a nice man." It was like he got a bad vibe off him and he went round the court and closed all the windows.'

When Eric Wilson returned there were four guards around him. The source told us, 'He's not that big a fella, but he just oozes evil. You look into the eyes and they're dead. There's a badness in him. You could feel the evil off him, you could see it in his eyes.'

Though it was the judge's responsibility to put the questions to Wilson, at times his English failed him somewhat, and eventually the list of queries was given to Wilson himself to read. It made little difference. His answer to each was, 'No comment.'

Gardaí then asked his guards to ask Wilson if he wanted them to pass on any message to his family, but he refused to deal with them. The Spanish told the travelling party that their prisoner lived a monastic existence in custody. The source added, 'They said, "He keeps to himself, he has his cell and he doesn't mix with any other prisoner, that's it."'

A few weeks later Eric Wilson was back in a courtroom once more, but this time to be tried for the murder of 'Tall Dan' Smith. The case against him was strong. There was the initial confrontation between him and Smith and the blood spatter retrieved by forensics from a T-shirt and on the motorbike at the farmhouse in Coín. However, the state had no murder weapon and the evidence stood or fell on a single witness who said he had recognized the man he knew as 'Eric' or 'Lucky' when he lifted the visor on his helmet to carry out the shooting.

Under Spanish law, the relatives of a murder victim are allowed to bring their own private prosecution alongside the state's. Both have the right to submit evidence, and to demand a particular sentence and monetary compensation, though

a–e: Brothers John, Eric and Keith (*above, left to right*), their cousin Alan (*below, left*) and nephew Luke (*below, right*) have racked up an astonishing number of arrests to the Wilson family name. None have escaped unscathed, however: John was murdered in 2012 and the rest are now in prison.

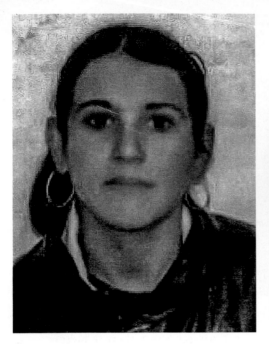

2a: Marioara Rostas, from the Roma community, went missing on 6 January 2008. She was last seen alive begging at a set of traffic lights in Dublin city centre.

2b: Alan Wilson was charged in connection with Marioara's murder, but was later acquitted at trial.

2c: The investigation discovered that Alan Wilson was the registered owner of a silver 01-LH Ford Mondeo at the time of her disappearance, the same type of car her younger brother saw her get into.

3a: A room with an external lock at 2 Brabazon Street examined as part of the investigation. The building was badly damaged in a fire just under two months after Marioara's disappearance.

3b: After a forensic examination, Gardaí concluded that a total of seven bullets had been fired into a wall in the first-floor living room.

c: An armchair in the house at Brabazon Street howing where bullets ad been fired into the urniture.

4a: The bunker that Fergus O'Hanlon led Gardaí to as part of their investigation into Marioara's disappearance.

4b: On 23 January 2012, the Garda Technical Bureau removed what appeared to be set of human remains from a shallow grave, before placing it, still curled in the foet: position, into a sterile body bag.

5a: Marioara's family were devastated by their loss; they left Ireland five months after her disappearance. (*Left to right*: her father, Dumitru Snr; her younger brother, Dumitru Jnr; his wife, Argentina; and her mother, Marioara).

b: Members of An Garda Síochána attended Marioara's funeral in Tileagd, Romania n February 2012 (*Left to right:* Garda Ofelia Hough, then Detective Inspector Michael Cryan and Sergeant Paul Murphy).

6a: Paul Reay was shot four times by Eric Wilson and died in Drogheda in November 2006.

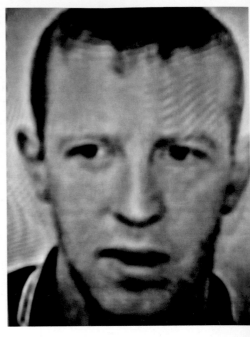

6b: Roy Coddington lived on the same street as Paul Reay; he was murdered by Eric four months later, in March 2007.

6c: David 'Boogie' Brett was shot in the head and neck in May 2007 outside Foilogohig national school in Cork.

6d: Underworld sources claim that Alan Napper (*above*) and David Lindsay were lured to an isolated bungalow in Down in July 2008 and murdered.

7aa & 7ab: In a hit ordered by the Kinahans, Paddy Doyle (pictured inset (*left*) with a young 'Fat Freddie' Thompson (*right*)) was murdered on the Costa del Sol in February 2008. He was shot 13 times by his assassin.

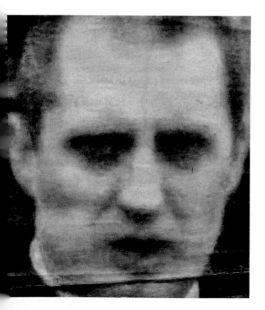

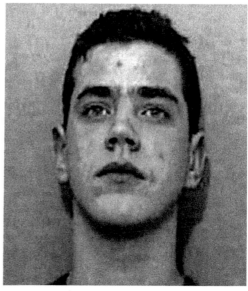

7b: The murder of Anthony Cannon (*above*) in July 2009 is believed to have been Keith Wilson's first gangland hit.

7c: Eric Wilson was sentenced to 23 years for the murder of 'Tall Dan' Smith (*above*); Wilson shot him outside a bar in Málaga in June 2010.

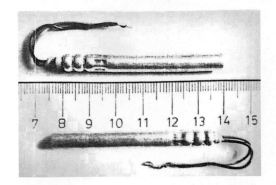

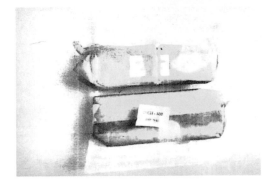

8a–f: Extracts from a technical study carried out as part of the Spanish authorities' investigation into Eric Wilson show an anti-tank grenade plus ordinary grenades, detonators, plastic explosives, smoke bombs and bullets.

9a–c: Sean Hunt (*above*), a veteran smuggler, refused to give in to the demands of Alan Ryan. In a retaliation hit, he tasked Keith Wilson with the murder of Daniel Gaynor. Gardaí scooped up the Sturm Ruger SP101 revolver (*top right*) and Keith's hoodie (*right*) near the crime scene.

9d: In the Criminal Action Force's first press release, they claimed that 'We are a big group and have lots of guns and men. All crime gangs are with us.' However, the *Sunday Tribune* reported that its garda sources believed the whole thing was 'a joke'.

1. you dont desereve all ~~there~~ this bad
in
~~to~~ our lives.
Things will trunaround for us but we have
to make it works its going to be a battel
but we can do it. so keep your head
clear and focus on what needs to be
dunne

2. I can ~~onley~~ be as good as what you can
do for me now so do what i ask ive
well tot about things

3. I well get a life sentence IF (n) lives
so lisen and we work this out.
For (n) ▇ will do it. ask (b) can he get
▇ (g) and car. Push ▇ to do this
tell him Ill give him 10.000 and what ever
he needs. IF or when this is dunne
things will fall in to place

4. Talks to solicitor play the game ~~offer him~~
~~to our see what he says~~ he ~~comes across~~
as haven a soft hart ~~play on that~~
(list) ~~evidence matters~~ | john ~~fatos~~ phone| car key
(b) is that other thing dunne|Erica |oona|
ask max to get ~~a list of~~ f girlfriend
~~and all~~ the times when he was ~~visited~~
~~to her when~~ ~~police~~ new
(list) runners track suit short socks
(be ~~happy~~ all the time ~~no matter~~ what)
I ~~that~~ money safe |how much have we
Got ~~lien~~ around = 8000
what about.

you and max are going to take the
box so uses need to look well going to te
use words not to use

10: A handwritten note that was addressed to his mother Mary Wilson and detailed plan to murder Herbert Kilcline was recovered during a search of Alan Wilson's cell at Cloverhill prison.

11a: Mary Wilson, mother of Alan, was caught attempting to flush a note that appeared to contain instructions on individuals who should be targeted down the toilet at a garda station.

11b: When Marioara Rostas disappeared, Maxine Wilson, daughter of Mary, was in a relationship with Fergus O'Hanlon, Alan's former right-hand man who is now in the witness protection programme.

11c: Convinced that Herbert Kilcline (*above*) was the most likely candidate to cooperate with the Gardaí, Alan Wilson dispatched Maxine to shoot him at his home. Kilcline says that Maxine pointed a gun at him, fired, but missed.

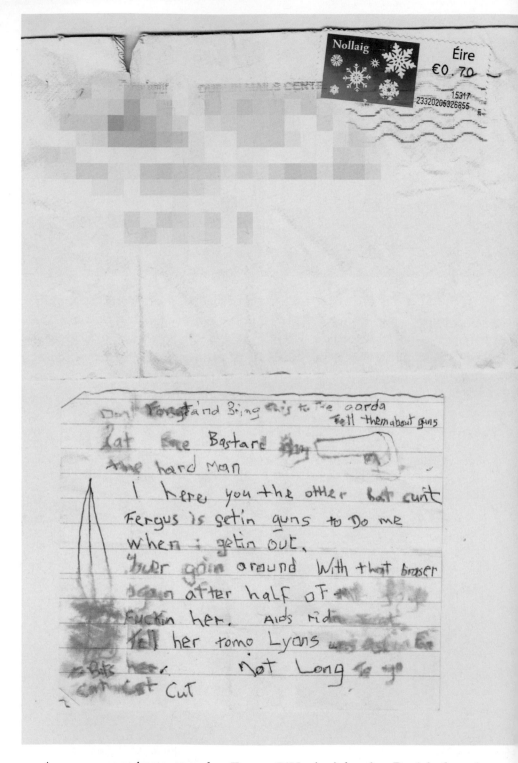

12: An anonymous letter posted to Fergus O'Hanlon's brother Patrick, featuring a hand-drawn picture of a pistol and dagger.

13a–c: Gardaí foiled the planned murder of Gary Hanley (*above left*) in November 2017. Thanks to surveillance, they knew that the black cloth placed on a lamppost (*above right*) was to assist the getaway navigation. The 9 mm Luger Beretta handgun and backpack (*below*) were found in the car with Luke Wilson and Joseph Kelly.

14a: Liam Brannigan received a sentence of 8 years for conspiracy to murder Hanley.

14b: Dean Howe pleaded guilty to conspiring to murder Hanley and was jailed for 6 years.

14c: Joseph Kelly, 'the getaway driver', got 12 years for his part in the assassination plot.

14d: Daniel Kinahan (*right*). Hints that Kinahan, head of the Kinahan organized crime group, was behind the planned hit on Hanley were heard through surveillance. (Here he is pictured with legendary boxing promoter Bob Arum. Kinahan has tried to go 'legit' through his involvement in boxing.)

15a: The investigation into Marioara Rostas' disappearance was launched under Superintendent Joseph Gannon (*above*), Senior Investigating Officer Michael Cryan and Detective Sergeant John Doyle.

15b: SIO Michael Cryan said that though the investigative team were disappointed in the outcome of the trial for the murder of Marioara, they were relieved they could return her to her family.

15c: Without the late Colm Fox's precautions around DNA evidence collection, Keith Wilson might yet be a free man.

16a&b: Detective Chief Superintendent Seamus Boland (*left*), Detective Superintendent David Gallagher (*middle*) and Detective Inspector Noel Browne (*right*) ran the investigation into the Hanley plot.

16c: Judge Tony Hunt officiated over a number of trials arising from the activities of the Wilsons.

16d: Assistant Commissioner Organised & Serious Crime, John O'Driscoll, is in charge of all anti-feud operations.

this is rarely actually paid. Crucially, however, both prosecutions have equal status in the eyes of the judges. The state requested eighteen years in jail upon conviction and compensation of €45,793 to be paid to the victim's mother, Karen Wetherell. Smith's family wanted a 25-year tariff, with €300,000 in financial restitution.

The state opened its case first, with prosecutor Maria Jose Criado telling the jury of four men and five women, 'This was a savage murder. The defendant left the bar after an altercation with the victim and returned armed with a pistol and with the sole aim of ending Daniel's life. He shot him repeatedly in a cowardly fashion from close range and injured him so seriously he died shortly afterwards on the pavement outside.'

Carlos Comitre, representing the dead man's family, added, 'As well as planning Daniel's murder, the defendant acted with cruelty by killing him in an inhumane way that increased his suffering. The defendant was just looking for a fight and Daniel was just trying to help a girl he was annoying.' Gesturing towards Mr Smith's mum Karen Wetherell, who was sitting in the public area, he told the jury she had depended on her son financially to make ends meet.

Comitre continued, 'I know Eric Wilson murdered Daniel, the state prosecutor knows it and so does Daniel's mum. Although there is no amount of money that can compensate a mother for her son's loss, it's important to take into account this was not a traffic accident. It was a malicious and savage murder. His mum can never see him alive again. The last thing she can do for him is be here in court today.'

Bar owner Steve Reynolds took the stand and nervously gave evidence as Eric Wilson eyeballed him from the dock. He told the court, 'I went out to deal with the row and it ended with the defendant leaving. It seemed to be about a girl who was suggesting someone had put their hand up her skirt.

'Eric had arrived at the bar on the powerful Yamaha motorbike he owned. I asked him if he was okay and he said he was calm. I saw him leave on his motorbike and the next thing was that later I heard some shots being fired.

'I didn't see who fired them. I spent the last minutes of Dan's life with him trying to stop the bleeding. People were suggesting the name of the killer. The name they were suggesting was Eric's.'

Following the fight Wilson had put up at the farmhouse, authorities were taking no chances in court. He remained handcuffed and was flanked by a member of the Guardia Civil throughout.

Eric Wilson, listening closely with the help of an interpreter, gave no reaction as the evidence against him was read out to the court. When the time came for him to speak, Wilson claimed he had been several miles away drinking in another bar when the murder occurred. He said he had decided to leave after Smith shouted at him for 'accidentally bumping' into a woman. He testified, 'He was a big man in a group that looked pretty drunk. I thought the best thing to do was leave and that's what I did. I never went back. When the shooting happened I was drinking in my local village pub nearly twenty miles away.'

Wilson said he had moved to Spain three years beforehand to start a new life after becoming addicted to gambling at home. He claimed he made his living buying and selling horses he kept at the Coín farmhouse and conceded that he had told officers he was someone else when he was arrested. He said, 'They told me they were investigating a bank robbery and asked to come into my house so I told them I was the person named on the rental contract.'

However, the key moment came when the man who had recognized Wilson gave evidence. Spanish judges have wide discretion when it comes to the protection of witnesses. Because of the historical threat from Basque separatist group ETA, for example, police officers are only ever identified by their ID number and often address courts from behind a screen. Protected Witness 1/2003/10, who had seen the killer with his visor up, was permitted to testify from a neighbouring room with his voice electronically disguised, but he was so terrified of Eric Wilson that this was not enough.

The man asked Judge Maria Luisa de la Hera several times if he could wear a motorbike helmet, even though only she and the jury could see him on a screen. It was only when he was persuaded that his evidence would be too muffled to be understood that he agreed to take it off. The witness, who had been an acquaintance of both Smith and Wilson, said he had seen the initial row between the pair earlier in the day and that Wilson had been 'very angry' when the two men squared up.

He continued, 'When Daniel saw the motorbike he told everyone on the terrace to get inside the bar. Dan stayed on the terrace. The killer had the visor on his helmet up as he appeared on foot a few moments later from a side street.

'I could see his face and I saw it was Eric. He shouted as he approached Dan and put the visor down. He had a pistol in his hand and shot Dan. Dan fell to the floor. I heard eight shots, fired in quick succession. Dan wasn't able to defend himself.

'The first shots Eric fired were from about twelve metres away and they got closer as he approached Dan. The last were all from close range.'

Asked if he was sure it was Eric Wilson, he replied, 'Perfectly.' Though several people had told police who arrived at the scene that the Irishman had carried out the shooting, the man was the only one who took the stand to positively identify him.

It was reported in advance of the trial that Irish-accented men had called to the pub following the shooting, warning those present not to speak to authorities. One barmaid who was working that day told the jury, 'I heard the shots, but I was behind the bar and I saw nothing.' A colleague said he initially thought bangers were going off when he heard the shots.

He then saw a man with his hand extended towards the ground in a firing gesture before he ran to a nearby lane and a powerful motorbike was started. He said, 'I couldn't say who it was because it was dark.'

Both prosecutors and the defence were allowed to address the jury a final time before they retired to consider their verdict. Maria Jose Criado, for the state, urged the jury to see through what she termed Eric Wilson's 'inventions and excuses' after thirteen months of silence in which he failed to give an alibi.

She reminded them that Wilson was being investigated by gardaí over a string of unsolved murders back in Ireland, and also of what had been found at the farmhouse in Coín. Summing up, she said, 'The accused killed Daniel Smith with several shots. He gave rein to his most basic instincts and terminated a row in the only way he knew how, by shooting a defenceless, unarmed man. Unfortunately, you can't undo the damage he's done. But you can see justice is done and that's what Daniel and his family deserve.'

Family prosecutor Carlos Comitre said Wilson had deliberately sought to increase his victim's suffering by shooting him twice in the testicles as he lay on the ground. He added, 'The defendant fled and left Daniel drowning in his blood on the ground in a lasting agony. An off-duty Guardia Civil arrived and Daniel was still alive. All the paramedics could do when they reached the scene was certify him dead. You can do something for Daniel now and ensure justice by deciding he is the author of the shots that ended his life and his mum's life.'

The last word, though, was given to Eric Wilson himself. Staring at the jury, he said, 'I speak to you today with a clear conscience and a clean heart. I came to Spain to live peacefully within the community of Andalusia and hopefully someday have a family here as well.

'We all know what happened to Daniel Smith. It's a disgusting, evil crime, but I did not kill Daniel Smith. I don't know who did. All I know is that when I woke up on 7 June 2010 I had no idea I'd be in jail for the next thirteen months and in a courtroom today accused of murder. I only ask you to allow me to resume my life in the community in peace, that's all. Justice.'

The speech had little impact. Twenty-one hours after going out, the jury returned a guilty verdict by an eight-to-one majority. The foreman said, 'We find the defendant killed the victim in a pre-meditated fashion and using extreme violence. He had the time to pre-plan the murder and acted in an inhumane way that increased the victim's suffering. We conclude the defendant didn't just come to Spain to live peacefully within the community as he has claimed, but also to end human lives as the weapons found at his home indicate.'

Following the guilty verdict, the state prosecutor immediately upped her sentence demand to twenty-three years, while the family stuck with their request for twenty-five years. Karen Wetherell was too distraught to give a reaction and was ushered from the courtroom by her partner, Russ Kelly.

However, their prosecutor, Carlos Comitre, told the waiting press, 'The gaping wound Wilson caused will always be open but at least now Daniel's mum has some sort of closure and might be able to sleep at night without the help of tablets.'

Wilson's defence lawyer Javier Mora said outside court, 'The key to all of this was the protected witness who gave evidence against my client. He was the sole witness to stand up in court and identify him as the killer. We will appeal as soon as the judge determines sentence.'

They would not have to wait long. In the meantime, however, some of the evidence, which had not been heard in open court but shown to the jury behind closed doors during the trial, began to leak to the local press: this included details of phone taps made as part of a separate investigation, during which Wilson's name had cropped up. The recordings had been summarized in Spanish rather than being left in their original raw form and detailed conversations between two Irish mobsters identified only as B and P. They read:

'B starts to talk about a third person who has been arrested in Spain [Eric Wilson]. B said the families are looking for the bodies to move on and that EW could arrive at an arrangement with authorities to say where the bodies are.

'B says that people are worried that if he talks, he could bring a lot of people down with him. P asks how many bodies there are. B says there are more than ten in Ireland alone. B says there are three in Drogheda and four or five in Dublin and two more in the countryside.

'B says he's the chief suspect in ten murders, but they don't have any proof. B says he's a madman, but they had never arrested him and now he's locked up abroad for murder and explosives.

'B says the guys are worried he'll betray them and they'll

get life and he'll be freed. B says the guys are chewing their fingernails right now. B said REDACTED has been in many scrapes and knows what to say, but Eric doesn't.

'B says everything he had done before was planned carefully but not this, this was because he was drunk and now he's fucked. B says that he's a ticking time bomb. B says that something was in the *Sunday World* and asks how they knew that.

'Because not many people knew that he sold them [guns] and didn't get rid of them. B says that surely REDACTED said it and that his holidays had been paid for by the police and that he had got a pass from the gardaí.

'B says the article didn't mention to whom he sold the guns.'

This was the first time Eric Wilson had been openly linked to the murders. Unbeknownst to him, however, he had narrowly avoided a much worse fate. Among those worried about Wilson spilling the beans were Micka 'The Panda' Kelly and Daniel Kinahan.

Kelly's nose was still seriously out of joint over Wilson's failure in 2008 to torch the house in Rathfriland as ordered, while Kinahan feared that details of the cartel's double-cross on Paddy Doyle might come to light – along with other matters. Garda intelligence indicated that both considered having Eric Wilson murdered in custody, but were stopped by one consideration, his brothers and cousin, who they feared were just 'mad' enough to come after both of them and seek revenge. A potential hit on the hitman behind bars was thus discounted.

Five days after being convicted, Wilson learned of his fate. Unlike in Ireland, defendants are not recalled to court for sentencing hearings, with judges instead issuing a written ruling, which is communicated to their lawyers. Here, Judge de la Hera handed down one of the stiffest tariffs possible. The maximum sentence for murder is thirty years but the crime normally receives between fifteen and eighteen years upon conviction.

However, the callous circumstances of Daniel Smith's death warranted twenty-three years in jail, the judge decided. Wilson was also ordered to pay Smith's mother €100,000 in compensation, while being given an equally meaningless ban on approaching her for the following thirty-five years. Eric Wilson would not be returning to Ireland for a very long time.

Back in Dublin the feud between the Real IRA and the city's criminals was continuing – and the dissidents were starting to get the upper hand. Micka 'The Panda' Kelly was the latest dealer in the sights of Ryan's mob, who had warned him to pay up or else the previous May.

Kelly had been basing himself between Spain and Dublin since the murders of David Lindsay and Alan Napper, but after his girlfriend had a child he decided it was safe enough to come home and stay with her for a while. When Kelly refused to pay up, the dissidents kept watch on his girlfriend's home and ambushed him as he arrived at the apartment block to visit her and the child. The Panda was shot six times with an assault rifle by a gunman who gardaí believe was Alan Ryan's brother, Vinnie.

As Vinnie Ryan got into the getaway car to flee, the driver deliberately reversed over their badly injured target. The drug dealer bled to death as he lay face down on a wad of cash he was carrying with him.

In November 2011 it was Keith Wilson's turn to face the music. The first day of that month, after an adjournment of a week, his trial for Daniel Gaynor's murder got under way.

In its opening statements, the prosecution told the court that, though the gunman had fired three times, only one bullet had hit Gaynor. The victim, the jury heard, had died from a 'single penetrating gunshot wound to the neck' and his death would have been 'almost instantaneous'. The other bullet had missed its target, while the third had misfired in the gun.

Gaynor's girlfriend Sarah Treacy took the stand and revealed how she initially 'thought it was someone messing' when they were confronted by a masked man pointing a silver gun at them.

'Daniel tried to turn his head to the left,' said Ms Treacy, who added that she did not know how many shots there were, as she was 'deafened': 'Daniel fell in front of me. I just heard a ringing in my ear.' The witness said she 'could just see a pair of eyes' but saw the man was wearing a peaked cap and a white glove 'like a magician's glove', and was carrying a gun. She described the gunman as of slim build, between 5 foot 8 inches and 5 foot 11 inches and said he ran off 'towards The Den'.

She said she went over to where Gaynor was shot and frantically tried to get her mobile phone to ring the emergency services. An ambulance came and Gaynor was taken to hospital but he was dead within half an hour of arrival. Keith's decision to discard his clothing would prove the clincher in his conviction.

The bullets taken from the Sturm Ruger SP101 revolver were made of pure lead. Without a harder metal casing around them, such as copper, they tend to mushroom considerably upon impact and this had happened with the fatal round, which had struck Gaynor in the neck. The result was a bullet that was useless for evidence purposes. 'It is not possible for you to definitively link it to the gun?' defence barrister Brendan Grehan asked ballistics expert Detective Garda David O'Leary.

'It was too badly damaged, but it's not possible to eliminate it,' Detective Garda O'Leary replied. Sarah Treacy had no training in firearms, but she had been correct in her assumption that the gun had appeared to jam. 'In my opinion the order would have been one misfire and three discharges – audibly a click and three bangs,' Detective Garda O'Leary told the court, adding that the shells discharged had been from that kind of firearm but it was not possible to say if it came from that particular weapon.

Detective Garda O'Leary said there were holes in the gun as the last digits of its serial number had been drilled. He told Grehan that drilling through the metal entirely destroyed the digits, whereas if they are filed off it is still possible to uncover the number. He said a gun with drill holes in it would leave an impression on the bullets it discharged. However, the best the prosecution could say was that the bullet taken from Gaynor's neck was 'similar' to the live rounds found in the gun.

The state also called forensic scientist Dr Clara O'Sullivan, who told the court the chances of someone besides Keith Wilson having the same DNA found on the discarded clothing were less than one in a billion.

As closing statements got under way, Keith's barrister attempted to attack what he called 'a striking void of evidence' in the case. There was no evidence Gaynor ever knew the accused, he said, or that Keith knew him. There was no proof of any motive and no positive identification of his client.

Meanwhile, John Wilson had devised his own strategy to try to get his younger brother off. He could be seen attempting to intimidate the relatives of witnesses who had come to court as moral support, slipping into seats beside them and staring overtly at them until gardaí intervened and began sitting beside the relatives instead. This led to a confrontation between John and one detective in which he made a reference to knowing where the garda lived. The incident was such a common occurrence when dealing with serious criminals that no further action was taken.

Meanwhile, prosecuting counsel Alex Owens had conceded that there was no testimony linking Keith to the shooting and the case relied 'very heavily on silent witnesses and circumstantial evidence'. However, he added, 'all of the circumstantial evidence points to the guilt of the accused. Either he's the unluckiest man in Ireland or he is drowning in a sea of circumstantial evidence.'

The jury unanimously agreed and convicted Keith Wilson of murder and possession of a firearm with intent to endanger life. A victim impact statement was read out to the court on behalf of Gaynor's family. In it, they revealed that Gaynor's two young sons, who witnessed the killing, were deeply traumatized and had required counselling. Sarah Treacy was also 'in regular contact' with a counsellor, while Gaynor's mother was 'inconsolable' and his family would never be able to get over it.

Judge Garrett Sheehan handed down the mandatory life sentence for murder and also imposed an eight-year term for the firearms offence to run concurrently. The conviction would not have been possible without a DNA match, which was unimpeachable in court, and the credit for that went to Detective Inspector Colm Fox.

Fox would pass away tragically in February 2018, but his former superintendent in Finglas, David Dowling – now a retired detective chief superintendent – told the authors, 'At the time of the murder, Colm was the detective inspector for the K District, the busiest district in the country. He worked with many grieving families over the years and showed his experience as a senior investigator when he instructed his team to retain any of

Wilson's cigarettes for the purpose of obtaining his DNA. It was one of the first times gardaí used the strategy of obtaining DNA from a suspect's discarded cigarette.'

Sean Hunt had now been shorn of Eric, Keith and Alan Wilson and was no longer prepared to use John's services. That made the dissidents bolder. While at the family home on Ramillies Road at the beginning of December 2011, he emerged to find a pipe bomb had been left under the front of his van. Most people would have called in the army to defuse it, but not Hunt.

A senior investigator with knowledge of the incident revealed, 'He disposed of it himself. He was extremely lucky. The bomb was a substantial device, it would have taken down the front of the house; the van was parked right up against the front of the house. He dismantled it and told gardaí he had thrown it in the canal.' Whatever else Hunt was, he was certainly not a coward. Threats were coming thick and fast, but Hunt stayed put rather than moving to Spain permanently to take himself out of the dissidents' reach.

Gardaí were regular visitors to his home to serve him with an official green Garda Information Message (GIM) about a credible danger to his life. On such occasions, gardaí are required to advise the recipient on his security, even if they know their instructions will be completely ignored.

'He wouldn't tell you anything about himself or his business,' the investigator said. 'He would say he could take care of himself. He would talk to us about it, but only to try and elicit information on exactly where the threats were coming from.'

Eric and Keith had now gone down due to acts of extraordinary carelessness. Their cousin Alan was about to show them he could match them in that department.

10. 'We found her'

The remains were taken out of the bag – he took the
body out and just rolled it into the hole
                                        – Fergus O'Hanlon

If Alan Wilson had access to a contraband mobile phone inside Cloverhill prison, he did not appear to be using it. Instead, he made the most extraordinary series of calls on the official prison phone, despite signing a consent form upon his arrival at the jail acknowledging that all outgoing communications on it were recorded by the Irish Prison Service.

Six days after his return behind bars, the *Sunday World* ran an article about the Marioara investigation. Without naming Alan, it cited the belief of garda sources that the chief suspect in the investigation was close to a 'nervous breakdown'. He would soon prove them right.

With his cousins in jail and his best friend Fergus O'Hanlon's loyalty no longer guaranteed following the split from Maxine, Wilson sought to take control of matters on the outside from behind the walls of Cloverhill.

In a chilling telephone call to his mother Mary on 30 August 2011, Wilson threatened to kill a *Sunday World* journalist, along with a senior detective from Kevin Street station. During the call, he told his mother, 'Listen, the damage the police and this paper person done to me, I'm going to resolve this whether I live or die. I'm going to take them to the next life with me. This, these people and this man that done this print is after taking my family away from me and I'm going to do the same to him, yeah, whether I live or die, no matter what it takes.'

In another call just a few days later, Wilson outlined his intentions for his best friend when he said, 'Tell them to call Fergus down somewhere and kill him.' Alarmed by the content of the calls from August, the Irish Prison Service was preparing to deliver the sinister recordings to detectives when they intercepted another one between Wilson and his mother at 11.13 a.m. on 16 September 2011.

He reiterated his threats, declaring, 'That man that wrote the newspaper article, yeah, a lot of people are calling us names over that.' Bizarrely, Wilson had also seemingly forgotten about his earlier attempts to have Fergus O'Hanlon murdered. 'Tell Fergus to give the best weapons over and do whatever,' he told his mother. 'Get in touch with John, Richard, everybody around you, tell Maxine too and tell them to do as much damage as possible.

'Just tell them to get the best yokes and get it dealt with and tell him, your man that wrote that, I'll give him €20,000 if he goes to that address and sorts it out. Tell them to attack any member of his family and kill them.' Gardaí suspected the names mentioned by Alan Wilson referred to his cousins John Wilson and Richard Cawley, who had also been recruited by Alan to shoot Fergus O'Hanlon.

Following the calls, gardaí also received intelligence that Cawley had previously met with O'Hanlon to discuss Alan's situation. During the meeting a woman is believed to have told O'Hanlon that Cawley was planning on shooting him because he owed a €3,000 drug debt to Alan. Cawley would never get the chance to target O'Hanlon because the latter was found dead from a suspected drugs overdose on 27 September.

The recordings were passed to detectives at Kevin Street and the Irish Prison Service continued to listen to Wilson's ramblings.

Two months on from the publication of the *Sunday World* article, Wilson was still venting his frustrations about the media and the gardaí, this time in a call to his girlfriend, Rachel Hamilton. In a telephone call on 4 October 2011 he launched a tirade of abuse against the same senior detective who he had threatened in an earlier call. 'That fucking copper, tried to set us up,' he said. 'Cunt, isn't he?'

In total, the Irish Prison Service recorded a staggering 123 phone calls of Alan Wilson's conversations between 21 July and 22 November that year. After considering the content of the calls, gardaí made their next move on 28 November when Wilson, his mother Mary, sister Maxine and Fergus O'Hanlon were all arrested on suspicion of conspiracy to kill the journalist and detective. Kilcline was also arrested on suspicion of withholding information, although he maintains his arrest was staged.

During the course of their interviews with Wilson, detectives played him the recorded calls. In response, he denied his threats were genuine: 'I wasn't serious about the threats. I don't intend to kill anyone. I was just frustrated.' While Wilson's relatives and his close associate were being questioned, the decision to play the recordings to O'Hanlon was also made.

Although O'Hanlon was aware he was in serious danger following the previous attempts on his life, hearing his former friend so callously issue orders to have him killed proved a turning point in the investigation. After months of battling his demons, O'Hanlon made the decision to work with gardaí.

Shortly before he was due to be released on 1 December

2011 O'Hanlon put in a request to speak to Detective Superintendent O'Gara and a meeting was duly arranged at Kevin Street garda station. Those in attendance included O'Gara, Detective Inspector J. J. Keane and Sergeant Sean McAvinchey. O'Hanlon opened the meeting by asking what sort of 'protection' he could expect to receive if he provided them with information on the murder of Marioara Rostas.

He was assured that gardaí would use every resource at their disposal to protect him and his family. Another reassurance was that Sergeant McAvinchey would maintain contact with him, by telephone and in person. Reassured, O'Hanlon asked to meet Sergeant McAvinchey on 6 December 2011. The officer was accompanied by his colleagues Ciaran Byrne, Brian Heaney and William Wright as they met with O'Hanlon in the city centre. From there, they drove to Orwell Park in south Dublin.

Upon arrival O'Hanlon guided them to a location close to the High School in Rathgar and pointed them to a spot where he claimed Wilson had stashed firearms and ammunition. 'I was shown where the spots were by Alan Wilson,' he said. 'He told me that the Wavin pipe with ammunition and the sawn-off rifle were there.' Garda search teams immediately launched a coordinated sweep of the area during daylight the following morning, but were unable to locate any weapons.

However, when the gardaí met with O'Hanlon at an ESB substation on Dodder Road on 8 December 2011, they had better luck when they recovered two 9 mm handguns and a quantity of 9 mm ammunition. The weapons were well wrapped in silver duct tape, covered with a plastic bag and buried in a deep hole. Garda ballistic experts later confirmed the firearms were in 'perfect condition'. During the search O'Hanlon also helped dig for the guns and when asked how he knew the weapons had been buried at the site, he replied, 'I knew that the two automatic handguns would be there because I seen them being put in a pipe and transported off. Alan Wilson transported them himself from New Street Gardens.'

As O'Hanlon worked closely with the state, officers received more useful information from Herbert Kilcline. He claimed Alan Wilson had been using a one-bedroom apartment in Clontarf, north Dublin, at the time Marioara disappeared. The property had been rented by Wilson in O'Hanlon's name, but used by Wilson so he could still get the €200 per week carer's payment for looking after his mother.

According to Kilcline, O'Hanlon would stay at the property after rowing with his then partner Maxine. Later, gardaí established that flat No. 5 on the middle floor of 23 Castle Avenue had been leased by Alan Wilson until 3 July 2009. The lease had only ended when there had been a fire in the bedroom.

Twenty-four hours before O'Hanlon's release, officers also interviewed Herbert Kilcline on suspicion of withholding information. Unbeknownst to Alan Wilson, Kilcline, a qualified solicitor, agreed to assist Detective Sergeant John Doyle in persuading Fergus O'Hanlon to give up the body of the teenager. Although it had started off as a missing-person case, gardaí were now dealing with a murder inquiry.

Kilcline recalled his behaviour in the weeks following Wilson's threats over the prison phone in an interview with gardaí. He explained: 'Mary Wilson contacted me to say that Alan needed to see me – the reason given was that he wanted assistance with a drug-driving charge that he was expecting. After much consideration, and conferring with Sergeant Doyle, I decided to go on the visit in the hope that he just might say something about the Rostas case.

'However, when I visited Alan, he was in a rage and grinding his teeth and clenching his fists. Instead of focusing on the imminent drug-driving charge – which is the reason I was there – his focus was on the recent *Sunday World* article. He was asking how can people be located and that they needed to be "dealt with" and that Fergus would have to do it.

'Alan then said could we go to libraries to look up old phone directories to find where people lived. He asked if I could check in the Land Registry to see if they owned houses, or did I know anyone in the ESB who could find people. I was taken by surprise by this so I just told him to leave it and that the story would blow over. He then quietened down a bit and said he would be out soon and look after business.'

Kilcline also maintains that his 'arrest' over the threats made to the *Sunday World* journalist and the detective was staged to convince Wilson of his loyalty. As he explained: 'I had to be arrested for my own safety but when Maxine was arrested she knew I'd set her up. These arrests were seen as a window of opportunity to get Fergus to start talking.

'When I was being held I said I was happy to stay to assist with putting things together in case I could assist with anything that emerged in interviews.

'I knew Fergus wouldn't have anything to do with this mad murder plan and when the recordings of Alan threatening to have Fergus shot were played to him, that's when he decided to finally go against Alan.'

Though O'Hanlon continued to work with gardaí, he found himself in trouble again on 28 December 2011 when he was arrested on suspected burglary offences and remanded to Cloverhill prison. On 30 December O'Hanlon's new girlfriend made contact with gardaí informing them that he now wanted 'to do the right thing' in helping officers to locate the Romanian girl's remains, but continued to insist that he had to speak to his solicitor Bridget Rouse first. Investigators made it clear to him there would be 'no promises' of 'favourable treatment', explaining the decision would be a matter for the DPP.

At 4.55 p.m. on 3 January 2012 Bridget Rouse contacted gardaí to let them know O'Hanlon was now prepared to bring authorities to where the Romanian teenager had been buried. Within minutes, gardaí were on their way to Cloverhill prison.

O'Hanlon was brought to a meeting room inside the prison at 6.02 p.m. There he outlined his version of events regarding the murder of Marioara Rostas. O'Hanlon claimed that after arriving at 2 Brabazon Street at 5.30 p.m. on 8 January 2008 he was 'physically sick' when he saw the body of a female lying in a top-floor bedroom.

He said he was convinced he could be charged with the killing as Wilson left the house. When Wilson returned at 8.40 p.m. O'Hanlon said he was carrying a 'large green lawnmower bag' and 'cleaning agents'. He said Wilson lifted a firearm, loaded the ammunition magazine, cocked the weapon and told O'Hanlon, 'Get that bag and come on.'

O'Hanlon continued: 'At this point, I wasn't sure what was going to happen; he was behind me with the weapon and I knew there was one in the breech. I was afraid to ask anything else. I presumed he wouldn't want to leave anyone to tell the story and I was afraid he'd kill me. It was after all this happened, within a few days I started drinking heavily.'

O'Hanlon was released on bail from the District Court on 9 January and met with two members of the gardaí. He directed them towards the Dublin mountains, a dumping ground for bodies often used by crime gangs as well as the suspected killers of several young women who had vanished in the 1980s and 1990s.

As the garda car drove along the R759 road, O'Hanlon

asked them to stop. Stepping out of the car at a locked gate to Kippure Forest, he told the officers he was certain that they were standing at the same gate through which he and Alan Wilson had carried Marioara Rostas's body.

Darkness was falling, so the trio left and returned the following morning. Once back at the same spot, they climbed over the gate and headed along a track on the left-hand side of the forest. O'Hanlon stopped at a point halfway up the hill, indicating an area covered by thick, dense trees, where he believed the teenager had been buried. The group were then joined by Senior Investigating Officer Cryan and Detective Superintendent O'Gara. The latter recalled, 'It was the perfect place to bury a body because it was in the middle of nowhere.' Once the possible burial site was identified, O'Hanlon was driven to Naas garda station to continue his interviews.

There, he told gardaí that Alan Wilson had claimed he murdered Marioara because she had witnessed her brother being killed at the flat in Clontarf. O'Hanlon insisted that Wilson had then 'taped [Marioara's] body from head to toe' before folding her into 'the shape of a horseshoe groove' and placing the body in the boot of the car.

O'Hanlon maintained that Wilson ordered him to lie down in the back of the vehicle. 'At this stage I was getting extremely nervous and I got on to the floor of the car,' he told gardaí. 'I had to compose myself and hold it together because if I showed any weakness, I was in fear that wherever we were going, I wasn't going to come back from.'

O'Hanlon said that upon their arrival at the forest Wilson began looking for a 'bunker' and 'signs of wood', but couldn't find them. Unable to locate the 'bunker', the pair started digging. 'I was thinking to myself that I could end up the same way and end up in the same hole,' O'Hanlon told gardaí. 'I was the only witness to this. When the hole was dug, the remains were taken out of the bag – he took the body out and just rolled it into the hole. The body was in the hole and Alan started slamming the head of the body with his foot, there was at least five or six slams.' In an attempt to cover their tracks, O'Hanlon told investigators they had spread pine needles to restore the ground to its original state.

O'Hanlon completed his interviews by claiming that Wilson instructed him to clean the room where he maintained the teenager had been shot. He said, 'I started off by myself but he dropped in from time to time over the next few days to see how well the room was cleaned. The second day he came in with a bell-sander for sanding wood. Bleach and ammonia were used to clean the wall.'

While gardaí began a search on the mountainside, the hunt for the weapons identified by O'Hanlon in Orwell Park was also stepped up. On 15 January the Defence Forces, using high-tech search equipment, discovered a pipe containing a large amount of ammunition including 9 mm rounds, shotgun rounds, .22 ammunition and a handgun close to the High School in Rathgar. Two days later, the army also recovered a three-foot-long Wavin pipe containing ammunition, a knife and balaclava in Bushy Park. Part of a wall beside the tennis courts in Terenure College was searched too and a Smith & Wesson revolver retrieved.

O'Hanlon, who had returned to Kippure on 16 January to again insist it was the area where the teenager had been buried, brought gardaí to the sprawling fields of Bushy Park, a 51-acre recreational area located in the Terenure area of Dublin, the following day. He led the officers to a wooded section of the park close to the River Dodder. Gardaí would later recover a .357 Magnum revolver, a sawn-off shotgun and a quantity of ammunition, all covered in silver duct tape. According to O'Hanlon, the Magnum had been used by Eric

Wilson to murder Roy Coddington in Drogheda on 22 March 2007. 'The Magnum was used in a murder in early 2007,' he said. 'I was serving a sentence in the Midlands Prison at the time. I was told by Alan when I was released the Magnum was used in Drogheda to kill Roy Coddington. That's what I was told by him.'

O'Hanlon also pointed to an area close to the bandstand, which he claimed contained Alan Wilson's 'ready-to-go kit'. According to O'Hanlon, his former close pal kept an emergency bag containing clothing and weapons to be accessed if he ended up on the run from gardaí, his enemies in the Real IRA or rival criminal gangs. Despite an extensive search, gardaí were unable to locate the 'emergency kit'.

The weapons had all been recovered, but there was, as yet, no sign of Marioara's body. The search, involving twenty gardaí from the South Central Divisional Search Team, the organization's Technical Bureau, the Garda Dog Unit and a mechanical digger operated by Garda Dermot Walsh, had begun on 13 January under the command of Patrick McMenamin, now a chief superintendent. Working in teams and armed with shovels and spades, the team had to dig trenches and test the shape and colour of the ground around them over a 200-metre radius. It was an arduous task.

Just three days into the search Garda Walsh was operating the digger when he spotted planks of plywood. Further excavations revealed a deep rectangular hole, measuring about 5 foot wide and 3 foot 6 inches deep. Gardaí believed it was the 'bunker' referred to by O'Hanlon. But despite its misleading name, they considered it more likely to be a pre-prepared grave. 'It just didn't make sense to store weapons there because they wouldn't have been easily accessible,' former Detective Superintendent O'Gara said.

As the search for Marioara's body entered its tenth day on

23 January, Garda Walsh was carefully removing soil when he noticed parts of a black plastic bag protruding from below the roots of a tree. Switching off the vehicle, Garda Walsh shouted for his colleagues to join him. Within minutes, the Garda Technical Bureau had removed what appeared to be a set of human remains from a shallow grave before placing it, still curled in the 'foetal position', into a sterile body bag.

As he sat in his office, Detective Superintendent O'Gara received the call he had been anticipating for three years. He walked the short distance to Superintendent Gannon's office and told him, 'We found her, Joe. We found her.' The pair, along with Senior Investigating Officer Cryan, later made their way to the mountain as they waited for Assistant State Pathologist Dr Khalid Jabbar to arrive.

The forensic scientist soon confirmed the discovery of human remains. Although no official identification could be made without a full examination, gardaí were in no doubt they had recovered the body of the missing teenager. 'There was an eerie silence on the mountain that day once the remains had been discovered and it's a day I will never forget,' O'Gara said. 'One of the first thoughts that entered my head was that the poor girl would have been lying in that makeshift grave all alone during the terrible winter of 2010 and under a tonne of snow. There were guards with bruises, blisters and cuts, but when those remains were discovered there was a dignified relief among everyone standing on that mountain. Once she had been removed, there was a rigid outline and indentation of where she had been resting for the last four years. If the search team had not found her, I don't think I would ever have got them off that mountain. There was immense relief that this poor and vulnerable girl could now get the Christian burial she deserved.'

Chief Superintendent McMenamin also paid tribute to

the work put in by his officers: 'It was just such a great team effort from everyone involved. It was tough, manual labour but everyone was prepared to keep going until we had achieved our objective. We weren't leaving that mountain without Marioara.' As the coffin carrying the remains left the Wicklow mountains at 2.22 p.m., arriving at Tallaght hospital mortuary a short time later, word soon spread of the discovery and the news broke on RTÉ that a body had been found.

Alan Wilson's reaction to the discovery would come two days later. A close associate of O'Hanlon, with no involvement in crime, was confronted by two men in the Rathmines area. During the altercation, one of the men said, 'Fergus is doing a lot of talking these days. You must read the papers. We know what he is doing. Watch your backs. Now you've been told.'

The discovery of the body topped the news agenda. Dr Jabbar's initial post-mortem findings concluded that the remains were female and she had been shot in the head four times with a .22 firearm. The body had been wrapped in eight black plastic bags, a bed sheet, pillowcase and one large, industrial-sized clear plastic wrap and bound with duct tape.

With the body recovered, gardaí now needed to tie Alan Wilson to the crime. One way of doing this would be to establish what telecommunications mast Wilson's mobile number, which they had obtained from his sister's phone, was pinging off on 8 January 2008. By identifying the area and time where the phone had been in use, detectives hoped to corroborate O'Hanlon's testimony. Their star witness also told gardaí he recalled seeing a receipt from Woodie's hardware store in the green lawnmower bag used to bury the teenager, and gardaí were able to establish that Wilson's phone had been pinging on the Long Mile Road, the location of one branch of the hardware store.

A press conference was arranged at Pearse Street garda station on 26 January, with Chief Superintendent Michael O'Sullivan telling journalists present that seasoned detectives had been 'shaken' by the murder.

He said, 'It was the most heinous of crimes, which shocked all the investigating officers and the search teams who found her body. I can say she suffered an appalling death that is incomprehensible in a civilized society. Marioara was a harmless, defenceless young woman. She was abducted, brutalized and murdercd for no apparent reason.' The following day journalist Brenda Power wrote of her horror in her *Irish Daily Mail* column: 'The last person to see Marioara alive was her 15-year-old brother,' she said. 'Their misery, neither of them much more than children, is unimaginable even in recession, never mind prosperity.'

Around the same time, a friend of Wilson's sister Maxine, who cannot be identified, also came forward to gardaí to provide more evidence of the conspiracy of silence around the murder. 'She told me that Alan Wilson, her brother, brought a Romanian girl back to the house,' the woman said. 'She showed me the house and I asked her why she was killed and she said because they had seen "the devil in her eyes".'

The Rostas family returned to Ireland on 29 January 2012 to reclaim their daughter's body. It was later repatriated to her homeland on 7 February 2012, with the €10,000 cost covered by the Department of Social Protection. Before leaving Ireland, Marioara's heartbroken father Dumitru said, 'All my hope lies in the Irish police. Whoever did this were monsters. I want to look into the eyes of the men who did this. I kept hope that my daughter was alive but after a while I knew she was dead.' Senior Investigating Officer Cryan and the garda family-liaison officer Paul Murphy, now a detective inspector, later travelled to Romania for her funeral while the teenager was simultaneously remembered at a vigil in Dublin city centre.

Alan Wilson was now frantically trying to prevent the case against him building further. With Fergus O'Hanlon under the protection of the gardaí, Alan sent his cousin John round to terrorize his former friend Herbert Kilcline instead.

'Fergus was out of the way so I was the number-one target because he knew I was working with the gardaí,' Kilcline said. 'There was one incident in which I was hit with a pick-axe handle in my back yard around the start of February 2012. The guy was wearing a balaclava but I recognized the eyes – they were John Wilson's. I was also later told that he had a gun buried somewhere in a lane at the back of my property but when it came to it I don't think he was brave enough to do it. I think John was more suited to being a lookout man rather than a killer. When I met him before he would stare at you and give the impression he would take no messing and there's no doubt he could be intimidating.'

O'Hanlon had his next appointment at Nenagh garda station and pointed out four more sites where possible weapons had been buried. One of those sites was a property in Rathdrum Road, Crumlin. The following day, 18 February 2012, O'Hanlon had his fifth, sixth, seventh and eighth statements with the investigation team at Ennistymon garda station. At 1.12 p.m. he began to provide details of the attempts on his life.

Referring to the incident in Dun Laoghaire, he said, 'We were on the Dart and Maxine was on the phone. When we got to the last stop, I seen someone coming towards me with a jacket up to his nose, one hand in the pocket and a baseball cap on. I thought this was suspicious, you know, a summer's day, so I jumped on the track, on to the other side.

'I called Herbie [Kilcline] to pick me up. Herbie came, but he was in a panic, he didn't even stop, he drove by me into another car. The back of the car was damaged. I went over to see if he was OK and he told me Alan rang him asking what he was doing, that he was getting in the way of business.' Throughout the afternoon, O'Hanlon recounted his information on the murders of Roy Coddington, along with David Lindsay and Alan Napper. At 7.21 that evening O'Hanlon also outlined his knowledge of the flat in Clontarf, detailing how it was often used by Wilson's associates to 'cut up cocaine' before revealing how Wilson had instructed Herbert Kilcline to pay the landlord €13,000 in compensation for the fire.

During his interviews O'Hanlon was also asked if he had seen any other firearms. 'Only a time when I was with Alan down the country,' he answered. 'I didn't know where we were and then Alan pulled into a garden. He told me Eric was there but I'd only seen Eric once before then.

'So when I was in I went to sit down on the couch. There was something hard, so I pulled it out. I thought at first it was an AK-47 but it turned out to be a replica. I turned to put it under the sofa but I couldn't, so I kneeled down and there were three or four shotguns under the sofa. There was another weapon upstairs, there was red writing on it – Heckler.' This was a clear reference to the house at Killerig in Carlow and was viewed by gardaí as further confirmation of O'Hanlon's information.

Five days after his last statements were made, officers recovered two handguns and ammunition inside a pipe buried under concrete in the front garden of a house in Rutland Avenue.

The following day O'Hanlon travelled north with Sergeant McAvinchey and Detective Sergeant Doyle to meet with the

PSNI. Just as he had done in 2010, he pointed out the site where it was believed Napper and Lindsay were buried.

On 6 March 2012 Alan Wilson appeared before Dublin District Court accused of burglary over the cleaver and shotgun incident at Lisa Murray's home in Blanchardstown three years earlier.

Meanwhile, gardaí involved in the Marioara probe continued to build their case.

11. Feeling the Heat

*I didn't want to go into the witness protection programme
because it would have turned my life upside down*
— Herbert Kilcline

While Fergus O'Hanlon's secret interviews continued at various locations outside the capital, gardaí decided to keep up the pressure on Alan Wilson's family by bringing in his sister and mother for a third time on suspicion of withholding information. At lunchtime on 9 March 2012 gardaí arrived at the family home in New Street Gardens and both women were arrested and taken to Pearse Street station.

Maxine had refused to identify the killer of the Romanian teenager when she was previously arrested, but this interview would be different. Without batting an eyelid, she named her ex-partner Fergus O'Hanlon as the murderer, although without offering any evidence. She had also bizarrely claimed she was being pursued by associates of notorious INLA godfathers Declan 'Whacker' Duffy and Dessie 'The Border Fox' O'Hare over an unpaid drugs debt. In her interview, Mary Wilson maintained a 'no comment' stance and both women were released without charge the following day.

On 23 March Alan Wilson was rearrested by SIO Cryan on suspicion of possessing a firearm with intent to endanger life at 2 Brabazon Street between 6 January and 29 February 2008. Three days beforehand a former female friend of his had confirmed that Wilson's mobile number ended in the digits 309.

During a 24-hour detention Wilson was interviewed fifteen times and made no comment on each occasion before he was released back into the custody of Cloverhill prison at 7.13 p.m.

Two days later Fergus O'Hanlon made his ninth statement to investigators at Newbridge garda station in Co. Kildare. This time they focused on phone records, his memory of the flat in Clontarf, the bullet holes found in 2 Brabazon Street and his visit with gardaí to Co. Down in February 2010.

'I wanted to bring them to the spot,' O'Hanlon said. Repeating the statement he previously made after bringing gardaí on a wild goose chase across the border, he added: 'I thought of my family. If the body was recovered, what would happen? Members of my family would have been killed. I heard bullets being fired before. It wouldn't have been the first time that Alan Wilson openly used guns and tested them with phone books inside a house.'

Gardaí worked the phone evidence as Detective Garda Brian Sheeran prepared their file for the DPP and established that Marioara had rung her brother on 7 January 2008 from a device with the number 085 8264309, the last three digits of which matched the ones in the statement given by Wilson's female ex-pal.

Connecting the number definitively to Alan Wilson was proving difficult, but gardaí received a breakthrough when it emerged that the SIM card for the number had been used in a device owned by Maxine Wilson. They also established that Maxine's number had been in contact twenty-nine times between 7 and 8 January 2008 with the number Marioara had used.

The phone used by Marioara to contact her brother belonged

to a pre-paid, unregistered user. However, gardaí were later satisfied it was Wilson's phone after Herbert Kilcline and another former female associate identified the number as his.

Officers also established that the number had been in use at three different locations, all central to the inquiry. The most crucial information outlined how the number Marioara used to ring her brother in Romania had been mapped by the telecommunications mast at Clontarf Castle. The phone evidence was the last piece of evidence contained in the gardaí's preliminary prosecution file to be sent to the DPP.

While the DPP considered what charge to bring, Alan Wilson appeared at Dublin Circuit Court on 29 March hoping to have his charge of aggravated burglary for the raid on the Mountaine family home in 2010 dismissed. His legal team's main argument was that the Section 29 warrant used by gardaí to arrest him on 9 February 2010 was no longer valid thanks to a controversial decision by the Supreme Court the previous month.

The Section 29 warrant had been introduced in 1976 to allow senior gardaí to authorize an emergency search, but the Supreme Court had recently accepted a challenge to its use by Algerian national Ali Charaf Damache. He had been apprehended after an international investigation into an alleged conspiracy to murder Swedish cartoonist Lars Vilks because of his allegedly blasphemous drawing of the prophet Muhammad. Since the ruling, dozens of cases and convictions had been quashed because of the 'unconstitutional' warrant.

Addressing the court, Wilson's barrister, Michael O'Higgins, explained how a woollen hat had been found in a neighbouring garden close to Mr Mountaine's home. Three DNA profiles had been identified from it, with his client's having the majority profile. Mr O'Higgins said his client had been arrested at his home and brought to a garda station for questioning and, crucially, to obtain a DNA sample.

The barrister informed the court his client had been held under a Section 29 warrant, which he claimed rendered his subsequent detention as 'unlawful' and any evidence taken from him was 'inadmissible'. After careful consideration, Judge Martin Nolan accepted the legal arguments made by Wilson's legal team and struck out the case. Although a victory for Wilson, he remained in garda custody as he still faced a charge over the Blanchardstown incident.

On 4 April 2012 gardaí visited Clontarf and spoke to a number of residents at the flat complex on Castle Avenue. All were shown twelve separate images of men and women and asked if they had been present at the flat. One woman interviewed that day immediately pointed to the image of Alan Wilson before suggesting his name was 'Fergus', while another resident pointed to Wilson's photo and said his name was 'Martin O'Hanlon'. The statements backed up Kilcline's previous statement that the flat had been organized by Wilson.

Just eight days after receiving the preliminary garda investigation file, the DPP contacted Detective Superintendent O'Gara to inform him there was enough evidence to charge Wilson with the murder of Marioara Rostas. The file had been sent before a separate request to access phone records of the suspects had been delivered to Garda HQ from Pearse Street station. In their application, gardaí said, 'Alan Wilson has connections to organized crime in Dublin.

'A profile was completed on him in Ballyfermot due to his association with the Rattigans and members of his family who are involved in firearms crimes. He is suspected of involvement in the sale and supply of weapons. He is described by informants as extremely dangerous and very violent. He is suspected to be a cocaine user.

'He changes cars quite a lot and intelligence would suggest that he changes his mobile number once a week. During the summer of 2008, he spent some time on holidays in Conne-mara, Co. Galway.'

In their summary of O'Hanlon, gardaí concluded, 'O'Hanlon is described by gardaí as being very violent and is also suspected of having access to firearms. He is a heroin addict and probably a cocaine user as well.' The reports would describe Maxine Wilson as having connections to ser-ious crime 'through her brother and partner', while Mary Wilson was described as being 'extremely protective of her son, believing he can do no harm'.

Following the DPP's decision, Senior Investigating Officer Cryan, along with four members of his team, were dis-patched to Cloverhill prison. At 4.15 p.m. on 5 April Alan Wilson was arrested on suspicion of murder. Clearly irri-tated, he replied, 'You have ruined my evening. I wanted to hold my daughter for the first time.'

Wilson was transferred to Pearse Street station and for-mally cautioned with the offence at 5.45 p.m. He replied, 'I didn't do this.' He was brought to a special sitting of Dublin District Court at 8 p.m., where he sat with his hands in his pockets while he was charged with murdering Marioara Rostas. As he was remanded in custody, his only supporter in the court, his sister Maxine, yelled, 'I love you, bro.'

By the time of the charge, the forensic report on the .22 bullet fragments lodged in the walls of 2 Brabazon Street had been completed. Detective Brian Barry from the garda ballis-tics section concluded that the ammunition discovered in the house was the same calibre, the same design and had the same characteristics as that used to kill the Romanian teenager. The weapons experts were unable to make a 100 per cent match because of the damage to the bullets in the walls.

However, gardaí had better luck with the .357 Magnum recovered after O'Hanlon pinpointed the spot where it had been buried. Though O'Hanlon said it had been used to murder Roy Coddington in Drogheda, an examination of the weapon found it had actually been used to kill David 'Boogie' Brett in Co. Cork on 21 May 2007.

Gardaí had told his inquest in 2008 that it was their belief the victim had been executed in a 'professional hit'. The weapon was found to be clean of fingerprints and DNA, but the revelation prompted gardaí to issue a fresh television appeal for information. Inspector Tony Sugrue told viewers, 'We are convinced there were a number of people involved in the handling and transportation of this weapon before the killers themselves used it. There wasn't just one person involved.' At the time of writing in 2020, the case remains under active garda investigation.

Investigators believe the Wilsons merely provided the weapon to be used in the shooting, but had decided to hang on to it afterwards despite the risks. One former associate of Alan Wilson, who cannot be named, told the authors Wilson did not dump weapons used in murders – even though they could potentially be used to prosecute him for killings not committed by him.

The source said, 'Because Alan was so fucking tight, the more money he got, the meaner he got. The barrels were being opened with a drill. He was running a drill up the barrel to change the lands and grooves. The gun would be wrapped up then, and buried.

'Just lashing a drill bit up and down the barrel, that's not going to destroy the striations, the lands and grooves. It's tempered steel and it goes way into the steel. You can't remove the lands and grooves. A lot of people are under the impression if you put a drill bit up and down the barrel, you'll destroy the lands and grooves and you can use it again and again. But if you do that, you make that barrel more unstable.

The bullet tumbles as it travels down the barrel. It destroys the accuracy.'

As detectives in Pearse Street prepared their Book of Evidence for court, they were also reminded of the threat posed to people associated with their key witness, O'Hanlon. They received a complaint that Wilson's mother, and a female associate of convicted Kinahan cartel arsonist Davin Flynn, had called to The Finches pub in the Neilstown area of west Dublin on 11 April.

There, they asked to speak to the stepfather of O'Hanlon's new partner. Upon being told that he wasn't in the bar, the women asked one of his friends to contact him by phone. When he answered, the man was informed he'd 'better' tell his stepdaughter to withdraw any statement she had made in relation to the Marioara Rostas case. The pair were arrested three days later on suspicion of the 'attempted intimidation' of a potential witness.

During her questioning at the garda station, Wilson's mother asked to use the ladies. She was accompanied by Garda Amy Kelly who, on hearing the sound of rustling paper, forced open the cubicle door, catching Wilson's mother red-handed, attempting to flush something down the toilet. Although the note was partially damaged, it appeared to contain instructions on individuals who should be targeted. As a result, gardaí obtained a warrant to immediately search Alan Wilson's cell at Cloverhill prison.

That raid recovered a handwritten note, the home address of former Justice Minister Alan Shatter and a map providing directions to an unidentified house, detailing a plan to murder Kilcline. The note, littered with spelling mistakes and addressed to Wilson's mother, is revealed here for the first time. It read:

'*You don't deserve all this bad in our lives. Things will turn around for us but we have to make it work it's going to be a battel but we can do it so keep your head clear and focus on what needs to be dunne. I can only be as good as what you can do for me now so do what I ask ive well tot about things. I will get a life sentence if h lives so listen and we work this out.'*

Also in the note were references to Kilcline with the letter 'h' circled: *'I will get a life sentence if h lives so listen and we work this out,'* it said.

Instructions followed with the name of the person tasked with murdering Kilcline: *'For h, ******, will do it. Ask can he get sun and car. Push ***** to do this tell him I'll give him 10,000 and what ever he needs. If or when this is dunne things will fall into place.'*

The note also gave further directions relating to Wilson's legal battle: *'Talk to solicitor play the game offer him 10,000 see what he says he comes across as haven a soft heart play on that. Evidence matters. Ask Max to get a list of F [O'Hanlon] girlfriends and all the times when he was violent.'*

Lastly, there were requests for clothes: *'Runners, tracksuits shorts socks. Be happy all the time no matter what. That money safe. How much have we lying around. what about 800. You and max are going to tick the box so uses need to look well going to use words not to use.'*

The note was only one key piece of evidence against Wilson obtained that day. On his way home from work, SIO Cryan received a call from a colleague at Pearse Street station informing him that a caller had contacted the station demanding to speak to him and insisting it was urgent. Cryan returned the call and recognized the voice from previous investigations.

Along with a colleague, he met the man in a McDonald's car park in the capital. The informant told Cryan that he had been offered cash to murder Kilcline, with John Wilson acting as a getaway driver on a motorbike. The man was adamant he had no intention of getting involved. In a final warning, the man told Cryan that the plan to kill the solicitor was at an advanced stage and it would only be a matter of time before someone else was recruited to carry it out. The armed Emergency Response Unit was immediately dispatched to Kilcline's home and he was taken out of Dublin.

Kilcline later recalled, 'The gardaí told me I was at risk and to take precautions by leaving my home. They didn't tell me who was plotting to kill me but I heard it was John because he was the only one of Alan's cousins who was left and he had also previously attacked me. There was also some kind of map and I think this was to my house. I was also aware of a previous occasion in which Mary Wilson put some notes down the toilet. She could just see no wrong in her son.

'I didn't want to go into the witness protection programme because it would have turned my life upside down. I had elderly parents and I was working at law as well. I was simply given safety advice and then I went away for two weeks.

'Obviously they had an idea I was working for the police and I also made it clear to Fergus in the middle of all this that whatever I knew, I would pass on. The whole thing was very intimidating and I was under serious pressure with some of my friends very concerned for my mental well-being and concerned that I would harm myself.'

That same evening gardaí returned to Cloverhill prison to listen to Wilson's telephone calls. In one to his sister, he could be heard ordering her to 'put that on hold'. Gardaí also received intelligence of Wilson's belief that his cell was being bugged after he showed his mother a note he had penned as she visited together with a younger relative. As Wilson's mother was illiterate, the information, containing details on his case, was taken down by his younger relative. A file was later sent to the DPP, but no charges were ever brought over the conspiracy plot.

The campaign of intimidation continued. On 28 May 2012 O'Hanlon's new partner was preparing dinner when there was a knock at the front door. Answering it, the young mother was confronted by Maxine Wilson and her new partner. The man, who cannot be identified for legal reasons, lunged at her and the pair attempted to force their way in, demanding to know where O'Hanlon was. With her terrified children screaming in the background, the woman managed to slam her door and rang 999.

Shortly after the incident Maxine and her partner were arrested in west Dublin and later charged with trespassing. The case was dealt with in the form of summary disposal by Dublin District Court, with the culprits ordered not to have further contact with 'any witnesses' in the case of DPP vs Alan Wilson.

Maxine also secretly met with a garda for coffee on a few occasions. The aim of the interactions was to persuade her to testify against her brother. 'She was very close to making a statement against her brother but she didn't in the end because she was terrified,' one investigator said. 'She had met with a female garda on a few occasions and was clearly troubled by what she knew but she just ended up following orders.'

Wilson was busy on the intimidation front inside too. He spent hours canvassing inmates at Cloverhill prison, asking them if they knew Fergus O'Hanlon or if there was anyone in the jail who was close to him. Towards the end of June 2012 a conversation with another inmate pointed him towards an incarcerated relative of O'Hanlon's. Wilson approached him several times, each time pressing him to give up O'Hanlon's current location. Concerned for his safety, the prisoner told his wife that Wilson had been putting him 'under pressure' to uncover O'Hanlon's whereabouts. She duly informed gardaí and investigators immediately contacted the Irish Prison Service to report Wilson's threatening behaviour. The inmate was later moved to a different landing

and an assurance was given there would be no further contact between them.

By the end of July 2012 the DPP had received the gardaí's
full file on their investigation into the murder of Marioara
Rostas. The 122-page document contained statements, forensic reports, crime-scene images and background information
on everyone connected to the case as well as a detailed account
of the investigation. Gardaí now turned their attention to
completing their Book of Evidence, which had to be ready by
August. Once delivered, Wilson would know the date of
when he was to stand trial for the teenager's murder.

In the meantime, Wilson had kept his head down in prison
after the attempts at intimidating associates of O'Hanlon
had failed, with his only visitors being his mother and sister.
On the outside, Wilson's main link continued to be his cousin
John, who was also under threat from criminals and the Real
IRA. John had been pulled in and questioned about intimidation attempts during the month too, before being released
without charge.

According to Herbert Kilcline, Alan Wilson had become
increasingly reliant on his cousin from 2011 onwards. 'When
Fergus pulled back from Alan after Marioara was killed, John
came into the picture more,' he explained. 'Alan never did
anything on his own. Before he was arrested, John was a show
of force when he accompanied Alan; he was the muscle.

'It was designed to show that if you did anything against
him, there would be comebacks. Alan also had a habit of
bragging about things. It was designed to send a don't-mess-
with-me kind of message. When he was in our company,
Alan would always sit there silently – he just didn't do
conversation.

'Looking back, he didn't do drink or drugs [then] but then
we hear in 2011 he had been introduced to cocaine. Before

his arrest and because Fergus had been keeping his distance, he had also surrounded himself with a few younger criminals and this was because he was manipulative and controlling. People looked up to him because he also had money but I'm not sure where he got it from.'

On 9 August 2012 Alan Wilson and his legal team appeared before Judge John Lindsay at Cloverhill District Court. During the brief hearing, a solicitor for the DPP told the court that the Rostas case had been given 'priority', with 192 interviews conducted and 300 statements taken. However, the state prosecutor asked for more time to prepare the Book of Evidence. Judge Lindsay granted the state two further weeks, but warned the DPP that time was running out and 'something needs to happen'.

The investigation team spent the next fortnight putting the finishing touches to the Book of Evidence. This was presented to the court by Detective Inspector Cryan on 31 August and Wilson was informed that if he intended to use an alibi in his defence he should notify the DPP within a fortnight. Wilson's mother was present and blew him a kiss as he was led back into custody, promising to see her son soon.

With charges against Alan Wilson finalized, there remained the question of what to do with Fergus O'Hanlon. In submissions to the DPP, the investigation team acknowledged the role played by O'Hanlon after the murder and proposed he should be granted immunity from prosecution and used as a state witness against Wilson. Detectives were 'forthright' in recognizing that O'Hanlon had a case to answer in relation to his role in the disposal of the teenager's body, perverting the course of justice, assisting an offender and withholding information.

However, they also outlined how Wilson's former best pal was 'committed out of fears for his own safety'. Gardaí asked the DPP to consider O'Hanlon's decision to assist them after the recordings from Cloverhill prison were played to him. Investigators argued the information provided by O'Hanlon had been 'crucial and invaluable' and how the crime had caused him 'significant distress' over the years.

Detectives said there were no 'pre-conditions' or assurances sought by O'Hanlon before assisting the investigation team and felt he had put himself in a 'perilous' position. While accepting there was 'clear evidence' linking O'Hanlon to the offence of withholding information and assisting an offender, investigators suggested justice would be 'best served' if O'Hanlon was granted immunity from prosecution. The state returned its decision a few weeks later, agreeing it was in the 'public interest' for O'Hanlon to be used as a key prosecution witness against Wilson, with the accompanying immunity. It was also decided to hold Wilson's trial before a jury at the Central Criminal Court and not the non-jury Special Criminal Court, which has been used more frequently in recent years, especially during the ongoing Kinahan–Hutch feud.

Back in jail Alan Wilson awaited news on his trial date for the shotgun and cleaver incident in Blanchardstown in June 2009 and spent most of his days examining the Book of Evidence to be used against him in the Rostas case.

One senior prison source said, 'He had very little interaction with the other inmates and seemed preoccupied with his cases, constantly reading over the material at his disposal. He was a completely different character after the gardaí searched his cell and he was always polite and courteous to staff. Staff were also aware that his mood could change at the drop of a hat and he could become very threatening. All he had to do was stare at people and they were afraid.'

*

While Alan Wilson languished in prison, on the outside, the Real IRA–criminal war had hit unprecedented heights. Over the previous few months, Alan Ryan had been extending his extortion activities even further. After an associate of his had been badly beaten up in a nightclub, Ryan and his crew stole €300,000 from a well-established drug dealer and armed robber from the northside nicknamed 'Mr Big'. The cash had been earmarked for funding a drug deal in Europe but Ryan's cohorts intercepted the loot as it was being transported.

On 3 May Ryan also abducted a former member of the Westies crime gang, Jason 'Jay' O'Connor, and snipped off two of his fingers with a bolt cutter in Fairview Park after O'Connor failed to meet his extortion demands. One of the missing fingers was found in Fairview Park that evening and gardaí were alerted. Doctors later sewed the recovered finger back on to O'Connor's hand, but the second was not found. Despite his injuries, O'Connor refused to identify his attackers.

Months later, Ryan made an overt reference to the incident during an off-the-record interview with *Irish Mirror* crime reporter Cathal McMahon, who he agreed to speak to on background about dissident activity.

McMahon later wrote, 'At the end of our meeting he held up his left hand and ran his right index finger across three digits. He stared at me briefly and quipped: "You know what happens to people who turn me over." '

Next, Ryan confronted Mr Big in a car park and warned him he would have to hand over more money or face serious consequences. The drug dealer, who was in loose contact with the motley crew who formed the Criminal Action Force, decided enough was enough.

At 3.30 p.m. on 3 September 2012 Alan Ryan and two Sligo-based men from the dissident 32 County Sovereignty

Movement named Aaron Nealis and Paul Stewart were walking along Grange Lodge Avenue in Clongriffin, north Dublin. Ryan was on his way to visit his mother, who lived nearby.

Suddenly a man described as 'tall', wearing what appeared to be a prosthetic mask, came running up behind Ryan and shot him in the back. The man then shot Nealis in the leg and fired another round at him which grazed his cheek, while Stewart dived behind a car.

The gunman turned back towards Ryan, who had fallen to the ground, and fired several more shots into his chest and head before making his getaway. Witnesses said Ryan appeared to be trying to say something to his killer before the *coup de grâce* was applied.

The hitman fled in a silver Volvo, which was later discovered burnt out at Balgriffin cemetery, before switching to a Fiat Punto, later torched at the nearby Bewley's hotel. Gardaí believe the assassination was carried out by a prolific hitman named Kenneth Finn, who was himself shot dead in 2018.

The shock in gangland circles was seismic. No criminal organization had ever dared to take on the paramilitaries in such a fashion before and Mr Big fled to Spain while gardaí awaited retaliation.

Armed members of the Special Detective Unit patrolled in Darndale and Coolock, where Mr Big was based, and overtly surveilled known Real IRA members to prevent revenge attacks against drug dealers linked to him.

The 32 County Sovereignty Movement, which is considered the Real IRA's political wing, issued a statement, saying, 'Alan was shot in the back in cold blood on the streets where he grew up, streets where he had worked tirelessly to tackle the scourge of drugs which he had always opposed with every fibre of his being. We cannot express in words the pain now felt by both the movement as a whole and individual activists now that he has been taken from us. Alan's murder does not mean the end of the cause for which he gave his life.'

However, Alan Wilson and his CAF cronies would not have long to celebrate the demise of their bête noire. For the first time, the Wilsons were about to get a taste of their own medicine.

12. Death of a Strongman

I will make it my mission in life to find out who did this to you
— Keith Wilson

John Wilson had been ducking and diving for over two years now, but on 28 September 2012 his luck ran out. The execution had been careful in its planning. On 26 September a brown Volkswagen Passat was stolen from the home of a man in Celbridge. It was brought to west Dublin and hidden away in a safe place.

John Wilson was then placed under surveillance. Unbeknownst to him, he was followed from early on the day he would die. At around 10.30 that morning, he pulled up outside a convenience store on Cherry Orchard Avenue on his motorbike and went inside to the deli counter.

Minutes later, two other men entered from a different door into the shop, watched Wilson and left again within seconds of his departure. Shortly before 1.00 that afternoon, Wilson went to pick up his seven-year-old daughter from school. His friend Leslie Herbert was in the front passenger seat and the girl got into the back. They then drove to Wilson's home on Cloverhill Road, where Wilson parked up and ran inside to fetch something, leaving the front door open behind him. A few seconds later the stolen Passat drove up and parked behind Wilson's car.

Herbert would later reveal that his 'natural instinct was to run' so he climbed out of the passenger seat and took off down the road. However, the two-man team in the Volkswagen were not after him. One of them, dressed in a black hoodie and with a scarf around his face, got out and sprinted up the path and in the doorway after John Wilson.

He caught up with Wilson in the hallway and fired wildly as his target turned to flee. Six shots were loosed off, but only two actually hit him. Wilson was struck in the back and in his left elbow and slumped to the ground. The other four bullets embedded themselves in the kitchen door and one was later found on the kitchen floor. Neighbour Robert McHugh had heard the gunshots from his living room and looked out the window in time to see a 'hooded figure' leaving Wilson's house. He ran outside and prevented the victim's daughter from entering the house, while trying to shield the frantic child from the sight of her father on the ground in the hallway 'struggling to breathe'.

Within twenty minutes, an ambulance had arrived and paramedics worked on Wilson for over an hour at the scene trying to revive him, but it was too late. The second bullet had penetrated his lung, spleen and stomach and he swiftly bled to death.

The Volkswagen Passat was driven a short distance away to Cherry Orchard Crescent, where it was set alight. However, it was barely ablaze by the time gardaí arrived and, once the flames were extinguished, some crucial evidence was recovered from it. More importantly, gardaí almost immediately had the name of the gunman. With 116 previous convictions by the age of thirty-seven, Keith O'Neill was well known to gardaí. The vast majority were for driving offences, though he had also been done for possession of drugs with intent to supply.

Initially, there was no sign of him. Investigators later

learned O'Neill had been dropped to the Borza chipper on the Ballyfermot Road, where he was captured on CCTV joining members of his family for something to eat. The killer had dumped the black hoodie he had worn for the shooting, but was still wearing the jeans and distinctive green T-shirt he had on during the hit. He took a bus to Liffey Valley shopping centre, where he bought a change of clothes in JD Sports and put them on.

O'Neill's home was by now under surveillance by gardaí and, when he arrived there, detectives watched as he walked with his daughter to a nearby skip and threw two JD Sports bags containing a pair of jeans, a green T-shirt and a pair of Nike Air Max trainers into it. These were retrieved and their contents sent for forensic testing. The gardaí who took them out could already get a strong smell of petrol from one of the bags. O'Neill was arrested and taken into custody, but refused to say anything.

When forensic tests found gunshot residue on the jeans and O'Neill's DNA in one of the pockets, gardaí received the go-ahead from the DPP to charge him with murder. On his initial court appearance on 6 October, when the charges were put to him he replied, 'Youse have got the wrong man.'

John Wilson was entirely aware of the various threats against his life and some investigators were surprised he had been fatally caught out at his own home. One said, 'It was kind of unusual for Wilson to get caught like that because he had plenty of enemies and was well aware of who was around him.

'He was always on the lookout to the extreme of paranoia that either the guards were watching him or someone else was watching him. But he'd gone into the house to collect something and they were straight in the door after him, he'd left it open so they didn't even have to break it in.'

It was also abundantly clear that O'Neill had not been acting off his own bat, but he refused to cooperate in interview.

Alan Wilson went ballistic following his cousin's murder and began ranting in his cell. Aware of his volatile nature, prison officers kept a close eye on him. Wilson was overheard vowing revenge to other inmates at the prison.

'He had been spending most of his time in his cell at that time but when he did come out he would only talk to a handful of inmates,' one senior source said. 'A lot of the inmates were afraid of him but there were a few who expressed their condolences to him.

'When they did this, the Prison Service received intelligence that he vowed revenge because John was family and one of the few people in the world he could depend on and trust. He was convinced it was the Real IRA and kept saying that if he got out of prison, the person who killed John would be dealt with. Alan was also very unhappy that he was unable to attend the funeral and it was clear the murder had a deep impact on him. To prison staff, it appeared the killing made him even more of a recluse.'

He was not the only one to erupt in rage, though. The dead man's mother, Kathleen Wilson, was subsequently charged with breaking into the home of Keith O'Neill's innocent eighty-year-old mother Margaret and attacking her as she prepared dinner. Mrs Wilson was intensively defensive of her boys and had previously clouted *Sunday World* reporter Niall Donald about the head when he called to try to talk to her following Eric's conviction in Spain.

Donald wrote that Kathleen had to be restrained by her grandson Luke, who told her, 'Get back in the house, Nan. Stop now.'

A charge of burglary over the incident at Margaret O'Neill's home was later struck out at Dublin District Court and the Probation Act was applied to charges of assault and criminal damage meaning the Wilson matriarch escaped conviction.

John Wilson was buried seven days after his murder, with both his brothers unable to attend. However, a letter from Keith was read out to the congregation in which he claimed his slain sibling was 'not a drug dealer or a gunman'.

It continued, 'I promise you, I will make it my mission in life to find out who did this to you.' Another message from Eric Wilson was also read out from the pulpit, in which he said John had lived for his wife and family.

The farcical nature of the CAF was further highlighted by two separate declarations to the media by individuals purporting to be members, one promising revenge and the other claiming Wilson had left the group and that there would be no retaliation.

Following the botched Players' Lounge attack, John Wilson had moved away from his old guardian, Sean Hunt, and would certainly not have been seen as under any protection Hunt offered. However, gardaí investigating John Wilson's murder did not believe it was a Real IRA revenge hit. Instead, intelligence suggested he had been gunned down by a rival criminal over a debt of €20,000. Though weakening, the Real IRA was continuing to pose a threat and would murder the veteran gangster Eamon Kelly as he returned to his home from a bookies a few months later.

However, the loss of Ryan would eventually be too much to bear. Mr Big had gambled that the dissidents were effectively a one-man band and it paid off. Following an ostentatious IRA-style funeral for Ryan in Donaghmede, the Dublin-based Real IRA basically fell apart. Without their charismatic leader, the Dublin faction became riven by disagreements and in-fighting. Ryan had been given a lot of leeway by the dissidents' northern command, but, when the money dried up, so did their patience.

Senior figures were again sent south and punishment shootings were issued to two members for allegedly skimming off the top of extortion funds supposed to be destined to buy weapons in Eastern Europe. Gardaí estimated that only around half of the money collected from drug dealers for 'the cause' had been sent northwards to the Real IRA leadership. The rest had been pocketed by Ryan and his cronies.

On 11 October 2012, Alan Wilson appeared in court charged with threatening to kill or cause serious harm to Paul Campbell and discharging a firearm with intent to endanger life at Mr Campbell's property on 12 May 2009 following the row between their children. Wilson pleaded not guilty to the charge. However, all accusations against him were later struck out when Campbell told the court he had 'no idea' who the gunman was.

For the second time in recent months, Wilson had serious charges against him dropped. He celebrated by sending someone round to fire more shots at a house, this time belonging to an innocent relative of Fergus O'Hanlon on 24 October. Intelligence later indicated the gunman had been Luke Wilson.

Luke Wilson was at this stage well down the path to following his uncles and cousin into the family trade. Now eighteen years old, he had run up a string of convictions for road-traffic and other minor offences. He had also inherited his uncle John's talent for getting into rows.

On 13 January 2013, following a furious bust-up with a

local criminal in a Ballyfermot pub, Luke went to the Memorial Park in Kilmainham to collect a shotgun from a childhood friend named Paddy McCann. Luke would have had no reason to mistrust McCann – which is precisely why someone had hired McCann to murder him. As the pair made their way through the park, McCann took out a pistol and fired wildly at his old pal. Luke was hit three times before the gun seemed to jam and McCann panicked and ran off. In his desperation to escape, the gunman took his victim's mobile phone but unwittingly dropped his own Samsung device.

Gasping for breath on the ground, Wilson dialled 999 at 2.50 p.m. and told firefighter Peter Gorman he had been shot three times, providing details of his location before naming McCann as the shooter. The line went dead so Peter Gorman returned the call, with Wilson again naming his attacker. An ambulance arrived and Wilson was rushed to hospital, where doctors satisfied themselves that his life was not in danger.

At the hospital the following day Sergeant Paul Murphy played him two voice recordings of 999 calls made by Wilson to Dublin Fire Brigade. Confirming the voice on the phone was his, Wilson refused to name the gunman 'out of fear for his life'. However, he later had a change of heart and made five statements to gardaí. In one of these, he said, 'I met a fella in the field and after a while searching for the shotgun we decided to head back.

'I turned around, I saw him pulling out a gun, it was a handgun, grey in colour, red writing on the back of the butt. He let one shot off and got me in the front of the neck, I said to him, "What the fuck?" I hit the deck in the bushes.

'I felt another shot hitting me in the arm, the right arm, then another shot, I felt it ringing in my head, but I didn't know he got me in the head. Then he went to shoot me again but I could hear the gun jam, I could see him take the clip out, he tried to shoot me again when he put the clip back in, but it was jammed. He took off running.'

Though Luke Wilson initially declined to name the gunman, he eventually changed his mind. 'I am certain that this person was Paddy McCann from Decies Road, Ballyfermot,' he said in a subsequent statement.

'I have known him for the last fifteen years and I more or less grew up with him. I was shocked when I turned round and saw him with a gun in his hand pointing at me, it was then that Patrick McCann shot me. There was nobody else there at the time, just the two of us.'

The younger member of the Wilson clan remained in St James's hospital until 28 January before discharging himself, suffering the loss of sight in his right eye and ongoing problems with his voice box.

Intelligence later revealed that, following the shooting, McCann and another man discussed what had happened at an apartment block in Clondalkin. There, one of them was heard saying, 'He deserves to get shot.' Gardaí believe McCann had been recruited by Mark 'The Guinea Pig' Desmond, later shot dead in December 2016, after the major criminal accused Wilson of threatening his relative. It was yet another moment in Desmond's up-and-down relationship with the Wilsons. He had threatened Eric over his relative Martin Kenny's death, then hired him to help kill Anthony Cannon. Now The Guinea Pig had tried to kill his nephew.

In their file submitted to the DPP, gardaí described the shooting as a 'cold, calculated and premeditated attack, which resulted in Luke Wilson receiving serious, life-threatening gunshot wounds.

'Luke Wilson believed that he was meeting a friend to help him put together a shotgun. Wilson states the meeting with

McCann had been planned two or three days beforehand. From CCTV footage it is clear that McCann and another man carefully planned this premeditated attack on Luke Wilson.

'Investigating gardaí believe there is sufficient evidence to indicate Patrick McCann brought Luke Wilson to a secluded area in Memorial Park with the intention to murder him.' McCann was charged with assault causing harm and possession of a firearm with intent to endanger life.

Alan Wilson had escaped prosecution over the violent burglary of the Mountaines' home on a legal technicality and had seen the charges against him over the Paul Campbell house shooting disappear when the victim failed to identify him. But there was a third issue from 2009 still hanging over his head.

On 7 February 2013 he appeared before Dublin Circuit Criminal Court to face the music over the shotgun and cleaver incident in Blanchardstown. Both Wilson and David Crowley were charged with assault causing harm and trespass, while Crowley was also accused of unlawfully possessing a firearm. On the face of it, it was a slam-dunk case. After all, both Lisa Murray and her father had known Crowley for years and identified him at the scene. She had told gardaí that night, 'I'm 100 per cent sure it was David Crowley and Alan Wilson I saw. Alan Wilson was wearing black gloves.'

But the court heard her memory was a little fuzzier now. Lisa Murray told Alan Wilson's barrister Padraig Dwyer that she now did not remember making the original garda statement. She had never seen Alan Wilson before she saw him in court this week, she said, though she would have heard of him through the alleged victim.

The witness further informed Crowley's barrister Gerry O'Brien that she had been drunk on the night in question and could not recall making any statement to gardaí. She had spent the afternoon at her sister's in Clonee and the two of them had shared a bottle of vodka in the garden as it was a sunny day, she said.

After returning home, she walked into the hall, heard the noise of an argument in the kitchen, and thought someone was breaking into her house. She told prosecuting counsel Fiona McGowan that she then ran to her father's house and did not see anyone in her house. Likewise, Murray did not recall having been told that Crowley and Alan Wilson had been arrested about a mile away shortly after the incident. The prosecution said her evidence was 'materially inconsistent' with her original garda statement, which was then read out to the jury following legal argument.

Four days later Lisa Murray's father Noel – who had told gardaí he had roared at Crowley on the night of the attack – was on the stand. Noel Murray now told Fiona McGowan that he had 'no memory' of giving a statement to Detective Garda Tom Cooney on the night and that he 'wasn't positive' that the signature on the bottom of the statement was his. He added that when his daughter came to his home he thought there had been 'a domestic', but that when he went around to Lisa's, 'everything seemed all right there, so I went back to me own house'.

Murray also told Crowley's barrister that he had not slept for two nights before the alleged incident and was under a lot of stress, as his wife of forty years had just been diagnosed with lung cancer.

He said he had taken a sleeping pill, had drunk four or five cans of cider and had been planning to go to bed at 8 p.m. before the alleged incident took place. Detective Garda Cooney was called to the stand and told the court that when Murray made his statement, he did not present as someone under the influence of drink or prescribed medication.

Judge Desmond Hogan ruled that both Murrays could be treated as 'hostile witnesses', a categorization used for those who give evidence in court that is substantially different from formal statements they have previously made.

More state evidence came from Garda Niall Phelan, who was one of two officers who had forced Alan Wilson's silver Corolla to stop. Garda Phelan said Wilson had been 'extremely nervous and evasive and seemed to be sweating profusely'. His colleague Garda Nigel Petrie, who arrested Crowley, described both accused as 'edgy and quite fidgety'. 'They weren't easy within themselves and were avoiding eye contact with us. Although they answered our questions they were quite evasive,' Garda Petrie said.

The jury was told two pairs of black leather gloves and another pair of gloves were recovered from the car, along with a screwdriver and two baseball caps. Metallic particles found on Crowley's grey hoodie and on Wilson's striped shirt gave 'very strong support' for the suggestion that the two men had been in contact with, or in close proximity to, a discharged gun, forensic scientist Dr Thomas Hannigan said. One of the pairs of leather gloves found on the driver's seat also revealed traces described as 'extremely' characteristic of gunshot residue, he said.

Detective Garda Pat Traynor said that he interviewed Crowley after his arrest and the accused denied having been at the house. Instead, Crowley said that he was arrested with Alan Wilson in the car after they had driven out of the city centre. He said he was wearing gloves in June because he always wore gloves and it was still cold outside. He admitted he knew Lisa Murray, but said it was because his brother was going out with her sister.

The trial ran for a full thirteen days and on the last, both men were convicted of all charges by the jury after just three hours and forty-seven minutes of deliberation. Wilson's sister Maxine tried to speak to her brother after the verdict but he ignored her. When journalists approached her for a comment outside the court, she said, 'Fuck off, he's all right.'

Sentencing was adjourned until the following April 2014 when Wilson was jailed for seven years and Crowley received eight. In his remarks, Judge Desmond Hogan said it was a very serious offence and there was no reason given. But he said there had to be some compelling motive as to why it was committed. The judge said he wondered if the men were acting as enforcers using intimidation and fear. The issue of the dispute involving a woman – outlined to gardaí by both Lisa Murray and her father – was not raised in court.

Details of a sinister incident, which occurred during the trial itself, now emerged. One jury member reported that he had been standing outside the building about to have a smoke when David Crowley came over and lit his cigarette for him. After some discussion between barristers, Judge Hogan and the jury, the jurors had said they were happy that the incident would not have any effect on them and the trial continued. Crowley had also had his bail revoked and was remanded in custody after being caught lying during proceedings.

He had turned up late to the trial and told Judge Hogan he had been dropping his child to school. However, Crowley had forgotten that schools were on their mid-term break and when the judge sent a garda to confirm the school was shut, he remanded Crowley in custody for contempt.

Seven months after his cousin was packed off to jail, Luke Wilson came to court to see his one-time friend face justice for leaving him blind in one eye. Detective Sergeant Michael O'Brien had told McCann's initial Dublin District Court that McCann 'had nothing to say' when the accusations were put to him. He had objected to bail, citing a fear of witness intimidation and saying more serious charges could be brought against McCann. It was a solid prediction. By the time McCann appeared before the Central Criminal Court, the charge of serious harm had been upgraded to attempted murder, while the firearm accusation remained in place.

This also appeared to be a slam-dunk case, but gardaí must have been nervous after witnessing what had happened in the trial of Alan Wilson and David Crowley. In the event, McCann eased their fears by pleading guilty to both charges during a short hearing in front of vastly experienced Judge Paul Carney. Sentence was set for November when the full facts of what had happened would be laid out.

On 11 November 2014 Judge Carney was told McCann had shot his former best friend because he owed money for drugs and feared he would be killed if he did not comply with orders.

'Was he told drug debts would be set aside if he could carry out an assassination?' Judge Carney asked McCann's barrister, Padraig Dwyer. Mr Dwyer said the attack was carried out as a result of fear and McCann's addiction to drugs.

He said his client came from a decent family but had been using drugs and alcohol since he was twelve years old. The lawyer added, 'He was threatened he would be shot if he did not shoot Mr Wilson.'

Luke Wilson declined to provide a victim impact statement to the court. Apart from the lost eye, his injuries from the shooting had included associated cerebral stroke, palsy in his right arm, permanent scars and damage to vertebrae. He might also require further surgery in future, the court heard.

There was a further week of adjournment while the judge considered what tariff to impose. But if McCann had thought that throwing himself on the mercy of the court was his best hope, he was in for a shock.

In his sentencing remarks, Judge Carney compared the incident to the RTÉ gangster series *Love/Hate*, which was gaining huge audience figures every weekend at the time. The show's creators had already seen life imitate art when one of their plots, which featured dissidents in a feud with criminals, was followed by the Real IRA–CAF gang war. Now lightning struck twice as the sentencing hearing was preceded by an episode in which a teenage character named Wayne was murdered by his childhood pal on the orders of gang boss Nidge.

Judge Carney had evidently been watching. 'I have a priority here that not everyone may agree with,' he said. 'Last weekend over one million people tuned in to watch the last episode of *Love/Hate* and the following morning something, which might as well have appeared in a *Love/Hate* script, was poured out in a sentencing hearing.'

The judge said the accused's drug and alcohol addiction and his dysfunctional upbringing afforded him no defence. Two explanations were given for the attack, he said. The first was that McCann's drugs debt would be set aside if he killed Wilson. A second was he feared he would be 'tortured and disappeared' if he didn't carry out the attack.

'It is not going to go out from here that figures in gangland can have an assassination carried out by preying on somebody vulnerable, in the expectation that if the enterprise fails there will be great leniency extended on account of that person's vulnerability,' Judge Carney continued.

He handed McCann a twenty-year term for attempted murder, with a concurrent ten-year sentence for weapons possession. The last three years of the twenty were suspended, but McCann had still received one of the toughest sentences for attempted murder in living memory. To put it in context, the average term of 'life' served for carrying out a murder is fourteen years.

The next day the *Irish Sun* revealed that McCann had been coerced into it by The Guinea Pig over a debt of just €300. Desmond had been furious when a violent pub row had broken out between his relative and Luke Wilson after comments were made about both John and Eric Wilson being garda informants.

In a subsequent interview with the *Irish Daily Star*, Luke Wilson – who had tried to shoot someone at the age of sixteen – made an impassioned plea to the country's youth to stay on the straight and narrow. 'Any young person reading this paper tomorrow, I would tell you that a life of crime is no way to go,' he said. 'You will either end up in a grave or in a prison, doing twenty years like the scumbag who shot me.

'I heard the gun being cocked and when I looked around, my so-called friend was pointing it at me. I asked him, "Are you going to kill me?" And then he fired. He opened fire on me and got me in the neck.

'I dropped to my knees and turned to the side and could feel another bullet hitting me just below the ear. My eyeball came out, I was holding it in my hand and he shot again. I put my hand up to block my forehead and it hit me in the arm.

'I was lying on the ground and taking a seizure. He said, "I'm not going to kill you", and went to fire again, but thank God the gun jammed. I thought I was dead.'

It had been another rough year for the Wilsons, but those they had been terrorizing were deeply relieved. By the time of his sentence, Alan Wilson's name was known to all gardaí in the capital.

'I know he was still in prison on remand over the Rostas case but any serious conviction directed towards him had to be welcomed,' Herbert Kilcline said. 'He avoided prison on two serious incidents in the past and this conviction was now going to keep him off the streets for a very long time.

'It's often the case that when people go into prison, life is very much different when they get out – they don't have the same power and allegiances change. Although he was now serving a seven-year sentence, we all knew the big trial was just around the corner.'

13. Off the Hook

Alan stood on her. He was dancing on her
— Fergus O'Hanlon

As Alan Wilson entered into the first year of his seven-year sentence, his legal team received notification that his trial for the murder of Marioara Rostas would be pushed back until 18 June 2014. It had initially been due to begin in November 2013, but was delayed owing to a backlog of cases at the Central Criminal Court. Wilson spent the intervening period serving his sentence. However, he was also arrested on 19 August by gardaí investigating the discovery of the weapons identified by O'Hanlon, and later taken to Kevin Street garda station for questioning before being brought back to his prison cell. He rarely integrated with other inmates and kept out of trouble.

When his day in court arrived, Wilson looked relaxed as the jury of ten men and two women sworn in were told the defendant would be pleading not guilty to the teenager's murder.

Following the short hearing to select the jury, the trial got under way exactly one week later. The case had drawn massive media interest and it was standing room only as prosecutor Sean Gillane began the state's case against the accused. True to form, Alan Wilson saw this as an opportunity to intimidate.

He began eyeballing members of the press in the benches, in particular one female reporter working for the news agency Ireland International, which supplies many of the country's newspapers with court copy. The unfortunate woman was so unnerved by his staring that she requested her byline not be used in any printed reports.

In his opening remarks, Mr Gillane told the jurors about the victim, outlining why her family had travelled to Ireland and why they found themselves begging on the streets of Dublin on 6 January 2008.

The prosecutor then spoke of the moment the victim and her younger brother were approached by a stranger in the car and the subsequent phone call, which the 'very upset and frightened' teenager had made to her brother in Romania. The accused, he pointed out, admitted owning the Ford Mondeo, but denied he was driving it on the afternoon Marioara disappeared.

The jury was told of the fire at 2 Brabazon Street, how the property was owned by Wilson's sister Maxine and how ammunition and bullet holes had been discovered there. Mr Gillane also outlined how the 'significant development' in the case came in the 'dying days of 2011' when O'Hanlon identified an area in a forest in Kippure where the teenager had been buried.

Gardaí had first found an empty 'ready-made grave or bunker', Mr Gillane explained, before discovering the teenager's remains in a shallow grave. There was complete silence in court as he revealed how the teenager had been shot four times in the head, had a pillowcase placed over her head and a knotted sheet wrapped around her legs before being encased in plastic secured by duct tape, 'mummifying her within'.

Mr Gillane gave a summary of the evidence Fergus O'Hanlon would provide. He said O'Hanlon would testify as to how he received a call to return to Brabazon Street on the week beginning 7 January 2008. He said the jury would hear how the accused came downstairs holding a firearm and wanted to show him something.

He said that the accused brought him upstairs and showed him a corpse, telling Mr O'Hanlon, 'She was a witness.' The accused then left and returned with cleaning material and a large bag. Mr Gillane said that O'Hanlon assisted the accused in undressing the victim. The accused put a pillowcase over her head, wrapped her in a sheet and placed her remains in the large bag. The accused then put her in the boot of his Mondeo and drove her to Kippure.

Reminding jurors of the lonely mountainside, Mr Gillane told the court, 'Mr Wilson appeared to be looking around for the bunker. That having not been found, the two began to dig the shallow grave. The teenager was buried and her belongings burnt nearby. The two men returned to the house on Brabazon Street and Mr O'Hanlon spent two days cleaning the scene.'

In his conclusion to the court on the opening day of the trial, Mr Gillane reminded the jury of conversations between the accused and Mr O'Hanlon when he explained, 'The last words from Mr Wilson to Mr O'Hanlon were, "You never saw what you saw." Mr O'Hanlon was also warned not to return to Kippure.'

On the second day of the trial, which had dominated the national news headlines, it was the turn of pathologist Dr Khalid Jabbar to give evidence. He testified how he had noticed a 'shallow grave' and a body wrapped in 'dark plastic bags' when he visited the mountainside on 23 January 2012.

Dr Jabbar also told the court how he had 'noted evidence of physical violence and trauma' with 'four gunshot entrance wounds to the front half of her head'. He said he had recovered 'multiple metallic fragments' from Marioara's head, including one almost complete lead bullet, which had 'mushroomed'. The cause of death, he told the court, was four gunshots to the head.

As the trial moved into its third day, the jury heard from the victim's father, Dumitru Rostas. Mr Rostas explained his reasons for moving to Ireland, his memories from the day she went missing and his frustrations in reporting his daughter missing on the first occasion.

A number of witnesses who saw the teenager begging that day then took the stand. One, Martha Murphy, said Marioara 'appeared very young, about thirteen or fourteen' and was 'very thin, with sallow skin'. In the closing stages of day three of the trial, Garda Daniel McCarthy was called to give evidence about the fire at 2 Brabazon Street.

'It appeared that there was a probability that an accelerant could have been used,' he said. 'On the top floor, there were the burnt remains of a fuel can. There were still fumes of petrol from it.' The garda also agreed with Wilson's defence barrister, Michael O'Higgins SC, that the house had been let to Fergus O'Hanlon and Maxine Wilson.

An image of a bullet recovered from a wall in the house and photographs of a hole in the wall of a living room on the first floor were shown to the court. The day concluded with testimony from members of the garda search team who recovered the teenager's remains.

The following morning, two of Marioara's brothers were up. Her older sibling Alexandru spoke of the horror call he had received from Ireland on 7 January 2008. He described how his terrified sister had begged him, 'Tell Dad to come and get me.' Alexandru said Marioara could see a 'little sign' and started to read 'some of the letters' from it before the line went dead. She had been 'crying and seemed frightened', he said.

Cross-examined by Michael O'Higgins SC, the witness

said he had reported the call to his father and Romanian police and agreed with the defence barrister that Marioara had initially claimed a man had dropped her 200 kilometres from Dublin. He also agreed that the sign from which his sister had read the letters could have been a street sign, but did not agree that he had told the police his sister had been taken from Romania by two men.

Dumitru Jnr, the last person to see Marioara alive, was next. He told the court that the man who offered to drive his sister to 'McDonald's for some food' had given him €10 before leaving. He described the man as being more than 'twenty-five years of age, skinny and white skin' with 'small black eyes and small spots on his left cheek'.

Dumitru Jnr also identified the photofit that gardaí had prepared after noting his description. Further evidence was taken from the owner of 2 Brabazon Street, who said there was no lock on the outside of the upstairs door or bullet holes in the wall when he rented the house to Maxine Wilson.

After four days the jury was removed as the case stalled following legal argument between the prosecution and the defence: the dispute centred around whether or not technical details about the number Marioara had used to call Romania could be introduced to the jury.

Gardaí had established that the phone number used by the dead woman to ring her cousin Alexandru was the same one used in calls to Maxine Wilson around the time of the abduction and that it had 'pinged' off a mast close to Lombard Street at 12.30 p.m. on 6 January 2008. Later that same evening it also pinged off a mast in Clontarf and then again the following day. Further records would also show the phone had connected to masts in Ballyfermot and the Long Mile Road in Crumlin after the call was made to Romania. The device had no signal from 8 p.m. on Monday 7 January until 2 a.m. on Tuesday 8 January.

A ruling by the European Court of Justice just three months earlier had raised concerns over convictions secured on mobile phone evidence. The ruling declared that a directive, introduced in 2006 requiring phone and Internet providers to keep customers' details for two years, was 'invalid'. Digital Rights Ireland had taken a challenge, claiming that the directive was a 'fundamental' privacy breach, and the European Court of Justice upheld their complaint.

Alan Wilson's defence now claimed the mobile-phone mast evidence should be excluded. They also argued that details of calls to and from the number to Herbert Kilcline, Maxine Wilson and Mary Wilson, plus confirmation from Kilcline that the number belonged to Alan Wilson, should be left out too. Such testimony would be crucial in establishing that Marioara Rostas had rung home to Romania on a phone linked to Alan Wilson.

However, the prosecution privately had concerns that if it was presented to the jury, his legal team could use the European Court of Justice ruling to successfully appeal any possible conviction. A decision was taken not to introduce the evidence. It would be a key moment in the trial.

The discussions ran on for almost three weeks before court resumed on 17 July. Judge Patrick McCarthy apologized to the jurors for the delay. He said that 'complex' legal issues had been discussed in the jury's absence with it taking 'longer than expected'. Asking the jury to return the following day, the judge concluded by saying, 'We're on the home stretch.'

Fergus O'Hanlon was due to begin testifying the following day. After the prosecution decision to avoid using the phone evidence, everyone was aware that the trial's outcome depended on what was coming next.

O'Hanlon was asked to take the court back to the night of 8 January 2008. He said that after returning to 2 Brabazon Street, he noticed a 'nervous and shaking' Alan Wilson coming down the stairs with a 'rifle in his hand'. O'Hanlon said Wilson then told him, 'Come here, I want to show you something.' O'Hanlon continued, 'There was the body of the dead girl there, in the centre of the room, lying on her back. She looked like she was wide awake. She had a hole in her forehead and blood running down her nose. I asked who she was and he said a witness to her brother being killed.'

O'Hanlon then detailed how Wilson had left the house before returning with the lawnmower bag. Once the remains had been wrapped in plastic and 'folded over into the shape of a horseshoe', they drove to the Dublin mountains, he said.

Upon arrival at the isolated spot, O'Hanlon told the court how they had been unable to locate the bunker before 'Alan started digging a hole'. When that was completed, Wilson had 'removed her from the green bag and pushed her into the hole'.

He said, 'She was stood on a few times. Alan stood on her. He was dancing on her.' They returned to the city and O'Hanlon said he cleaned the upstairs bedroom, which had contained 'heavy blood staining on the floorboards, skirting and window ledge'.

Upon completion of his evidence, O'Hanlon admitted to Michael O'Higgins SC that he was a convicted criminal but denied being in the house when the teenager was alive. When asked why he had refused to participate in an identification parade in October 2008, he replied, 'I always refuse to go in an ID parade.'

Now the barrister switched tack. He asked O'Hanlon if he had ever been violent to a woman. The witness replied, 'I wouldn't call it violence.' O'Higgins asked O'Hanlon if he had ever broken his girlfriend's ribs. O'Hanlon answered, 'I did so accidentally.'

The defence then queried whether O'Hanlon had a problem with dark-skinned people, Muslims or non-nationals. He replied 'no' before adding, when it was put to him, that he didn't recall calling hospital security staff 'Paki bastards and Muslim racists' in August 2009. He denied threatening to shoot them and later firing shots at them from the van.

O'Hanlon also rejected claims by witnesses who said they heard him say he was going to shoot the men. He insisted it was a 'coincidence' the men were shot twenty-four hours later. He conceded he had 'handled' a lot of firearms, but maintained he had never discharged one. O'Hanlon was asked if he had threatened to shoot another girlfriend's brother and admitted he had, but contended the remark had been made 'in the heat of the moment'.

Next, the barrister focused on 2 Brabazon Street. He questioned O'Hanlon on whether the property had been used as a brothel and as a place where people went to take drugs. O'Hanlon insisted it had not, but admitted a girl had died from a drug overdose at the property. He said he was unable to comment on bullets being found in a wall and when asked about an area of red paint on a wall, he replied, 'My partner painted the wall. She thought it would be a good idea to do a bit of decorating.'

Mr O'Higgins told the court it was the 'worst' decorating he had ever seen before suggesting that gardaí had asked if the wall had been painted to cover up blood. O'Hanlon replied, 'I can't comment on that.'

The star witness agreed that he had been on methadone programmes and had been receiving daily doses at Trinity Court, located close to Lombard Street. When asked if he was there on 6 January 2008, O'Hanlon replied, 'I couldn't tell you whether I was even on the programme at that time.' Details of the silver Ford Mondeo were brought before the court and O'Hanlon agreed that he was the registered owner at the time of his arrest, but maintained it had been given to him by Wilson in April 2008.

When it was put to him that he had been stopped while driving the car on 1 February 2008, he admitted it was plausible but emphatically denied he was behind the wheel on the day of the teenager's disappearance.

O'Hanlon accepted he was 'far from an angel', but said this did not render him a 'lesser witness'. Michael O'Higgins retorted, 'You're a lesser witness because you're a compulsive liar.' The jury was sent home for the weekend, with O'Hanlon set to resume his position on the stand the following Monday.

On the second day of O'Hanlon's court appearance, the cross-examination started with Wilson's barrister suggesting that the accused 'closely resembles' the photofit of the man seen driving the Romanian teenager away. 'I wouldn't agree,' O'Hanlon said. Mr O'Higgins claimed his client was not a 'good likeness' to the photofit and asked O'Hanlon, 'Is that because you picked her up and Mr Wilson didn't?'

'I didn't pick her up,' O'Hanlon answered.

There was little more of interest heard that afternoon, but a third day of cross-examination was set to begin the next morning. The defence queried whether O'Hanlon 'hated' Wilson and wanted to 'fuck him over'. 'No, I don't hate him,' the witness said.

But Mr O'Higgins was leading him into a trap. He referred to an encounter between a garda and O'Hanlon in March 2011 and read out loud from the garda's note of the interaction. 'He has fallen out with Alan Wilson. He spoke freely about his hatred of Wilson,' he said.

In response, O'Hanlon said, 'I didn't speak freely. He probably interpreted in his own way.'

Next, Mr O'Higgins read out a transcript of a call between O'Hanlon and his girlfriend, which read, 'I waited four years to fuck him over for what he deserves.' O'Hanlon denied ever uttering the words. As the cross-examination continued, Mr O'Higgins asked O'Hanlon if his description of the murder was 'movie-like'.

'I would agree,' O'Hanlon said. 'It's like a blockbuster. It's not every day someone comes home to find someone dead in their house.' Mr O'Higgins read notes of a meeting between the witness and his solicitor to the court. He said, 'You told your solicitor you arrived home after a murder took place and saw Alan Wilson with the gun still smoking.'

'I didn't mean literally still smoking,' O'Hanlon said.

Pressed on his accounts of the accused's possession of a gun when he was asked to clean the scene, O'Hanlon replied, 'I knew I had to help him. It was damned if you do and dead if you don't.'

The barrister moved on to who had secured O'Hanlon immunity from prosecution. O'Hanlon said he 'might' have mentioned it but denied making any deal. Mr O'Higgins then referred to a transcript of the phone call with his girlfriend while he was in prison. In the call, the court was told she said, 'Hopefully you won't be going back to prison', and O'Hanlon replied, 'Obviously yeah, I know.'

O'Hanlon was then asked why he was so sure he would not return to prison, given he was an accessory after the fact to murder. He said, 'Sure I'm in prison now, serving a sentence for drink-driving and burglary.'

But Michael O'Higgins kept hammering away. The defence read out the contents of another recorded call from prison to the court, where the couple discussed a sentence hearing he was awaiting and what the gardaí had been telling them. The jury heard that O'Hanlon's partner told him, 'They said they'll have you down in the hotel in a week. Yer man's boss is working on it as we speak.'

O'Hanlon had said back to her, 'They got the truth. The truth is all that could be given and it's up to them now.'

Mr O'Higgins could scent blood in the water. He put it to the witness that everything he had stated in court was a lie.

'It happened,' O'Hanlon insisted. 'Why would I want to fuck my life up and never see my kids again just to stitch someone up?' Before court ended for the day, the jury further heard how O'Hanlon had found his position in the witness protection programme 'stressful', leading to him vandalizing three different apartments provided by the state.

With O'Hanlon's credibility put on the line, it was the turn of the gardaí to come under the defence spotlight on day twenty-one of the trial. First to appear in the witness box was Detective Superintendent J. J. Keane. He denied that the state's main witness had received 'preferential treatment' or 'demanded immunity' in exchange for a statement against Wilson. 'At no stage was immunity ever mentioned,' the senior garda declared.

Another officer involved in the investigation, Sergeant Sean McAvinchey, told the court O'Hanlon 'didn't care' about the consequences for himself. 'We were offering no deals,' he told the jury. 'We were offering nothing in return for information.'

The final officer to take the stand was Senior Investigating Officer Michael Cryan who was asked if 'alarm bells' had gone off when it was realized O'Hanlon had previously faked a shooting and described another shooting as having happened at two different locations.

The defence suggested the claims went to the 'heart of his credibility'. Quizzed as to whether O'Hanlon's claims should have been followed up, Detective Inspector Cryan replied, 'If he's making it up, yes.'

O'Higgins had done some significant damage to the case against Alan Wilson and the pressure was on the prosecution to repair it. O'Hanlon's solicitor Bridget Rouse took the stand and told the court her client had been determined to make a statement against Wilson despite knowing he could also be charged.

A memo suggesting gardaí told her that O'Hanlon had asked them for immunity if he made a statement against Alan Wilson was read to the court. The jury also heard how the memo went on to recount that the officers said they weren't in a position to offer this, and that it would be a matter for the DPP after considering any statement made.

Under cross-examination by prosecutor Sean Gillane, the solicitor said that it was made 'very explicit to her' that there could be no deals and that O'Hanlon should know that. She said, 'I made it very clear to him that no offer was being made, that if he wished to make a statement, it was up to him. He said he wished to do that, notwithstanding my advice.'

Asked if this advice included that he might be charged, she replied, 'Yes.' Following Ms Rouse's appearance in court, the next two days of the trial would feature both the prosecution and defence's closing speeches.

On the morning of 28 July 2014 the Central Criminal Court was just as full as it had been throughout the duration of the trial for prosecutor Gillane's summing-up. He reminded the jury of the day the victim stepped into a stranger's car and added, 'Marioara is never seen again by anyone that cared for her.'

Mr Gillane pointed to O'Hanlon's decision to help gardaí

recover the dead girl's remains and said, 'I make no bones about that. He is the case. The jury's job is to tie the facts of the case. That involves a journey through the heart of darkness.

'O'Hanlon was involved in the burial of a young girl, who was savagely killed. The witness kept quiet about the crime for four years and that speaks to an almost unimaginable withering of his own humanity. But the prosecution says that a core humanity won out at the end of the day. The evidence on which the prosecution relies was never going to be from an altar boy or choir boy.

'But standing on the side of that mountain in January 2012, with the words of his solicitor ringing in his ear, he helped the guards find Marioara Rostas. She was executed in a manner that was cold, calculated and precise. This was no crime of passion, of temper or loss of control. It was the exact opposite.' Lastly, he recalled the evidence that had been destroyed before asking them to find Wilson guilty of murder.

Michael O'Higgins now stepped forward. He cast further doubt on Fergus O'Hanlon's character, describing all the testimony from him as 'lies and contrived lies' and a 'masterclass in perjury'. O'Hanlon, he claimed, had lied to gardaí and continued to lie in the witness box. The witness was characterized as a 'domineering, controlling, bullying person' and his refusal to take part in an ID parade because he was afraid of Alan Wilson was dismissed as 'complete and utter rubbish'. Mr O'Higgins directed the jury's attention again to the photofit compiled with Dumitru Jnr's help and said, 'It's a very strong likeness to him.'

He concluded, 'She [Marioara] was in Brabazon Street prior to the eighth when she was murdered. It's Fergus O'Hanlon who lived in Brabazon Street. It's a connection to him, like the photofit.'

Before dismissing the jury, Judge Patrick McCarthy was required to warn the ten men and two women that O'Hanlon was an accomplice and a beneficiary of the witness protection programme and said it would be 'dangerous' for them to convict on the basis of his 'uncorroborated' evidence.

It took the jury just two hours and fifty-three minutes to reach their verdict of not guilty on 31 July 2014, after a five-week trial. Gardaí were despondent but reminded themselves of what had been achieved. 'The main objective for everyone involved in the investigation was to recover her remains and we did this,' Detective Superintendent Cryan said.

'There was tremendous dedication and professionalism from everyone involved in the investigation and we were obviously disappointed with the outcome. We were relieved we could return Marioara to her family so her family could properly grieve and the investigation also helped us forge close links with members of the Roma community.'

The murdered teenager's family were escorted from the courtroom in tears following the verdict. Alan Wilson himself showed no reaction as he was brought back to prison to complete his seven-year sentence for the meat-cleaver attack.

14. Ups and Downs

I leaned back and looked out the window and seen
a hooded figure come out the door
— Robert McHugh

Alan Wilson's acquittal meant nobody would be brought to account for Marioara's murder. Gardaí were not looking for anyone else in connection with the killing and the Rostas family were deeply frustrated at having to return home without justice.

Before leaving, the family spoke of their 'bitter disappointment' with Ireland's justice system. 'We go home to Romania not knowing who killed my daughter,' Dumitru Rostas said. 'The person who did this should be killed, hanged or given a life sentence. If it wasn't Alan Wilson I want to know who? How can I forgive and how can I forget?

'On the one hand we are thankful she was found by O'Hanlon but on the other we didn't get justice and somebody killed her. If it had been an Irish girl who was killed, how would the justice system have reacted? She was the fifth-eldest of our children and we all miss her.'

Mr Rostas also supported the publication of an image of his daughter wrapped in plastic on the front page of the *Irish Sun* four days after Wilson's victory. He said, 'It's important for the people of Ireland to realize how my beautiful girl was treated. We support the image because it shows the awful nature of my girl's killing. The only time I will come back to

Ireland is if the gardaí re-open the case and pursue the criminal who killed my daughter.

'We are bitterly disappointed with the outcome and go back to Romania with heavy hearts. We will live with this nightmare for the rest of our lives – we can't get her out of our mind. It's been hard for all our family but it's been very difficult for Dumitru who was the last person to see her alive and Alexandru who spoke to her on the phone.

'Her absence is always felt by everyone in the family but no more than at dinner time when we as a family would always sit down together and talk about the day. Marioara would always take care of her brothers and sisters – they miss her every day. Our youngest daughter Rosalinda still asks after her.'

The teenager's father also thanked the people of Ireland for their support when he said, 'While we are disappointed with the justice system, we appreciate all the support from the people of Ireland. I can't thank the gardaí enough for everything they have done for us. We even had the Irish people stop us in the street this week to express their sorrow and also appreciate the support of the Department of Social Protection for arranging my daughter's burial.' This was a reference to the €10,000 the government department had paid to cover the cost of the teenager's repatriation.

Meanwhile, Herbert Kilcline was still in shock following Alan Wilson's acquittal. 'We were all convinced that he was going to be found guilty and we put our lives on the line making statements to the gardaí,' he said. 'When the verdict came in it was a devastating blow because I knew I would be one of the people he would be coming after.

'I stayed in different locations at the time and was constantly looking over my shoulder. Alan had the upper hand because he still had supporters on the outside; he only had about another five years to go of his sentence and that time would fly in. I remember being under a tremendous amount of pressure at that time. Some of my friends were worried about my mental state and this was all because of our decision to come forward.'

Kilcline insists he will always be 'frustrated' at the decision not to include any phone evidence. 'Eight expert witnesses were due to give evidence but they were never needed because there was no phone evidence,' he said. 'I was also willing to get into the witness box and tell the jury that the number Marioara had used to ring her brother in Romania was Wilson's because I and others knew it was his, but, unfortunately, I never got the chance.'

'Phone evidence was used in the trial of Joe O'Reilly for the murder of his wife Rachel in 2004 and also in the Graham Dwyer trial for the murder of Elaine O'Hara in 2012,' he said. 'It will always be a source of frustration for me because things could have turned out differently. With no evidence to corroborate Fergus's testimony, it was going to be difficult to get over the line.

'I will always think that if the trial had taken place before April 2014 things might have turned out differently. When I and others were making statements we weren't made aware of any European Court ruling and because of our decision I will always be in danger from that psycho Wilson. It's an ongoing worry for me and for the O'Hanlon family, who assisted the prosecution in this most heinous crime.'

Kilcline continues to live in fear of his life, while Fergus O'Hanlon was now residing at a secret location in the witness protection programme. Alan Wilson himself quickly forgot about the murder trial and concentrated his efforts on getting his seven-year sentence for the Blanchardstown cleaver attack overturned.

A hearing was set for the Court of Appeal in Dublin on 18 December 2014. Wilson applied to the court for bail pending the appeal against his conviction and sentence. Judge Michael Peart said the court was 'not happy' it was in an 'appropriate position' to determine Wilson's application before reading the submissions from the DPP and without having a transcript of Wilson's twelve-day trial.

However, Judge Peart said he was 'anxious' to facilitate an early date to minimize any 'potential prejudice' to Wilson. Once a date for the hearing had been set, Wilson's barrister, Padraig Dwyer, told the court how his client had only one previous conviction at the District Court for possessing a screwdriver before receiving a seven-year sentence for the incident in Blanchardstown.

He said the latter had been imposed despite no evidence from the 'injured parties' and no victim impact reports. In his final submission, Mr Dwyer argued his client did not receive a 'fair trial' because the jury had heard that Wilson was wearing a bulletproof vest on the day of his arrest. He argued that the 'obvious inference' was that his client was involved in gangland crime, and he was a person of bad character.

Wilson's appeal, along with the appeal of his co-accused David Crowley, got under way on 23 March 2015. In his opening remarks to the court, Crowley's counsel James O'Brien said the judge should have discharged the jury at his client's original trial because his client had approached a juror outside court and 'innocently' and 'generously [given] him a lighter'.

The incident, he argued, had been described by the jury as a 'jaw-dropping moment'. Mr O'Brien also argued that the victim's former partner, Lisa Murray, had said almost 'fifty times' that she had no memory of the events at her then partner's home.

He was quickly followed by Wilson's barrister, who told the court there was 'no evidence' of his client trespassing, no evidence of an assault and also how Lisa Murray's statement was 'wrong'.

Mr Dwyer also raised the issue of Wilson's bulletproof vest when he said the item 'played no role in the factual matrix of the events'. He added, 'It could only stand as a deeply damning piece of prejudicial evidence to put before a jury in a criminal trial.' In further submissions, Wilson's barrister told the court his client had been arrested for a firearms offence and was questioned in relation to that, but later charged with the burglary offence.

Both men returned to the court the following day as the appeal hearing continued. In response to Wilson's legal team, counsel for the DPP, Paul Burns, argued Wilson's bullet-proof vest was 'probative of joint enterprise'.

He said, 'People don't go around wearing bulletproof vests in their normal day.' The barrister also reminded the hearing how the trial judge in the case went to 'considerable lengths' to direct the jury on how to approach statements made by witnesses who later 'resiled' from them.

Mr Burns was asked by the President of the Court of Appeal Judge Sean Ryan how the men got into the property when there was 'no evidence' of a break-in or forced entry. He replied, 'The door could have been open and it wasn't necessary to conclude they were invited to the house because there wasn't a break-in.

'If the jury was satisfied that the purpose of going to the house was to carry out an unlawful attack on the victim, it was clearly trespass and they could never have had permission from anybody to do that. If the jury were satisfied it was a joint enterprise for both of them to go to the house to assault the victim, they were entitled to hold that it was a trespass.'

Following submissions by all sides in the two-day hearing, a date for 5 November was set for a ruling.

That was several months away, but Alan Wilson had something to focus on in the meantime: the case against the alleged killer of his cousin John. 'Wilson was still keeping his head down but to the small number of people he did associate with, he would always bring up the forthcoming trial of Keith O'Neill,' a prison source said. 'He kept saying how lucky O'Neill was that he had been caught and if Eric and Keith had been free he would have been a dead man.'

On 6 May 2015, nearly three years after the murder itself, Keith O'Neill finally came before a jury over the killing of John Wilson. Prosecuting counsel Conor Devally told the opening day at the Central Criminal Court that the shooting was 'an execution of sorts'. 'Mr Wilson was shot in the back – six bullets were discharged but two of them hit him,' he said.

The statement made by Wilson's seven-year-old daughter was then read out in court: 'My dad picked me up from school. My dad's friend was with him. I got into the back of the car and was sitting behind my dad. The three of us went straight to my house. My dad went into the house. When the man went into my house there were two people. One person stayed in the jeep. I just heard "bang bang bang". I could see my dad rolling around. I called my da. I feel a little bit sad and a little happy because my dad is away from the bad boys now.'

Neighbour Robert McHugh testified that he was in his sitting room on Cloverhill Road when he heard the shooting at around 1 p.m. on 28 September. 'I remember hearing gunshots and running out and meeting his young daughter,' he said.

'I leaned back and looked out the window [in my house] and seen a hooded figure come out the door. I couldn't see his face. His face was covered. I made my way towards the house. His daughter was trying to get into the house. She was upset and I stopped her going into the house. John was lying on the ground struggling to breathe.' McHugh added that it took 'around fifteen to twenty minutes' for an ambulance to arrive.

Garda Christopher O'Sullivan, the first member of the force to arrive at the crime scene, said the victim was not breathing and had no pulse by the time emergency services got there. He said, 'Dublin Fire Brigade attended within a matter of minutes. An advanced paramedic from the HSE took over and made a number of attempts. I observed a bullet on the kitchen floor. There were a number of bullet holes throughout the door leading to the kitchen.'

The court heard that resuscitation was continuous at the scene for over an hour and when there was no change it was decided to cease resuscitation. State pathologist Dr Marie Cassidy said John Wilson had been hit near the elbow of his left arm and in the left side of his back, near the armpit. The latter wound had been the fatal one, travelling diagonally across the chest and damaging the lung, stomach and spleen and causing the victim to bleed to death.

The circumstantial evidence against O'Neill was strong. Dunnes Stores employee Paula Molloy gave evidence that she had been on the till at the Mill Shopping Centre in Clondalkin on the day before the shooting and remembered one customer in particular. She said, 'I recall one gentleman I was serving – he bought ladies' gloves, men's scarves, more ladies' gloves, a men's hat and a paper bag. The person I served was sweating on his forehead.'

Similar items were later recovered from the partially burntout car by gardaí. O'Neill, wearing a distinctive green T-shirt, had been spotted with another man following John Wilson into the store on Cherry Orchard Avenue on the morning of the shooting and leaving when Wilson walked out again. Devally, for the DPP, told the jury, 'The gunman made good his escape, jumping into the back of a vehicle. Items were found in a nearby burnt-out vehicle, which included items that had been purchased by the accused.

'Shortly thereafter the accused, having shed one garment, got a lift back to Ballyfermot where he joined his family in a local chipper. He then went to Liffey Valley shopping centre – having changed in the shopping centre, when he got home he endeavoured to dispose of runners, jeans and socks and was seen disposing of them in a skip. Examination affirmed there was gunshot residue on the jeans. There was evidence that there was petrol vapour emanating from the socks. Mr O'Neill was detained and he denied his involvement.'

Defence counsel Anthony Sammon tried to make hay of the fact that nail guns used by carpenters emit some of the same material onto clothing as gunshot residue – and that the jeans, green T-shirt and Nike trainers recovered from the skip had been in an unsealed bag.

'Surely, as a scientist, what was in the skip that might have contaminated whatever was found would have been of interest?' he asked expert witness and forensic scientist Dr Thomas Hannigan. 'Did you not think it of any significance to inquire what had been in this skip? Would you accept from me that, as a forensic scientist, usual practice when a member of An Garda Síochána comes across an item of significance, they bag it, seal it?

'When did you become aware these items were brought to the station in an unsealed fashion? We are all here because a man is accused of the most serious crime. Surely the best standard should be attained?'

Dr Hannigan answered, 'The ideal solution is sealing – I

don't think it follows from that if it hasn't been fully sealed that the sample is contaminated. I'm suggesting the probability of contamination even if the bag isn't sealed is low.'

The jury of five women and seven men evidently agreed. After deliberating for only three hours and thirty-nine minutes, they returned a unanimous guilty verdict. Judge Tony Hunt told the jury he would make no observations on their verdict. 'It is entirely sensible based on the evidence I heard,' he said. 'I am not going to speculate as to what the background of this case is. I will proceed to pass the mandatory life sentence and express sincere sympathy and condolences to the family and friends of Mr Wilson and in particular his daughter.'

The judge might not have wished to speculate on the background, but it was clear to all and sundry that O'Neill was little more than a patsy in all of this. The *Irish Independent* later reported that a €40,000 price had been put on John Wilson's head, but that O'Neill never saw a cent of it.

However, the man gardaí believe was involved in the killing would be named in the High Court four years later during a case taken against two Ballyfermot criminals. The *Irish Times* reported that in a sworn affidavit, the Criminal Assets Bureau (CAB) told a judge that gardaí believed they had enough evidence to charge David Reilly over the shooting, but that the DPP disagreed. The CAB's case was presented to the High Court in October 2019 after they identified how Reilly was part of a gang who threatened builders at a social housing project in Ballyfermot in mid-2016 and who had earned a fortune from extortion.

As well as being a notorious enforcer for Derek 'Dee Dee' O'Driscoll, who had visited Eric Wilson over the murder of Martin Kenny all those years ago, Reilly had also previously been in a relationship with Sean Hunt's daughter Celine, with whom he had several children. Reilly was one of a number of west Dublin criminals who had been feuding with John Wilson. To this date, he has not been charged.

Alan Wilson was 'thrilled' with O'Neill's conviction, a senior prison source said. 'He was like a new man when O'Neill was convicted. He kept saying that justice had been served and how the prison authorities better ensure that O'Neill wasn't sent anywhere near him. He definitely had a spring in his step after O'Neill went down.'

However, Wilson's joy was short-lived as his mother Mary, aged sixty-three, dropped dead from a suspected heart attack at their family home on 13 September. The mother of two, who gardaí suspected of being involved in a sham marriage to a Libyan national in 2001 so he could obtain Irish citizenship, took her secrets of the Romanian teenager's murder to the grave.

Three days after her death Wilson was brought under armed guard to a funeral home in Dublin's Aungier Street to say his goodbyes between 9 a.m. and 11 a.m. But the loyal son was banned from going to his mother's funeral the following day at the Carmelite Church in Whitefriar Street in Dublin city centre. Only a handful of people attended. Wilson's mother had been arrested three times by gardaí investigating the murder of Marioara Rostas, who also believe she acted as a courier for notes from her son when he was in prison.

Herbert Kilcline maintained Mary Wilson's 'priority' in life had been to protect her son 'at all costs'. 'Alan and Maxine were the most important people in Mary's life,' he said. 'There's no doubt that Maxine would have confided in her about Marioara's murder but she wasn't moved at all. It was all about protecting her clan. She married into criminality and would never have betrayed her children. She knew about the teenager's murder, was aware of plots to have people killed by passing notes to Alan's associates and even told her son that the father of her grandchildren had to go because he knew too much. This is the type of person gardaí were dealing with – there was no humanity and zero empathy.'

A former neighbour of Wilson's mother told one of the authors she remembered a 'hard woman'. 'She was a tough woman and didn't have a lot of friends because she fought with a lot of her neighbours. Mary had her children and that was it. When they were all arrested for the Romanian girl she was telling people that they were all innocent. A lot of people were afraid of her because they were starting to hear stories about her son.'

Still in mourning for his mother, Alan Wilson came back to the Court of Appeal on 5 November 2015. Once again outlining the circumstances of the incident and Wilson's trial, Judge George Birmingham said the original statements by Lisa Murray and her father, later retracted in court, were entitled to be accepted by the trial judge.

He declared, 'In this case, there was information available to the trial court, which enabled it to conclude that statements in issue had been made by Ms Murray and that her evidence in court was materially inconsistent with them.

'It was reliable in the sense that it was clearly established that the statement was made and the circumstances in which the statement was made were that it was taken in the immediate aftermath of an incident, in her own home and before there was an opportunity to concoct or fabricate a statement.'

Wilson's brief had challenged his identification by Lisa Murray, but on this Judge Birmingham was quite firm. 'This was not a fleeting observation of a stranger at a bus stop or anything of that nature,' he said.

'The statement of Ms Murray was very specific in that she

recognized Alan Wilson straight away and that she knew him because her sister was going out with his cousin and she had seen him around the estate. It was a recognition effected in her own kitchen.

'Furthermore, some support for the statement is to be found in the fact that she commented that Alan Wilson had a pair of black gloves on when this occurred on 3 June, and the car in which Mr Wilson was travelling when stopped was found to contain gloves.

'The court is of the view that this was not the usual case of visual identification at all. Those who participated in this incident made no attempt to hide their identity. Instead, one must conclude that they were confident that those who were in the house and those who observed them, would, for whatever reason, be reluctant to give evidence. The fact that Ms Murray and her father resiled from their statements and that Mr O'Brien never gave a statement at any stage shows that their confidence was not misplaced.'

One rather far-fetched ground of the appeal was the possibility that any injuries to David O'Brien had arisen as a result of 'self-defence' by Crowley and Alan Wilson. But Judge Birmingham insisted, 'This court takes the view that the account given by Ms Murray rules out any question of self-defence. Particularly significant is the fact that the meat cleaver-type weapon described by Ms Murray did not come from her house.'

The Appeal Court also referred to the fact that the weapon was also a 'relevant consideration' for the jury to 'adduce' that Wilson and Crowley were trespassers. In conclusion, Judge Birmingham, who sat with President of the Court of Appeal Judge Sean Ryan and Judge John Edwards, confirmed the convictions of both men and dismissed the appeal.

*

Defeated in his quest to have his conviction overturned, Wilson was back at the Appeal Court four days later to appeal the sentence he had received for the same incident. This time, he had better luck.

His barrister Padraig Dwyer argued that the seven-year tariff was 'excessive' with regard to his client's 'antecedents' and because his client had never been in prison before. Mr Dwyer also submitted that there had been no victim impact statement in the trial although he conceded that the victim, David O'Brien, 'did sustain injuries'.

Judge Birmingham partially agreed. He ruled that Wilson's sentence would be reduced because 'he was effectively deprived of his liberty for twelve months' while on remand for the murder of Marioara Rostas. This meant Wilson had also been denied the opportunity for bail on the Blanchardstown attack because he was in custody on a 'more serious charge', the judge said. Once more, Alan Wilson showed no emotion as the judgment was delivered to the court and he was returned to his prison cell.

His determination to have the conviction quashed was matched only by his certainty that it would happen. Evidence of that came in an anonymous letter posted to a close relative of Fergus O'Hanlon. The letter featured a hand-drawn picture of a pistol and dagger amid a scrawl littered with spelling mistakes and read, '*I hear you and that other cunt Fergus is getting guns to do me when I get out. Your going around with that brasser. Aids ridden cunt. Not long to go. Cut, Cut Cut.*'

The mystery writer concluded by stating, '*Don't forget to bring this to the Garda. Tell them about the guns that bastard has. Some hard man.*' Although the letter was raised with detectives at Kevin Street station, it could never be proven who penned it.

Herbert Kilcline had few doubts, however. 'I've seen Alan's handwriting over the years and this certainly looks like it,' he said. 'I also think it was his because of his poor spelling and grammar. The drawing of the gun and the knife is clearly an indirect threat.

'On the one hand, it shows a level of paranoia because it appeared Alan thought Fergus was plotting to kill him. Did he think Fergus was going to come out of the programme to get Alan? On the other hand it showed a level of intimidation directed towards Paddy even though he wasn't involved in the case. The only reason he was being targeted was because of who he was related to.'

Despite continually falling short, Alan Wilson was now planning a Supreme Court appeal. But though he was going nowhere for the moment, he was paying close attention to what else was happening outside the walls of Mountjoy prison. There, events were unfolding which would eventually draw him in and lead to his downfall.

15. Practice Runs

*I'm just gonna fly upstairs with the machine gun, point
it at two of them, shoot them, get out, back into
the back seat of the car and drive off*
— Alan Wilson

By the middle of 2017 the Kinahan–Hutch feud, which had
broken out following the murder of David Byrne at the
Regency hotel on 5 February 2016, was in full swing. The
cartel had quickly gained the upper hand in the struggle,
which had turned into an extermination campaign against
anyone connected to the Hutch gang or family.

Wilson was on first-name terms with cartel figures such as
'Fat' Freddie Thompson, Thompson's first cousin Liam
Brannigan and young south inner-city gangster Dean Howe.
Prison authorities, who kept a discreet but close eye on
Wilson, noted how he would watch every news bulletin after
there had been a feud murder carried out.

'Wilson was very interested in events on the outside
because he had a personal relationship with senior members
of the Kinahan cartel,' a prison source told the authors.
'They were all from the same area. He kept his thoughts to
himself about the feud but would always watch the breaking
stories of all the murders on the news.'

The death toll from the feud stood at thirteen, all but two
of them killed by the cartel. But the huge garda attempt to
shut them down was beginning to have an effect and there

had been just one killing that year – the Hutch slaying of active cartel member Michael Keogh, whose brother Jonathan was later jailed for life for the murder of Gareth Hutch, that May.

The Garda National Drugs and Organised Crime Bureau (GNDOCB) had also succeeded in shutting down the cartel's logistics operation in a raid on Greenogue industrial estate in west Dublin the previous January in which a Kalashnikov assault rifle, a Mac10 sub-machine gun, handguns, semi-automatic pistols and ammo were recovered. The operation took the gang's quartermaster, a hitherto unknown figure called Declan Brady – nicknamed 'Mr Nobody' – out of circulation.

Thousands of miles away in Dubai, Daniel Kinahan needed someone to replace him on the ground. With 'Fat' Freddie Thompson already on remand for the murder of David 'Daithi' Douglas, the cartel leader looked to Thompson's first cousin, Liam Brannigan, who in turn recruited Dean Howe.

Brannigan was at that stage thirty-four years old and, like Alan Wilson, had managed to avoid any serious convictions – this was despite him being a key player in the Crumlin–Drimnagh feud. Gardaí believed he had acted as a logistics man in several of the murders. He was also unlike his peers in that he was a history buff who was one year into an archaeology degree at UCD. Howe, meanwhile, had been a player since his late teens. He was a runner for Freddie Thompson in the Crumlin–Drimnagh feud and had undertaken weapons training in Eastern Europe. In 2008 Thompson had subcontracted a hit on Martin 'The Viper' Foley to him after it was requested by Christy Kinahan.

Foley survived the hit only through sheer luck after he dived to one side in his car and managed to drive a short distance away even though he had been hit four times. Howe continued working for the cartel and had been arrested following the attempt on the life of John Hutch, Gerry 'The Monk' Hutch's brother, in September 2016. He had been the spotter for the murder bid and upon being detained, had pulled the SIM card out of his phone and swallowed it. Howe spent the rest of his seventy-two hours in custody refusing to eat or go to the toilet to avoid passing the SIM in his stool.

Both men picked up where Thompson and Brady had left off: identifying targets for murder and organizing the storage and transport of the weapons that would be used to try and kill them.

On 13 July 2017 Alan Wilson had another day out from Mountjoy to hear his Supreme Court appeal in front of five judges. As always, devoted sister Maxine was there to offer moral support. Wilson had challenged his conviction in the Court of Appeal on the basis of his identification by Lisa and Noel Murray and had lost. His Supreme Court gambit was based on raising 'issues of general public importance concerning the proper interpretation' of Section 19 of the 1984 Criminal Justice Interpretation Act. The clause allows gardaí to caution a suspect but also to draw 'adverse inferences' from a suspect over their failure or refusal to answer questions before or when they have been charged with an offence.

The thrust of Wilson's challenge was that he had been arrested and cautioned over the unlawful discharge of a shotgun at the house, but had eventually been charged with trespass. Another, more serious, charge of assault causing harm had later been added by the DPP, but that was not at issue here. It was very much a technicality, but as far as the Supreme Court was concerned, a crucial one. It ruled, 'The inferences caution must relate to the same offence as is involved in the proceedings ultimately brought and thus the same offence as that with which the accused is charged.'

Upholding the point of law raised by Wilson's barrister, the three judges quashed the conviction and ordered that he be retried over the Blanchardstown incident. They were promptly informed by the DPP that it was not worth bothering with. Wilson had – with remission included – already served most of the six-year sentence he had received.

Wilson had won. He was a free man for the first time since 2011, though the victory seemed rather pyrrhic given he had already done the time. However, the ruling would prove to be quite significant down the line.

Detectives from the GNDOCB and Kevin Street and Crumlin stations watched the ruling with concern. Pat Leahy was the Assistant Garda Commissioner for Dublin, with responsibility for policing in the capital. Now retired, he recalls the unease among his colleagues over Wilson's release. 'Our organization had taken a collaborative approach to tackling the Kinahan and Hutch feud,' he told the authors. 'We had some tremendous successes with everyone pulling together, especially against the Kinahan organized crime group, throughout 2016 and into 2017.

'However, despite the arrests and the seizures connected to the feud, the Kinahan group were still gathering intelligence and identifying targets for murder. I was having a meeting once a month with the specialist units regarding the feud and I remember Alan Wilson's name being mentioned. I remember thinking this wasn't good news for us and that we could be in trouble because there was real concern that he could get involved in this feud due to his connections to organized crime over the years. We were out there trying to save lives and we now had someone of Wilson's calibre thrown into the mix.

'However, this wasn't our only concern, as there were other feuds ongoing in the capital and that's why I had to spend €57 million on overtime to keep communities safe. We knew he would once again be a thorn in our side. Turns out we were right.'

But detectives were not the only ones who were apprehensive. 'The decision by the Supreme Court meant that Alan only had a minor district court offence to his record,' Herbert Kilcline said. 'It was bad enough him having a year taken off his sentence but this was a completely different ball game because he was now back living in the community.

'I remember the day of his release like it was yesterday because the gardaí phoned me up and told me he had been released; a crime prevention officer would be in contact; and for me to take sensible precautions. Once again, the pressure that I had previously been under returned and I kept a low profile and often changed my routine because I feared he could be waiting for me somewhere.

'I know he blamed me for telling Fergus to work with the gardaí and he would never ever let this go. Thankfully, Fergus was in witness protection but other members of his family were worried about intimidation even though they had nothing to do with the case. It was a very stressful period over the summer of 2017.'

Wilson had only been out of prison a matter of weeks when investigators from the GNDOCB received intelligence that he had offered his services to Liam Brannigan and Dean Howe.

On 29 August 2017 Detective Inspector David Gallagher, now a detective superintendent, held a meeting with a number of his colleagues at Dublin Castle. He outlined how they had received information about a 'navy/grey'-coloured SEAT Leon, bearing the false registration plates 08 D 127373, which had been parked in the Goldenbridge area of Inchicore in south Dublin.

The vehicle, he said, had been left there by the Kinahan organized crime group to be used as a getaway vehicle in the murder of one of a number of as yet unidentified targets. That same day, an undercover team was dispatched to establish the car's location and within a few hours the vehicle had been placed under surveillance.

At the same time, gardaí established the car had originated in the Birmingham area, with the false plates belonging to a Vauxhall import. Although never proven, gardaí suspected the SEAT was sent to Ireland by associates of senior cartel member Thomas 'Bomber' Kavanagh before his arrest by the UK's National Crime Agency for running a massive cocaine and money-laundering operation.

The following day, those identified as having access to the car were drug addict Joseph Kelly and Alan Wilson. On 31 August, Brannigan and Howe were also named as suspects, with intelligence now indicating the group had control of another four vehicles: a 3 Series BMW estate, a Nissan Primastar van, a Renault Laguna and a Mazda 6. The Mazda had also been brought into the country from Birmingham.

The Kinahan war on the Hutch gang and anyone connected to them had seen a number of hit teams recruited from across the city. The set-up was loosely based on the cell-type structure of the Provisional IRA active service units used during the Troubles. Each cell member would be assigned specific tasks in the planning of murders. The list of duties included everything from providing phones and safe houses, sourcing weapons and conducting surveillance on targets to securing vehicles, planning escape routes and deciding who would pull the trigger. But for security reasons, only one figure would communicate with the cartel leadership in Dubai: for this particular cell, that would be Liam Brannigan.

*

On 1 September 2017 the operation to bring down the cell swung into action. Surveillance would be a vital component. Four days later, gardaí applied to the District Court for warrants to allow electronic surveillance of the suspects. In their submission, gardaí stated, 'Specific investigations are being conducted into the activities of an identified structured criminal organisation referred to as the Kinahan organized crime group.

'Resulting from investigations conducted, a number of persons are linked to this criminal organization. They are Alan Wilson, Joseph Kelly, Liam Brannigan and Dean Howe. Liam Brannigan had access to a number of specific vehicles and it is our belief a number of these vehicles were to be used by Alan Wilson and Joseph Kelly in committing criminal actions.

'It is our belief that these vehicles were to be used by Mr Brannigan and/or other members of the Kinahan organized crime group in the participation in or contributing to activity intended to enhance the ability of the criminal organisation to commit a serious offence. The serious offences being engaged in and planned by this organized crime group, included unlawful possession of firearms and murder.' Once warrants were issued, the huge operation to bring down the sub-cell was up and running.

The following day the gang added further to their fleet of vehicles by purchasing a white Volkswagen Caddy van for €2,700 via DoneDeal. The name used to fill out the logbook in order to complete the sale was 'John Kavanagh' from Coolock in north Dublin. Gardaí would later establish it was Kelly – described by the seller as 'looking like a drug addict' and with a 'brown man bag' – who had bought the vehicle. Although gardaí had been monitoring the movements of the suspects since 1 September, they badly needed to eavesdrop on their conversations too.

On 9 September they got permission to do this, with further warrants authorizing 'the use of audio surveillance devices for the purpose of conducting surveillance on Mr Alan Wilson, Mr Joseph Kelly, Mr Liam Brannigan, Mr Dean Howe and/or their criminal associates as members of the Kinahan organized crime gang'. Within forty-eight hours, all vehicles under the control of the gang had been accessed and had hi-tech listening devices secretly installed on them by the gardaí's National Surveillance Unit and Crime & Security teams.

Unaware that they were under observation themselves, the sub-cell was also conducting its own surveillance in the north inner city, though gardaí had as yet no indication of who they were after.

At 6.12 a.m. on 11 September Alan Wilson got into the back of the Nissan Primastar driven by Kelly. The van moved off and the pair first went to Stephen's Lane, a small residential street in Dublin 2 sandwiched between Mount Street Lower and Mount Street Upper. This had been designated as a possible location for the 'switch', the spot where the car used to flee the murder scene would be burnt out and the hit team would get into another vehicle and drive away before eventually splitting up.

Wilson told Kelly, 'I'll show you on the way back first, but we'll just go from this laneway to our destination and then we head back to this laneway and head back to our destination and do it again, just so you get familiar with the turns. We'll time it. Now you're talking . . . there's a good few sets of lights and we've an illegal right-hand turn here as well.

'When we're heading back, we'll be heading back this direction . . . we'll need a third driver for when we destroy the car and get into the switch. We need to step into the back of a van and drive off and then probably we'll get out on the canal somewhere up there.'

Next, Wilson began giving directions towards the north inner city, occasionally pointing out other possible switch sites in the Store Street area for them to abandon their getaway vehicle and change to a new one.

At 6.24 a.m. Kelly asked about the possibility of luring their as yet unidentified target to a spot where he could be murdered. 'What happened to this fella being brought to us?' he asked. The reply indicated both Wilson's seniority within the cell to Kelly plus the fact that the unknown mark knew he was under threat. 'It's not happening,' he answered. 'He's wide to it.'

The pair drove onwards to the Fairview area, Wilson continuing to issue instructions to his driver about driving in different lanes. At 6.34 a.m. he gave both his junior colleague and those listening in more of an indication about what was in the pipeline.

'We're going to have to do it about ten o'clock at night as well to check that route,' he said in what gardaí believed was a reference to the roads they had earmarked to flee the murder scene.

Wilson was next overheard counting the number of traffic lights they passed and timing the progress they made as the duo engaged in a real-time dry run. 'That's twelve sets of lights,' he told Kelly. 'This is the route coming back in. The police will have an all-unit call by now. But we still have to drive at an easy pace. We can't race it on the road. We're after pulling off what we're doing at the flats or the pub, we're coming this direction. It's nearly nine minutes now, the place will be covered in police.

'When you pull in there, I'm gonna douse the car in petrol. Baseball caps is going to be too suspicious walking off. We won't have to worry about cameras on our route back because we'll be in the back of the van, yeah? We need to walk away clean and get someone else to burn the car for us.'

The following morning Kelly again collected Wilson, this time at 5.12 a.m. Once more they discussed the route, the burning of vehicles after the murder and this time, the issue of DNA. In one conversation, Kelly described their 'contract' as having a 'bit of an aul risky side of it, isn't there?'

'Very, very risky,' Wilson replied. 'That's it . . . it's a high-risk job.' The pair set off towards Fairview once more, Kelly complaining along the route about the delay in traffic lights going green. 'I wonder why they're so fucking long?' he moaned.

Wilson had other concerns. 'Yeah and see at ten at night, you have the prostitutes round here. You have a unit in the area watching everything. And if we skip these lights it could make a big mistake for us.'

'You wanna get out of the area quickly,' Kelly chipped in, to which Wilson replied, 'We'll do it nice and swiftly, we will. It's just what's gonna catch us, the illegal right-hand turn and the twelve sets of traffic lights . . . that's our big problem.'

Up until this point, gardaí did not know the exact spot planned for the murder. Flats and a pub had been mentioned. But Wilson now alarmed cops as he began chatting about shooting two people at a pub he did not name.

'They're gonna be sitting upstairs, yeah?' he said. 'I'm just gonna fly upstairs with the machine gun, point it at two of them, shoot them, get out back into the back seat of the car and drive off, heading this route.'

Anxious to be seen as fully committed, Kelly offered to back him up. 'I was gonna say, do you wanna even go in on your own?' he asked. 'You're on your own, like, do you want me to go in with you?'

But Wilson felt he did not require any assistance. 'No, you wait in the car,' he told him. 'I'll go in meself. I won't be a minute in there. I'll be less than thirty, forty seconds in there and we're gone. I'll be in the back seat of the car and we drive straight off, yeah?'

Carrying out a murder in a public place always came with the possibility of bystanders intervening. 'You don't want any hero bastards,' Kelly pointed out.

'Yeah, that's gonna be a problem,' Wilson conceded.

'That's why I'm gonna point at two of them, pull the trigger.' Returning to their escape plan, the pair again discussed having their bosses hire another driver, allowing them to jog home once their getaway car had been abandoned in the south inner city.

'He could have someone else there who can douse the van and torch it,' Wilson suggested. 'And we jog off down there and when we get to the road you split one way to your house, I split the other way to my house.'

The conversation then took a bizarre turn into the world of personal fitness. 'We went for a jog, you know, for two miles,' Wilson added. 'We done fifty press-ups, fifty pull-ups and two miles. You know Sandymount? We jogged the whole beach. I'm nearly thirty-nine now, fucking getting old. I have to try and stay a bit fit, you know?'

In just two days of recordings, gardaí had gathered information on the gang's preferred method of carrying out the shooting, their surveillance of the target or targets and their escape plans. With warrants in place until 7 December, they had time to listen in some more before having to make their move.

Kelly and Wilson returned to their mission the next evening of Wednesday 13 September, this time waiting until 10.03 p.m. before setting off for the northside once again. The conversation started off on inanities, with Wilson informing his sidekick that he was 'fucking stuffed' after a trip to an 'all-you-can-eat Chinese'.

Kelly replied, 'They're fucking lovely, aren't they? A1,' before Wilson quickly moved on to more serious matters. 'Remember I was saying to you before about something?' he asked Kelly. 'This fella . . . I have someone there that he said he's gonna, you know, bring him to a house party. He's gonna walk him into the front garden with his arms around him. And we just shoot him.'

This was a further piece of the puzzle for gardaí listening in. The suspected criminal was a former member of the Westies crime gang: evidently, he would cooperate in luring the target to a spot where he could be murdered.

However, the issue of who the gang were planning to shoot remained maddeningly unclear. Whoever it was though, the cartel were obviously prepared to pay top dollar. 'I think it's fifty thousand now,' Wilson continued, in an obvious reference to the money being handed over for the hit. 'I'm gonna see him on Friday.' Kelly, for his part, had reservations over the participation of the west Dublin gangster.

The man in question was a volatile character, known for his belligerence. He was involved in a number of criminal feuds and had been arrested and questioned by gardaí over the 2013 murder of Lithuanian crime boss Gintaras Zelvys in an industrial park at Rathcoole, Co. Dublin.

'I don't think he is the person we should be going for because he has loads of surveillance on him,' Kelly remarked.

'There's not really . . . not really,' Wilson answered dismissively. Kelly quickly changed the subject back to the issue of another driver coming on board. 'We'd say to him, "Right, pal, fucking sit here, we're going to do a bit of work, we'll be back." No problem.'

Wilson was not against the idea, but felt whoever it was should receive a lesser share of the cash. 'If we had €100,000 it's not going to go three ways,' he responded. 'See the switch driver? Give him €10,000 or something.'

'Even, c'mere, at the most, give him twenty – forty each,' Kelly agreed. He perked up at the mention of money and suggested they multiply their fee after the hit by investing it in drugs.

'We buy a nice bit of brown [heroin] between us, right?' he said. 'But also we're gonna buy a nice bit of applejack, I'm telling ya now, it's the hottest thing on the street.' Applejack is a slang term for crack cocaine.

Wilson gave only a vague 'yeah' in reply, but in other conversations, he could be heard boasting about how much he planned to make from selling on cocaine sent back to Ireland by the Baldoyle drug trafficker who had initially set his cousin Eric up with an apartment out in Spain.

'Friend of mine, yer man . . . you know from Blanchardstown, him and yer man got in a load of stuff and they let us make six thousand on each key,' Alan Wilson told Kelly. 'So I made a good bit, you know on five keys, so was able to cover all the bills and you know, whatever else I needed.'

Wilson later told Kelly that the Baldoyle trafficker was bringing in another ten kilos the following month and that he was expecting to make the same amount again per kilo. 'For doing nothing,' he bragged. 'Not a thing. Like, I didn't have to do nothing. I just go count all the money.'

The pair drove onwards and discussed strategies to confuse those investigating the hit by burning out their getaway vehicle close to Store Street garda station in the north inner city. 'When you think about it here, they're gonna be saying, "Right, that's a northside job, look where it was done, right at Store Street station,"' Kelly said.

They arrived in Fairview where Wilson got out to look at possible routes back to the city centre on foot. In doing so, he touched a gate outside a house. Wilson was obviously acutely aware of the fact that they might be under surveillance and his slip-up gnawed at him after he got back into the car and they headed back towards the southside again.

'We come over here at five o'clock in the morning,' he told Kelly. 'We clean that gate. I don't know where I put me hand. I'll bring a spray bottle of bleach. Have you got a yellow reflector jacket? I don't want to be suspicious cleaning the gate.'

Kelly seemed obsessed with the idea of getting someone else involved as an extra driver. Whoever it was should wear a shirt and tie to 'look respectable', he said. 'They need to look like they're not . . . have one eye or big scars.'

This time, Wilson was less negative in his response. Pointing at a street they were passing, he told Kelly, 'If he drives down that road he can burn the van there and make his way home, yeah? All our clothes is gonna be in this van. We're gonna take all our running stuff, our tops off, we're gonna have two cans of petrol in the van. Enough for it to go up.'

Kelly answered enthusiastically, 'Now, before we get out of the van we douse our clothes in bleach, loads of bleach, loads of petrol. When me an' you is in the back of the van, we'll be stripped, douse loads of bleach, loads of lighter fluid, loads of petrol and tell your man, "Right, our clothes are doused, so that when you [the driver] get out of the car, take your shirt off and put them on the passenger seat."'

Wilson said he believed the shooting should happen on a Saturday night. Kelly answered, 'I think I should go in with ya, back you up. You're going to where there could be a big party and there could be a gang of them. Someone starts throwing stools . . .

'I know you have a machine gun. Use that, riddle them, like, but if you go in do them two, if anyone tries to give, you know, straight away you just turn around, bang, one into the leg, "Put that fucking chair down. Anyone else moves, I'll take the fucking head off ya."'

'I'll be only five seconds in there,' Wilson said casually in response.

Despite the pair having just reconnoitred a residential area of Fairview, it was evident the spot for the shooting had not been yet agreed upon. There had been talk of the upstairs floor of an unidentified pub, flats, and a house party, and now the discussion had returned to a pub again. The actual identity of the target or targets remained elusive. But a break in the case would soon be made.

16. Target Identified

You know Gary Hanley, do ya?
                  – Alan Wilson

Though the five men were actively plotting to kill an as yet unidentified figure, it did not occupy their every waking moment. All of them took a day off on Thursday, 14 September 2017. There was no such luck for gardaí watching them, who spent the day tailing them as they visited their families or went to the pub.

But the following morning, the conspirators were all back at work. Once more Wilson and Kelly were the early birds, with Kelly picking up his partner in crime at 5.06 a.m. The pre-dawn starts were beginning to grate.

'Didn't get much sleep last night,' Wilson moaned. 'Bleedin' wrecked, I am. Only going to get an hour's sleep and then I've to collect the kids. Better not leave me stuck with these for the bleeding day. Once I get them, I won't get asleep, you know.'

'Same as meself,' Kelly answered. 'I'm fucking exhausted.' The topic would be a running theme for the day, with gardaí summarizing hours of legally irrelevant conversation between the pair by stating that they were 'giving out about women thinking they're up to something, giving out about partners giving them hassle'.

The Nissan Primastar took off for the northside, before returning back to Wilson's home at New Street Gardens in

Portobello, Dublin 8, at 6.23 a.m. Wilson went inside before re-emerging nineteen minutes later and they spent the entire morning driving around the city. At 11.41 a.m. the van stopped at the 74 Talbot Street pub and Wilson walked inside for two minutes before coming out once more.

There was no discussion about why, but gardaí who were tailing them felt the venue could be the bar in which Wilson was planning to shoot his unnamed targets upstairs. Certainly, the pub had an upper floor, though it was not a known hangout for any particular targets of the Kinahan cartel.

A strong indication that it was came when Wilson got back into the car and Kelly yet again raised the subject of him taking part in the planned attack. He told Wilson, 'While you're upstairs, the barman could be on the phone downstairs, "There's a bloke shooting people", and by the time you get back down, he's hung up and pressed the panic button. So when you walk in, someone else is standing behind you, they're guarding downstairs.'

'I went into three pubs before to shoot people,' Wilson replied defensively.

'No, I know, but you're going in to do two people on your own, know what I mean?' Kelly said. 'The minute you walk into the pub, you know, there's going to be screams, pint glasses, bottles getting thrown up into the air, people diving, you know, all that. Especially when they see someone with a fucking ski mask and a machine gun, yeah, and they're going to see you walk right by, every one of them.'

Kelly's idea began to grow on Wilson despite his earlier reservations. 'See if two of us went up, someone just held the door open for me,' Wilson said. 'I'd go in, shoot them, then straight back down the stairs. We'll only be a second upstairs.'

Next, Kelly had a sudden – and ironic – fit of panic about

being under surveillance. 'You know, the Old Bill, watching to see who you're meeting since you got out, all that shit,' he said. 'Keep the head down. Don't go meeting the usual people, you know mates, friends like.'

Wilson agreed. 'I'm gonna keep a low profile for the next two weeks,' he said. 'See, sometime probably this Monday or Tuesday, we'll drive the route again and just check the burn spot for the second vehicle.'

Another fixation of Kelly's up to this point had been the hiring of an extra driver. Now it became clear that Wilson had been musing about it himself over the weekend. Referring to a man who cannot be identified for legal reasons, he said, 'What do you think of your man Mark? Mark can't drive. Poxy driver, he is. He's bleeding six feet four he is, a big stocky thing, he is. That's too big, big stocky fella squashed in the car.' Another man, a former prisoner, was also mentioned but this time it was Kelly who expressed doubts about his viability. He informed Wilson that the ex-jailbird was 'heavily into gay porn' and was nicknamed 'Secrets' behind bars due to his habit of shooting his mouth off about other inmates.

Kelly then queried whether their 'employers' could themselves supply another man to take part in the murder instead. 'Yeah, they have a lot of money,' Wilson answered. Kelly sounded indignant about what he seemed to regard as penny-pinching by the cartel. 'Come on, they have all over Europe, know what I mean?' he said. 'So you're telling me they can't get us a solid man?'

At the same time as Wilson and Kelly were driving around the north inner city, Liam Brannigan and Dean Howe were under surveillance at Dublin's Phoenix Park. Gardaí watched from a distance as the two men walked up Chesterfield

Avenue, the main road bisecting the park, at 9.15 a.m., Howe pushing a bicycle.

They reached a spot known as the Wellington monument between the large obelisk, the entrance to the zoo and the entrance to the cricket grounds and hung around there. At 9.40 a.m. an unknown man arrived, driving a Toyota Avensis. The man got out of the car and Brannigan held out what gardaí could see was an electronic device of some type and pointed something out to the new arrival. The three men examined the object for a few seconds, before Howe gave the third man something else and cycled off.

Gardaí feared the gadget the men had been looking at might have been a tracking device. Investigators went to work and within a couple of days, received information from a confidential informant that their hunch was correct.

On 17 September Detective Inspector Gallagher, who was running the investigation together with Detective Superintendent Seamus Boland and Detective Inspector Noel Browne, told his colleagues on the investigation team that they now knew who the cartel was after. The tracker had been fitted to a white Range Rover driven by a Fairview resident named Sinead Murphy. Ms Murphy's partner, and the father of her young toddler, was a veteran criminal named Gary Hanley.

Hanley was far from a model citizen. He was just fifteen when he joined a pal named Richard Lynch in holding up an off-licence in Portmarnock in 2004. His trial heard he had picked up a gun and pointed it at the shop owner before the pair escaped with €1,200 in cash and cigarettes in a stolen car driven by Hanley.

He only got a year for that, but took part in a mass riot while serving it inside St Patrick's youth detention centre, landing him two more years. Hanley was not long out from incarceration when he stabbed a woman named Martina Kelly in the face with a set of keys outside Clontarf Dart station on 15 March 2007.

Hanley had blamed his victim for causing the death of his girlfriend because the two women had had a row, after which his girlfriend had driven off in anger and crashed. The fact that Ms Kelly was holding her baby at the time of the assault and pleaded to be left alone did not stop him leaving her with facial scars. In 2009, Hanley got four years in jail for the attack.

In 2017, gardaí in Clontarf considered him a 'trusted associate' of the Hutch gang, though not everyone agreed. 'Everyone is saying that Hanley was a member of the Hutch gang but he wasn't,' one north inner-city local said. 'He would have known some of them, but that was it. In 2017 he was doing his own thing and wasn't aligning himself with any faction. They were probably afraid of him and that's why they went after him.'

Regardless of the truth, Hanley had enough connection to the Hutch gang to make him a worthy scalp for the cartel. They may well have been influenced by his close loyalty to his cousin, an inner-city hitman named Jason 'Buda' Molyneux, who was also considered a Hutch ally.

There was another factor, however, which might have landed a price on Hanley's head. The Kinahan murder campaign had slowed almost to a halt because gardaí were so closely monitoring the main Hutch targets. Members of the Hutch family, including Gary Hutch's father Patsy, were receiving round-the-clock armed protection and accompanied wherever they went. Targeting was still going on and several other hits had been interrupted as they were about to take place.

The arrest of Declan 'Mr Nobody' Brady with a cache of

arms in January had been followed by the capture of Estonian hitman Imre 'The Butcher' Arakas in April following his arrival in Dublin to murder Gary Hutch's old pal, James 'Mago' Gately. There had been a further interception of a murder plot on the Kylemore Road just a month beforehand in August, in which an attempt to kill cartel target Michael Frazer was cut off. The two-man hit team had been arrested and their weapons seized. This had forced the cartel to be more creative in their choice of quarry. Thus, Hanley it was.

Following the meeting in which the information about the tracker was relayed to the rest of the team, Detective Sergeant Martin Mahon and Detective Garda Ronan Doolan set off to find the Range Rover and confirm if the devices were underneath. They eventually came across the vehicle on Beaumont Road and crawled under the chassis. Two magnetic GoTEK trackers were visible just under the central beam of the undercarriage. The items were removed and handed over for technical analysis, where data revealed they had been first activated in the south inner city before being transported to the Phoenix Park on the same morning and at the same time as Howe and Brannigan met with their mystery colleague.

From there, the devices went dark until they were reactivated at 4 a.m. that morning outside Hanley's home. 'Members of this group have conducted their own extensive surveillance of Gary Hanley's home,' gardaí noted in their investigative file. 'While doing so, they have made attempts to conceal their identities. They have moved a number of different vehicles on an almost daily basis as part of this activity.'

Over the course of the next week, Joseph Kelly embarked on solo runs to the north inner city without Alan Wilson. He was accompanied in the Nissan Primastar by Dean Howe on 25 September before another unidentified man joined him on 26 September as the scouting missions continued.

Dean Howe was a far harder taskmaster on Kelly than Alan Wilson's relatively laid-back style Howe ripped into Kelly over what he saw as his erratic driving. At one point Kelly drove dangerously close to a pedestrian. Howe, who had obviously not seen the incident, asked, 'Who's roaring?'

'Some bloke crossing the road,' Kelly responded.

The sound of a car horn beeping could then be heard in the background before Howe started shouting, 'Joe! Joe, wake fucking up, will ya?'

'I put it into first,' Kelly mumbled in response.

'You did in your bollix put it into first, you fucking mongo, ye!' Howe roared back. 'You're going to get us fucking nicked – take your fucking brain and wake fucking up.'

'Sorry, pal ... I meant to put it into first. I put it into reverse instead of first,' Kelly said.

But Howe would not be pacified. 'Fucking right, you meant,' he snapped. 'You're going to get us tore out of it. Take your fucking time, you're just flying. Joey, genuine everything you do you're making a bollix of it. Just fucking chill out ... chill out. You're after nearly killing us twice. I know where the yoke is, you're driving fucking by it. You better have your gloves, because I have mine on me. Joe, you need to wake up, mate. No mistakes, just nice and easy.'

It also became apparent that Howe was already irate at Kelly for failing to show for duty because he had received a court summons over leaving the scene of a crash while on his motorbike outside the entrance to a Jury's hotel car park.

Kelly had complained about being fined most of his dole money in order to have the offence struck out. 'Only I had me scratcher on me ... 150 poxy euro into the court poor box. The judge says "Right, execute the warrant."'

But Kelly's excuse that he had no means of getting in touch with Howe or Brannigan cut little ice. 'You fucked up, we had to do your job,' Howe snarled at him. 'That's bollix, Joey, the day you went to court, you fucked up. Look, we all fuck up, just don't let it happen again, pal. When you've got a job to do, you need to do the job. I don't want to be giving out, but we all have our jobs to do. That's the way everything works, we had to do your job because we couldn't get you.'

The pair next spent around half an hour discussing moving, parking and fuelling the four vehicles they had engaged for the hit. It was clear one of Kelly's main duties was to ensure the cars were properly located in various potential switch spots around the city.

After a while his motoring had improved to the point that Howe felt obliged to pay him a compliment. 'Now you're driving well. What the fuck was going on with you earlier?'

'I was just a little nervous, pal . . . sorry,' Kelly answered.

Unfortunately, it would not last. As Kelly tried to park behind a Nissan Micra, he almost ran over a pedestrian. 'Take your time,' Howe urged him, 'don't kill yer man. Fuckin' hell, Joey!'

'Ah, he's all right,' Kelly responded defensively.

'Apologize to him, Joey!' Howe ordered angrily.

Kelly could then be heard shouting, 'Sorry about that, pal', to the man who had evidently walked off.

Three days later, on Friday 29 September, Kelly again picked up Alan Wilson, who got into the back of the Nissan Primastar outside his house at 1.39 p.m. He told Kelly, 'So we're going our usual route, but this time we're going to Fairview. You know Gary Hanley, do ya? I know him very well. So, the same route we're going to use on the pub.'

It was the first concrete confirmation gardaí had that Hanley was the main target. Wilson then gave a hint as to the reasons for his absence some days earlier. 'See Friday night? No, sorry, see Wednesday night . . . for the first time in seven years I took a bit of coke,' he told Kelly. 'Fuck's sake, very strong. Asleep all day yesterday, the whole day. It was proper stuff, yeah. I didn't actually like it.' There were also indications that the murder plot had been speeded up. 'These want these done as quick as possible, I'll tell you the situation while you're driving.

'We'll check out the spot now. He goes to the gym about 5 p.m. If we get him at five o'clock, the inward-bound traffic is actually free-flowing.' Then there was a mention of the street and number at which Hanley lived and a reference to the white Range Rover.

Referring to the house, Wilson added, 'We watch it in the van, right, go out and do what we have to do, kill him and we jump straight into another car, drive off and someone else can drive off in the van.'

The area of Fairview where Hanley resided is a warren of small residential streets and Wilson was clearly worried about getting lost trying to escape afterwards. There was a lengthy chat about the problems of finding a particular right turn to get out of there. 'We'll tie a rag on that pole tomorrow night,' he informed Kelly. 'Have ya something like, you know, an orange bag or something so you won't miss it, or an orange cloth or something?'

At 2.49 p.m. the pair drove past Hanley's home. 'That door won't go in, that's a security door he has,' Wilson said as they eyeballed the house. 'I was told the windows are bulletproof as well. He has bulletproof windows, security hall door, so the thing I don't like, waiting around for anybody because that's how you get caught, you're waiting there with a weapon.'

Kelly agreed. 'That's what I'm saying, so like for us to get there at fucking . . . if he goes at five every day, yeah?'

Wilson responded, 'Me and you sit in the back of the van and let someone else sit in the driver's seat, we give it an hour, we see him coming out, we go and give it to him, get back in the van, we drive around the corner and we get into our car and drive our separate ways and your man goes off in the van, yeah? Wherever he is going to go, we don't know, but he has to burn that van, 'cause our DNA is all over it.'

The conversation returned to one of the candidates identified as a possible getaway driver. 'Ah here, I bumped into Mark,' Kelly said. 'He's made for a bit of work, I says to be honest I only go what I'm given myself.'

Wilson still had doubts about the big man, though. 'I think he's all talk, he is,' he said. 'I put him to the test a few times and he fuckin' . . .'

Kelly then dropped Wilson back to his home.

It had been a massive day for those monitoring the hit team. For the first time, gardaí now knew beyond doubt that at least one of the targets was Gary Hanley and that the gang were leaning towards trying to kill him at his home. But they were also acutely aware that the plot was moving forward with even greater urgency. Detectives had to balance the overriding concern of preventing a murder against the requirement to arrest the five conspirators red-handed so that they would have enough evidence to send them away for a long time.

Wilson took another day off and returned to his mission on 1 October. He was picked up once more by Kelly in the Primastar at 7.10 p.m. Without even saying hello, Wilson told him, 'We'll tie the black bag around the pole, yeah? Just mark the corner so when we do finally do this you know which turn to make.'

Somewhat put out, Kelly replied, 'How are you pal, all right?'

Wilson answered, 'Just rushing around all day. We'll just do a run past his house.' Another test run to Fairview was carried out before the pair drove back to Dublin 8 and went back to Fairview again.

There was further discussion of the escape route before Wilson was dropped off at 8.16 p.m. That same day, a crime prevention officer from the gardaí served Hanley with a Garda Information Message (GIM) about a credible threat to his life along with advice about his personal security. It was only one of a number of such warnings Hanley had received over the years and he displayed his usual bravado in refusing to accept or sign the form.

On 2 October, as the prospective date of the murder moved closer, Liam Brannigan and Dean Howe took the Nissan Primastar to carry out some reconnaissance of their own on Hanley's home. At 1.53 p.m., both Howe and Brannigan got into the back of the van and began pouring petrol into different containers. Brannigan wondered if they had enough, but Howe assured him they had 'bleedin' loads of it' and there was a brief chat about spray bleach too.

Howe then began to outline his problems with Joseph Kelly, who he and Brannigan referred to as 'Joker'. Brannigan took out his phone and rang Alan Wilson and the pair engaged in a lengthy chat.

He told Wilson, 'I'm just sorting out the juice and stuff like that here now, like I'm separating it because we need three of them and all, but I have a fellow to do that other little job as well, like, to take the thing away, whatever, yeah. I can't get this Joker fellow, his phone is off there, were you with him last night, yeah? Okay, okay, no problem, there's no panic, 100 per cent.' Gardaí took this as an indication that the long-sought extra getaway driver had finally been organized. 'We're nearly ready, so like we'll be able to do a couple of hours this evening, please God. We should have it wrapped up, I'd say. Well, not wrapped up but if we do a couple of hours, there's a good chance, unless the fellow's not . . .'

There was a pause before Brannigan continued in an evident

reference to Gary Hanley, 'We should see him this evening, because I've seen him myself with my own eyes like a few days ago, you know what I mean? That's what I'm saying, you need to pick . . . I thought you did that last night? You need a quiet little spot that you can sit, like you can just hide, sit in the back of the other yoke just waiting, you know what I mean, okay?

'Well, listen pal, if we're not . . . if you haven't the spot picked out, you can get all that spot and everything picked out tonight, get the things over into place and then we'll go to work then tomorrow. We'll get the motors that we need to get over there, you know what I mean? I'm going to get these few bits and bobs done into the van and that and let me know if you hear from Joker. I'm trying him, I only have this number, this phone for him, though. I haven't got the other number for him.'

Brannigan then hung up and told Howe, 'They didn't pick out a spot where they're going to wait.' Brannigan's unhappiness with the situation had clearly registered with Alan Wilson by the time he got into the back of the Nissan Primastar with Kelly driving at 8.08 p.m.

He told Kelly without preamble, 'We have to pick a spot where we're going to park up and wait.' Kelly, meanwhile, had obviously received instructions of his own. 'I was talking to our man earlier, yeah?' he answered. 'He's gonna have someone else watching him. We're not gonna be sitting on his road. I don't think there's a good place to wait, see, especially when you have a gun.'

'I know, but we need somewhere where we're going to wait,' Wilson insisted.

Kelly answered, 'Yeah, but he says there's going to be someone telling you, "Right, bang, he's after leaving." You have a spot sussed out, but obviously them people over there should know the best spots for us, shouldn't they?'

'We'll have to find our own one,' Wilson repeated, clearly exasperated. 'We both need a spot where we can park, me in the back seat, you drive, sitting in the driver's seat. Say an hour, the driver sitting at the house, then we get a call on the mobile that he's at the door, then we drive around, you tell me, "Look, he's at the door", and I'll slip out and kill him.'

'At the door?' Kelly asked. 'Will we not catch him walking down the road?'

'I don't think so,' Wilson answered. 'He's always in the garden talking on the phone.' However, Kelly was adamant it could be done if they sneaked up behind Hanley while he was strolling.

'I done that loads of times, you're right,' Wilson finally conceded. 'You just keep your eye on me, you know, where to pull in for me, yeah? Is that a can of petrol in the back of this? It's all going over me. We need a few of them with petrol in them. Loads of houses with cameras on them. See if we do a spot like that, people will get suspicious and call the police.'

The following day, 3 October, was largely uneventful as both Kelly and Wilson went over the same ground as before. Kelly received a phone call confirming another driver had been organized by Brannigan and Howe, though without any names being mentioned.

The day was significant only for one rambling remark of Kelly's summarized by gardaí as follows: 'Talks of Daniel and Christopher and joints of weed.' Although no surnames were involved, gardaí were pretty sure he was referring to Daniel and Christopher Kinahan.

If any further proof of the cartel's involvement was required, it was coming.

17. No Christmas Bonus

Baby, no baby – I don't give a fuck
— Luke Wilson

Howe and Brannigan began to take an increasingly hands-on role in preparing for the planned assassination. Over the next three days the pair were spotted driving around the city in the Renault Laguna and visiting various service stations, where they filled more canisters with petrol. The men used the canisters because they didn't want to keep driving into petrol stations to fill up the cars and, unlike law-abiding motorists, it was not in their interest to be caught on CCTV; neither did they want to spend their budget on filling up a car.

During these trips Howe often wore a distinctive tweed flat cap and warned Kelly to cover his face as he visited the Applegreen service station on Parnell Road in Dublin 12. 'Right, mate, put your hood up,' he told him. 'Grab a canister out of the boot, cruise in, keep your hood up, mate, I don't want any silly mistakes.'

There had been an incident in which Kelly, clearly under the influence of some substance, had shown up for an early-morning meeting with both men and been told by Brannigan, 'You're out of your bleedin' banana, pal. You knew you were meeting me at eight o'clock for work and you're out of your bleedin' box?' So when Kelly came back, Howe could not resist checking that his orders had been complied with.

'Good man, you kept your hood up, your face down and away from the cameras?' Kelly's answer was not recorded.

One thing that did come up was where the orders to carry out the plot were originating. During a discussion with Howe, Brannigan made reference to 'D', a verbal shorthand used by many criminals for Daniel Kinahan. 'I had a bit of craic with D last night,' he told him. 'He was saying, "How are you?" and I was saying, "What's the story, pal, how are things?" I was telling him, "This is where we're at, blah, blah, blah." He goes, "Mate, relax yourself. Don't push it. It'll happen, don't push it," he said. "As long as everyone stays safe, I don't give a fuck how long it takes, ya know what I mean."

'So he says, "How are ya anyway, what's the craic?" I said, "Ah, mate, still doin' a bit, a good bit, plenty of running," I said, "a bit of hot yoga," I said, "flat out," I said, "bleedin' feeling great," I said. "But goin' rallyin' this weekend. Goin' to a wedding at the weekend," I said. "What are you going to do, mate? If you feel good . . ."

'He says, "I keep meaning to go back training, goin' back next week." So I said, "How are you, mate, how's you doin', how's married life post-wedding?"' Brannigan was referring to Kinahan's wedding to Micka 'The Panda' Kelly's ex, Caoimhe Robinson, which had taken place the previous July.

A report on the nuptials – complete with details of Kinahan's drug-dealing activities – had appeared on the website Lovin' Dubai on the fifteenth of that month. However, the editors of the site (which usually covered matters such as the best brunch deals available to expats) were evidently unaware of the Emirates' stringent defamation laws. Libel is a criminal rather than a civil offence in the UAE and carries up to two years in jail upon conviction. Lovin' Dubai were later forced to issue a grovelling apology to 'Mr Daniel Kinahan' for 'any suggestion' the cartel leader 'was involved in an alleged international drug syndicate'.

On 5 October 2017 Howe drove the Laguna to Winetavern Street in the city centre to pick up Liam Brannigan and then onwards to Marino Park, a circular green area with seven streets coming from it like spokes on a wheel. Joseph Kelly was there waiting for them and both men wanted to supervise him on the parking of the SEAT Leon – set to be used to flee the murder – close to Gary Hanley's home. What followed bordered on farce.

Gardaí discreetly watched as Kelly drove the Leon and made several attempts to park it up. He first tried to place it at Fairview Terrace, but could not get it into the space, before moving to Brian Terrace around the corner. Brannigan and Howe drove by it to check it out, with Kelly sitting in the back. Neither was particularly impressed with how it had been left sitting on the road.

'Right, okay, just go back by it again,' Brannigan instructed Howe, who was driving. 'We may as well. We're having a great time here, buddy. I just have to say, mate, it seems to me that I always have to keep saying things to you. Like, I may as well be doing this myself here now.'

'He may as well be, mate,' Howe chimed in. The frustration in Brannigan's voice was clear as he continued, 'Mate, I could be doing this myself. I don't know what you're in for, because everything I try to do here to keep you safe, you just don't do it, you just don't do it.

'So I could have done a lot smoother myself if I'd just done it myself. Like, the reason I tell you to park there is so no one can see when you're at the car. This is what I'm saying to you, you see those bushes there? Those are protecting you from people seeing you, yeah? Are you fucking facing that way?'

An embarrassed Kelly answered, 'I'll just do a U-ey.' Brian Terrace is a narrow one-way street with barely enough room for two cars to pass side by side. Anybody attempting to observe what was going on would stick out like a sore thumb at either end, so members of the National Surveillance Unit were unable to see exactly how badly Kelly had screwed up his task. Judging by the rant Brannigan was on, it was pretty bad.

'But mate, what I said to you, *reverse in*,' Brannigan continued. 'I said to you, *reverse in the first spot there*. So mate, tell me now how are you going to get out of there when the call comes in?'

'I'll make that,' Kelly offered.

'Fuck off, mate, will you, seriously, mate,' Brannigan said. 'Try to let him come and fix it now because it's not good enough. For fuck's sake, you see that? You were to reverse into that spot there, right at that tree there, yeah?'

Brannigan then left while Howe continued to supervise Kelly moving and parking cars on the streets around Hanley's house. There would be no respite for Kelly though, as Howe began to question his motives. 'You're just making everyone's life harder, you're not making anyone's job easier,' he told him. 'You fucked up the whole job today, do you want this to happen?'

'Yeah, I do, pal,' Kelly maintained.

'I don't think you do,' Howe answered. 'Now, fuck off. I've a pain in my fucking hole with you now, I do. I'm doing your work. What are you getting paid for?' When there was no response from Kelly, Howe ordered him to join him in the back of the Nissan Primastar, filling yet more containers with petrol.

Apparently infuriated with Kelly's failures, Brannigan and Howe took over much of the surveillance duties themselves over the next three weeks. Alan Wilson was again absent for reasons which would become clear later and Howe and Brannigan were observed moving both the Laguna and the Primastar onto the street where Hanley lived.

The van was captured on the cameras on the front of Hanley's home on 26 October. Brannigan and Howe spent between 5.45 and 7.45 a.m. that day watching the house and discussing how to set up a dashcam in the front of the vehicle, which would allow them to observe the scene remotely.

Howe was still venting his spleen over his previous encounter with 'Joker'. 'Jesus, Bran, he's just the worst driver ever,' he told his colleague. 'Jesus Christ, he can't drive nails, fucking hell. I lifted him, earlier, fucking lifted him and then I felt a bit bad. I don't want to be giving out, but what the fuck?'

Howe was not happy with the comfort offered by the back of the Primastar either. 'Do you know what the back of this van needs?' he griped. 'A bleedin' ground mat for camping, hammer, take the air lumps out of it.' But Brannigan did not offer much sympathy. 'Right, mate, just stare at the fucking gaff,' he said.

Howe and Brannigan watched as Hanley's girlfriend left their house for work and then finished up for the morning. That afternoon, a garda who was not involved in the investigation but who was passing the Primastar became suspicious of it and began to peer inside. He could see a chair in the back and a small hole in the black covering in the rear window and realized it had been set up as an observation post. He reported his concerns to bosses, but was told to steer clear of the van in case he interrupted an ongoing operation.

The following morning's events made that irrelevant anyway. As Joseph Kelly and a mystery associate drove the Primastar past Hanley's house, he spotted their target standing in his front garden. The pair instantly became concerned that they had been clocked, but Kelly tried to put a positive spin on it.

'That's a good thing, that's a very good fucking thing, do you know that?' he insisted. 'See that drive-by there, that was better than a week's wait, if you ask me.' The man did not respond. Three nights later, the Primastar was burnt out elsewhere in the city – gardaí believe the vehicle was torched because Hanley had watched it being driven past his home.

From then onwards, the Volkswagen Caddy, which Kelly had bought on DoneDeal, came more and more into play, forcing gardaí to break into and bug it too. Though it had first been noted in the gang's possession on 2 October, it was not deployed for use until 2 November. On that day Luke Wilson entered the picture for the first time when he was observed getting into the Caddy with Kelly at 6.39 a.m. and they set off towards the northside. Gardaí remain unsure why Luke was brought into the plot at such a late stage, but suspect it was because Alan Wilson convinced Liam Brannigan it was necessary.

Even though it was Luke Wilson's first appearance within the conspiracy, it was obviously not his and Kelly's first meeting. It was equally clear that Luke Wilson also had a serious cocaine problem. Despite the early hour, the twenty-three-year-old's first words to Kelly were, 'We're gonna do a sniff or two. I can't fuckin' see. Have you got a torch, no? In your . . . ah, just turn the light on.'

'Just snorting it to wake myself,' Kelly said. 'Bollixed, I am. I wouldn't mind, I'm fucked, I am. I have to go to the bleedin' labour.'

Luke Wilson soon began complaining that he was 'bursting for a piss' and demanded Kelly pull over so he could relieve himself. Kelly, meanwhile, could be heard farting audibly. After one attack of flatulence, Wilson remarked,

'That's that coke, isn't it?' It became apparent the cocaine use was having unintended consequences in the cramped confines of the van.

As the conversation progressed, gardaí became aware Luke had been fully briefed by his cousin on what was happening. More importantly, they learned Luke had been selected as the gunman and Kelly – despite his numerous screw-ups – would drive the getaway car afterwards.

Luke asked if Hanley was 'up and about' but Kelly warned him, 'This fella is a paranoid cunt. This fella takes precautions big time. This fella won't leave his gaff, like.' Regardless, Luke seemed optimistic about the murder plot's chances of success. 'He doesn't even understand why our people want him gone, because he's such a fuckin' idiot,' he told Kelly. 'That's what I'm saying, like, you know? Eh, I've a couple of ideas. Like, you could sit in the back of the van and just wait for him to come out. Do you know what I'm saying?'

Now it was Kelly's turn to advise his new partner. 'This fella mightn't come out at all,' he said. 'That's the type of fucker this fella is. It's a big security door, right? You're not gonna get the door in.

'You're into that garden at him while he's at the door? He's gone. If he's standing at the door when you're running, you're not going to get him. He's just gonna slam the door. I know this fella, like. I was locked up with this bloke. If he hears us coming in that door, he's going to that back window.'

But Luke would not be dissuaded. 'Well then, why don't both of us tool up and one goes to the back and I clear the house?' Kelly gave a non-committal response and the conversation switched to the planned escape route. Luke was audibly snorting something and left those listening in with no doubts as to what it was. 'Ah, that coke is nice,' he sighed. 'Ha ha, fuck it.'

If Kelly had taken cocaine to make him more alert, it was not working. Despite having visited the area on numerous occasions, he soon became lost. 'See, it's all these little fuckin' stupid roads, look,' he told Luke.

'And what's putting me off is, I've been over here on fuckin' two different bits of work, do ya know what I mean? It's wrecking my fuckin' head. Sorry, pal, this is bollix, like.' Luke – still complaining of a need to urinate – rang someone to seek directions before they eventually stumbled on the target's home.

Both men agreed that trying to force open Gary Hanley's security doors with a crowbar would be a 'kamikaze job'. 'I think going over with a crower and all is fuckin' crazy,' Kelly asserted. 'I think that's crazy too, yeah,' Luke concurred. 'I have no problem camping in the back of the van and waiting for my opportunity to get him. Because he is going to step out at some stage.'

To the horror of listening gardaí, he added, 'Baby, no baby – I don't give a fuck.' The younger Wilson was brimful of ideas and suggested he approach the house dressed as some kind of workman in a hi-vis jacket. 'I knock on the door with a clipboard, try get an answer,' he suggested. 'Once I get an answer, I go in and I do what I have to do.'

'Bare-faced?' Kelly asked. 'Bare-faced,' Luke confirmed. 'You can't fuckin' go bare-faced,' Kelly spluttered. 'You can't put your face up like that. Your own face is your own face.'

But Luke insisted, 'There's disguises you can get, there's things you can use, you know? Is there nobody that can draw him out? For instance, if we get through the door, yeah?' he continued. 'There's gonna be his missus there, there's gonna be a child there. If they get in the way, they're gonna be killed. There's . . . I'm not fucking giving them, I'm not, like she's obviously gonna try and get in the way, there's a child gonna be there.'

This was too much for Kelly, who was not on board with the idea of killing anyone other than Hanley. 'Ah no, c'mere,' he reasoned. 'Listen, the way it is like, under strict orders, no birds have to be hit. If a ricochet happens, a ricochet happens. Accidents happen.'

But Luke was unrepentant. 'I was told by our friend across the road from you that if she gets in the way, give it to her as well,' he said. 'Say it takes five minutes for us to enter, the police will be all over us.

'I ain't fuckin' . . . I'm going, even if they get the door open, I'm going in, I'm doing the job, police are on top, I'm gonna start fuckin' shooting the police as well. There's an easier way to do this. He has to come up for air. So he's a gym bunny?'

'He's a fuckin' clown,' Kelly grunted back. 'It's all about getting him. This fucker's going nowhere. This fat bastard doesn't move.' 'That's the main thing,' Wilson said. 'We're at least gonna catch him with two before he closes the door, do ya get me?' Despite the fact that he was only in the door on the operation and had never – to gardaí's knowledge – successfully killed anyone, Luke Wilson had no problem expressing his dissatisfaction with how it had been run so far.

'It's a load of bollix, there's not enough homework done on this,' he told Kelly. 'I think the two of us should be armed. I really think that's the way forward. More homework needs to be done. We might as well be standing pissing into the wind with information we have at the minute.

'I'm not in this game to be fucking caught. We want fucking money, not jail. I've no problem, I'll even get on the phone and talk to them. They would respect you more for saying it. We need to put out there what we want, what we want to fuckin' do. Not what they want to do. There's an easier way to get him. They need to do their homework.'

Kelly, who said he had done 'eighteen out of the last twenty [years]' in prison, was in full agreement.

The following day, 3 November, Alan Wilson was back. Kelly picked him up at his home in the Caddy at 6.24 a.m. and brought him up to speed with what had happened in his absence. The reason behind it soon became clear.

'Jesus. Tell ya what happened to me two weeks ago,' he informed Kelly. 'Drank a bottle of whiskey, took a load of pure coke. I took a fit, right, so I went on a walk to calm down. I opened the bag and took more coke and I sat at the top of a set of steps and tumbled down head first. Took another fit and I ended up in hospital. I didn't use something to snort it with, just opened the bag, sniffed a load of it out of the bag.

'Only got out of hospital there two days ago. Brain scan and all. Lost me phone. Dunno whether the police got it or not. Getting used to the drink meself. Got out of hospital, drank a bottle of vodka. Police came into us in the hospital, says, "Are ya back on the cocaine?"

'They said, "What happened to you? We have a report you fell down a set of steps and you were knocked out and the ambulance driver says to us, bag of cocaine beside you that you thrown away." 'Cause you, you know, when I was coming round in the ambulance, I pulled a bag of coke from the ambulance driver, you know, ripped it up and fucked it everywhere.'

Despite his lengthy stay in hospital, Wilson was planning something similar with his partner for the evening ahead – whether she knew it or not. 'Going to get a litre of vodka, twelve cans of Red Bull, few DVDs, an eighth of coke, two Viagras and stay up drinking and taking coke till about three in the morning,' he told Kelly. 'We either do that or we could go see a film or go for dinner.'

Then, as if acknowledging it might be a bad idea, he added, 'Viagra and coke don't work together. I get paranoid on coke.' He further explained that he had taken cocaine a few weeks earlier and then followed it up with some Viagra, but that the erectile dysfunction medicine 'wouldn't work'.

He wondered whether he should just stop taking cocaine and stick with Viagra instead. Clearly out of his depth in the discussion, Kelly answered, 'I'm not really sure. Just take the Viagra and get into the humour with the missus.' Trying to be helpful, he suggested the cocaine might be 'killing it' or 'overloading it'.

'I let myself get too paranoid, checking this and that . . . that's what it is,' Wilson said. 'It's [coke] ruining it.'

Kelly agreed. 'You can't concentrate on enjoying yourself.'

Wilson then laughed as he told Kelly about an incident when he had opened up a pornographic website on his laptop by accident while his partner was sitting in another chair. He admitted she had caught him in the act, but he had insisted, 'I clicked that on by accident', only to be told, 'You have to tap that into Google.'

The chat switched back to Hanley. 'He's a lazy cunt,' Wilson opined. 'Thinks he's it, he does. This fella is all over Facebook making threats to people on the computer. Whatever way this goes down, I know the routes. If she came out and he came out there with the baby, I'd slip open the door. Duck down there and fly straight over, be in that garden in fucking seconds. He wouldn't know what's happening.'

The gang's increasing willingness to contemplate shooting Hanley even if he had a baby in his arms was by now causing serious anxiety among eavesdropping gardaí. This only heightened when Kelly told Alan Wilson that 6-foot-4-inch Mark agreed with the Wilsons' analysis that the hit should go ahead in such circumstances.

'He was getting into his jeep with a baby and your man Mark turned around and said "I wouldn't give a fuck about a baby in his arms,"' Kelly revealed. 'If someone gets hit with a reflection or a deflection that's out of our hands. That's in God's hands, isn't it? I can't understand how this ugly fat bastard is getting around without being seen.'

The murder plot and garda surveillance of it had by now been running for over two months. But despite all the bluster from the watching hit team, detectives did not believe they yet had the weapons in their possession to carry out the shooting. Guns were usually only handed over shortly before the appointed hour, as, at the time, being caught in possession of one carried a minimum five-year prison sentence. Moving in to arrest the conspirators now risked blowing two months of round-the-clock work for very little reward. Fearful as they were, gardaí had to sit tight. Three days later, their patience would be rewarded.

Brannigan and Howe were out first the afternoon of 6 November. Though 'D' had told Brannigan a month earlier that there was no deadline on the murder plot, it seemed he was running out of patience over in Dubai.

Brannigan rang Alan Wilson to plead with him to get a move on. There was also a reference to Kelly's home in Drimnagh. 'Buddy, you're bleedin' breaking my fuckin' heart, ya are, man,' Brannigan whined. 'I'm getting it up the arse off my man, ya know? He's giving me death, ya know what I mean?

'Ah mate, I was up at Drimnagh and I seen that the car was gone and all, like now. I'm after being at the gaff, I drove by it half an hour ago. Yeah. Right, mate, get onto this young fella. Get him. We need to have a chat later on, yeah? Right? Mate, tell him to get ready and go do the shift tonight. Exactly, pal, and if not, we'll come up with something else in the morning.'

That afternoon the National Surveillance Unit had watched as Kelly and Alan Wilson drove the SEAT Leon and Volkswagen Caddy in convoy towards Stephen's Lane. Kelly parked the SEAT on Power's Court around the corner and left a key in the wheel arch.

The pair then moved off in the Caddy again. Alan Wilson had previously boasted he knew Gary Hanley 'well', but there had obviously been some physical changes since they had last met. 'I seen a photo of him,' Wilson told Kelly. 'He's gone a big sloppy cunt. He's about eighteen stone.'

At 7.24 p.m. the Caddy pulled up outside a chemist in Rialto, where Luke Wilson – who gardaí believed was the 'young fella' earlier mentioned by Brannigan – got into the back. Alan Wilson's phone rang and he could be heard telling the caller, Liam Brannigan, that they were 'just picking this other fella up' before asking, 'If this doesn't happen, where does this toy go to?'

At one point he passed the mobile to Kelly, who engaged in a brief chat that mentioned Glasnevin cemetery. Kelly hung up then and asked, 'Right so, if we get a chance at this fella tonight, we're going to go for him, and if it doesn't happen, what are we doing?'

'If it doesn't happen tonight, you're just going to have to park the van in the Blackpitts and get a taxi up, collect the SEAT,' Alan countered. 'That way, we can place back again next time, and . . . what about the piece of steel?'

Gardaí considered both this and the talk of a 'toy' to be references to the murder weapon, something which was virtually confirmed seconds later when Wilson turned to his cousin and said, 'So you've got to go to Phibsborough to collect the yoke now. Do an hour or two at your man's house. The other car and all is in place. Joker there has the key and all ready for it. It's a fast SEAT Leon, a turbo one.

Just jog straight over and give it to him and that's it, in the car and drive off, the route is perfect.'

At 7.31 p.m. Alan Wilson got back out of the van at John Street and made his way home. Kelly and Luke Wilson drove on to Glasnevin, where they parked outside the Lidl across the road from the cemetery. They were soon approached by an unidentified man on a bike.

The three men went through what sounded like a bizarre charade of pretending to not know each other. 'You want to knock your lights on, pal?' the cyclist asked.

'Sorry, pal, no, just pulled out there,' answered Kelly.

'Did you, yeah?' the cyclist asked again.

'Just pulled out,' Kelly repeated.

Apparently satisfied, the man on the bike handed over a backpack. 'Put your lights on,' he told Kelly. 'Here, you can take the whole bag, right? Talk to you in a while.' He then cycled away.

Inside the van, Kelly and Luke Wilson were quite excited about finally getting their hands on a weapon. After the courier had gone, Wilson opened the backpack and Kelly asked, 'Well? Is she automatic? Revolver?'

'Beretta with a pipe!' Luke responded, before adding as if by way of explanation, 'Beretta with a silencer.'

'Lovely,' Kelly enthused as he started up the van and began driving in the direction of Fairview at 7.58 p.m. 'Ah man, we can bleedin' crack him a hundred times. You don't want to hit this fella, if he survives we won't get paid. This fella survives, we get no pay. Just shoot him straight in the [inaudible].'

Luke Wilson was not to be outdone in the bravado department. 'Just leather him out of it in the chest, then he's getting it in the crust of the head,' he said. 'Be easier to get this out of the fucking way, get paid. That time of year when you need a few quid. Kids to be worrying about.'

'Yeah, enjoy the reap of the rewards,' Kelly answered, unintentionally messing up the phrase. Luke's uncles had been in the habit of taking cocaine to ease their nerves ahead of carrying out hits, but Joseph Kelly had a different approach. 'While we're waiting, we'll have a little joint or something,' he said.

Once the initial thrill of getting their hands on the gun had dissipated, both men realized this was a dangerous moment. 'The only thing I don't like, we're sitting around with the toy in the car,' Kelly said.

'Big fucking risk with this toy in this bleedin' car,' Luke answered.

'Silencer is what's going to be perfect,' Kelly continued as they neared Fairview.

Luke joined in the more upbeat mood as the sound of a bag being unzipped was picked up on the microphones. 'Might as well get this fucking ready, will I?' he said. 'Yeah . . . she's fully clipped, all right. No, we're laughing with this, we're laughing.'

At 8.08 p.m., the Caddy turned onto Philipsburgh Avenue, a short distance from Gary Hanley's house. Gardaí had heard and seen enough. Members of the Special Tactics & Operations Command (STOC) based at Kevin Street station moved in and blocked the progress of the van, surrounding it with weapons raised.

'Old Bill, Old Bill, we're set up,' Kelly cried as a member of the STOC pointed a Heckler & Koch MP7 sub-machine gun at him and shouted, 'Armed gardaí, show me your hands!'

Luke Wilson was equally crestfallen. 'Aw no, aw no,' he wailed. 'Open the door.'

A search of the van revealed an adidas rucksack, a 9 mm Luger Beretta handgun, an 'improvised sound suppressor' and fifteen rounds of 9 mm ammunition, plus three canisters of petrol. Luke Wilson was found to be wearing gloves and had a ski mask in his pocket.

While his colleagues moved in on the would-be hitmen, Detective Garda Ronan Doolan was tasked with establishing a perimeter further up on Philipsburgh Avenue to secure the scene. In the most supreme of ironies, Gary Hanley – intrigued by the racket and the flashing blue lights – came strolling down the street from his house nearby to investigate.

Detective Garda Doolan spoke to him and advised him to return home. The man the hit team had patiently stalked for so long was now standing out in the open like a sitting duck while the men who meant to kill him were carted off in handcuffs.

At 8.24 p.m., sixteen minutes after gardaí moved in on his co-conspirators, Alan Wilson was arrested by the GNDOCB while driving with his partner and two children in a Toyota Corolla along the Crumlin Road in south Dublin.

At exactly the same time, the gardaí's Armed Support Unit breached the iron gates to Liam Brannigan's apartment block in Hanover Court in south inner-city Dublin, causing a 'loud thud noise'. Brannigan, who was walking towards the gate wearing running gear and a baseball cap, spotted gardaí coming into the courtyard and turned tail to flee.

Gardaí yelled for him to stop, but he managed to throw an object over the back wall of the complex before he was brought down by a member of the Armed Support Unit. Four of the five main figures were now in custody; it remained only to track down Dean Howe.

At 8.50 that night an Audi A4 linked to Dean Howe was also stopped by armed gardaí but there was no sign of Howe himself. His family home and two other properties were searched, but he was not there either. Gardaí later discovered he had brought his children to a concert by *X Factor* pop group Little Mix at the 3 Arena. A team was sent to the venue to search for him, but Howe had already been tipped off by this point and disappeared.

As four of his co-conspirators were brought to different garda stations around the capital, Howe was on the run. A source close to the investigation commented, 'It just shows how normal murder was for these guys. He had spent weeks planning to kill someone, and on the night set up to do the shooting, he brought his children to a pop concert.'

Though gardaí had searched the area into which Brannigan had launched the object on the night of his arrest, they had been unable to find anything in the darkness. Two days later Detective Garda Declan Moloney and Detective Sergeant Paul Curran from the GNDOCB returned to Hanover Court to comb the area again, but found nothing.

In the end, the answer was simple: CCTV had shown that what sailed through the air before going out of shot was an 'illuminated item', obviously a mobile phone. Detective Sergeant Curran took out his own handset and dialled the most recent number associated with Liam Brannigan. On the third call the ring was traced to a spot under a tree in the grounds of St Nicholas of Myra church on Francis Street. The device – an encrypted BQ Aquaris handset – was almost certainly the one being used by Brannigan to communicate with the cartel in Dubai. However, gardaí could not access it as it required a password, and it was immediately switched off to prevent it being wiped remotely. One more piece of evidence was in the bag.

Liam Brannigan, Alan Wilson, Luke Wilson and Joseph Kelly were held in custody on suspicion of conspiracy-to-kill offences. Analysis of the various pay-as-you-go or 'burner' phones seized from them proved they had been in regular contact with each other and had each other's numbers stored under different pseudonyms. Brannigan had Alan Wilson down as 'Lefty' and 'Weirdo' and Kelly was stored as 'Jok'. Kelly had Alan Wilson's number stored as 'Sid' and Brannigan as 'A'. Alan Wilson took a minimalist approach to inputting contacts: Brannigan was 'C', Kelly was 'J' and Luke was 'L'. Luke Wilson, the last to join the conspiracy, had only his cousin under three separate identities: 'Al', 'Lia' and 'Jackie'. All four suspects were interviewed on several occasions, but repeatedly answered, 'No comment' to all questions put to them.

On 13 November, a week after their arrest, the two Wilsons, Kelly and Brannigan appeared before Dublin District Court charged with conspiracy to murder Gary Hanley between 15 September and 6 November. They would have been joined by Howe, except he was in the wind.

18. Guilty as Charged

I regret aiding the gang and should have known better
— Alan Wilson

On 13 July 2018 two men were arrested by the Drugs and Organised Crime Bureau while transporting over €42,000 of cannabis, crack cocaine and 'ordinary' cocaine plus a Smith & Wesson .357 Magnum in a shoebox.

The pair were pulled over as they travelled in a taxi through Killester, a seven-minute drive away from Gary Hanley's home in Fairview. The weapon was bound for yet another Kinahan murder attempt against a member of the Hutch family, though Hanley clearly thought it was intended to be used against him. *Just found these pills to cure all Kinahan lovers*, he posted on his Facebook page, alongside a photo of a box of bullets. Though wrong, it was a timely reminder of how close he had come to being another feud statistic.

Two weeks later, on 30 July 2018, Luke Wilson was the first of the two conspirators to come before the Special Criminal Court. The evidence against the now twenty-three-year-old was extensive and the trial was set to run for up to ten weeks because of the amount of CCTV, phone-tap and bugging-device evidence.

But as he had been caught so bang to rights, Luke decided to take a leaf out of his former pal Paddy McCann's book and go for the poor-mouth approach. As the charges of plotting to murder Gary Hanley and possession of a Beretta pistol were read out to him and he was asked for a plea, Wilson stood and told the three judges in front of him, 'Guilty.' Formalities out of the way, the court adjourned for sentencing the following day.

The next morning Detective Inspector Gallagher took the stand and provided the court with the usual pre-sentence outline of the evidence against the defendant. He emphasized that Luke Wilson had been in the back of the van with a silenced pistol, fifteen rounds of ammunition, gloves and a ski mask, along with canisters of petrol.

Engaging in damage limitation was hard, but Wilson's barrister, Michael Bowman, did what he could. He told the court that a 'tremendous dossier' had been built up by gardaí in the months prior to November 2017, including twenty-three transcripts in the Book of Evidence. This displayed a 'vertical chain of command', Bowman said, and Detective Inspector Gallagher agreed that Luke Wilson had no hand nor act in the 'organizational part' of the endeavour. There was also reference to a financial award for Wilson, who the court heard only became 'visible' to gardaí on 2 November 2017.

Under cross-examination Detective Inspector Gallagher further agreed that even though Wilson was an essential part of the organization, he was also 'expendable' in the overall scheme of things. Mr Bowman said his client – who now claimed to be 'drug free' – could be heard snorting cocaine on a number of occasions in the audio recordings, which he attributed to Wilson's 'chronic drug difficulty'. Mr Bowman asked the court to take into account the fact that there was very significant trauma in Wilson's life when he lost his right eye at the age of eighteen, after having been shot in the face by his 'lifelong best friend' as part of an attempted murder.

The defence had handed in a psychiatric and probation

report revealing the impact from his mother's early death. 'Cocaine and alcohol led to a fairly dysfunctional family. His personal circumstances are tragic and one would hope he can break that cycle going forward,' his barrister said. Mr Bowman also said Wilson had developed post-traumatic stress disorder and fell into a deep depression as a result of the attack on him by Paddy McCann.

He said along with the injury to his client's right eye, the sight in his other was 'disappearing rapidly' and Wilson was due to have an operation to prevent him being left completely blind. The court also heard Wilson was broke, had gambling debts and was motivated entirely by money.

Mr Bowman conceded that the only mitigating factor was his client's admission of his involvement and the fact that he had owned up early in the prosecution. Wilson, the barrister said, was 'enormously relieved' that gardaí intervened when they did as otherwise it would have resulted in 'far worse consequences' for him.

Presiding Judge Tony Hunt remanded Luke Wilson in custody for psychological reports to be submitted to the court.

The defendant was back again on 9 November to learn his fate. Passing sentence, Judge Hunt said the court accepted Luke Wilson was not involved in the chain of command and had only featured on two of the twenty-three available audio transcripts. However, he pointed out that Wilson had been described by gardaí as 'an essential cog in the wheel' and had performed an important role. Judge Hunt added that it was without doubt that Wilson had a difficult start in life. He had thirty-six previous convictions at District Court level, including theft and road-traffic offences.

Possession of a firearm with intent to endanger life carries a term of between ten years and life in prison depending on the circumstances. Judge Hunt said the 'headline sentence' – or analysis of where Wilson's offence lies between the two – was sixteen years.

However, he accepted there were factors in Wilson's favour, the 'most weighty' being his early guilty plea, which reduced this by 25 per cent. The possession of a gun took place in 'very proximate' circumstances and the planned murder would have occurred without the intervention of gardaí, the judge said.

'Very serious harm was intended and it was only prevented by good police work,' he added. '[Wilson] is now facing a long custodial sentence at a relatively young age and his constant medical condition will make life difficult for him in prison and upon his release.'

He sentenced Wilson to twelve years with the final year suspended. The judge emphasized that Wilson could 'rest assured' that if he had gone to trial, he would have received a sentence of sixteen years. 'The plea of mitigation saved him a significant period of time in custody,' he said.

Remarkably, planning to murder someone in Ireland only carries a maximum ten-year sentence. Judge Hunt said the headline sentence for this particular case was eight years, 'but as both offences arise out of the same transaction, it results in a concurrent sentence of six years on that count.' Luke Wilson's eleven-year term was backdated to his arrest on 6 November 2017. Unlike Paddy McCann, his gamble had paid off.

Before the court rose, Judge Hunt addressed Wilson, saying, 'It's a long sentence but we have no choice in that matter. You have saved yourself four or five years.'

Wilson replied, 'I appreciate that, your honour.' For gardaí, it was a case of one down, four to go.

Speaking outside the court, Detective Superintendent Seamus Boland from the GNDOCB welcomed the outcome of the case. He said, 'Today's conviction is part of An Garda Síochána's relentless focus on those who are intent on targeting individuals for assassination. An Garda Síochána will continue to invest all necessary resources to protect our communities from those who would use firearms to take life for financial gain.'

Assistant Commissioner John O'Driscoll, who is in charge of anti-feud operations, added, 'Through a considerable number of recent convictions, including that of Luke Wilson, we have entered a phase where significant achievement is being made in bringing those engaged in organized crime, who wreak havoc in our communities, to justice.'

In May 2019 it was the turn of Luke's cousin Alan to come before the non-jury court. In the meantime, the number of conspirators charged over the murder plot had been extended to five with the appearance and remand of Dean Howe.

After nearly two years on the run – mostly spent holed up in Birmingham with the assistance of Kinahan godfather Thomas 'Bomber' Kavanagh – Howe had contacted gardaí via his solicitor in April 2019 and been arrested by appointment at Irishtown garda station on 13 May. Two days later, despite repeated 'no comment' responses during questioning, he was in court charged with the same offence as the others.

Joseph Kelly also pleaded guilty on 27 May to conspiring to kill Hanley and possession of a Beretta pistol, so it was no surprise when Alan Wilson went the same way three days later. Compared to his cousin, Wilson had only faced one charge and, after Judge Hunt's remarks at Luke's trial, had a fair idea what he could expect in terms of sentence. He might not have anticipated what else was coming down the line, though.

On 6 June 2019, a week after his first appearance before the Special Criminal Court, Alan Wilson was back there again. This time, it was to be told he was accused of three counts of attempted murder at The Players' Lounge in Fairview nine years earlier. Wilson was further charged with the possession of a .38 Special Calibre Smith & Wesson revolver and a .32 Auto Calibre Zastava semi-automatic pistol with intent to endanger life on the same occasion.

Inspector Ian Donoghue of Clontarf garda station told the three-judge court that he met Wilson that morning within the court complex and handed him a copy of the charge sheet, which was explained to him. Inspector Donoghue said Wilson was cautioned and replied, 'I've absolutely nothing to do with these allegations.'

Wilson, who was wearing the same blue jacket and blue jeans, stood as requested when the court registrar read the five charges to him, but did not enter a plea. An application for legal aid was made on his behalf and this was granted by the court.

On 29 July 2019 Alan Wilson was back once more for sentencing. Kelly was to be sentenced on the same date, though for security reasons he and the two Wilsons had been tried separately.

Kelly was dealt with first. The judges heard he had sixty-four previous convictions, and had previously received a lengthy sentence for possession of a pipe bomb. He was also jailed for hijacking a car during which a woman was removed from the vehicle and assaulted.

Kelly's barrister, Giollaíosa Ó Lideadha, said his client had been sent to Oberstown detention centre when he was fourteen and had spent the vast majority of his adult life in prison. Counsel added that while Kelly accepted he was 'no angel' at fourteen, his life went into a serious downward spiral after his release from the centre. Kelly had written a letter to the court, Mr Ó Lideadha said. He did not ask for pity or sympathy, saying he knew he deserved neither, however he did ask for leniency.

Joseph 'Joker' Kelly could not be characterized as an organizer, but he had clearly been prepared to assist significantly, Judge Hunt said. Kelly's principal mitigation was also his guilty plea. He was given six years for conspiring to murder Hanley and twelve years for possession of a firearm with intent to endanger life, both sentences to run concurrently.

Next up was Alan Wilson. He was lucky to be present in court at all. On 26 June, following his guilty plea, he had been set upon by three other inmates in Mountjoy and given a beating as well as being stabbed in the upper body with a makeshift blade. The attack was seen as a warning from Wilson's former employers in the cartel.

Gardaí later received word that Wilson had been demanding his 'fee' for the hit – estimated to be around €40,000 – despite the fact that Hanley was still alive. After a couple of verbal warnings, the cartel decided to engage in a more stringent form of sanction. Wilson spent a couple of nights in hospital. The injuries were not serious, but the message was received loud and clear.

In a lengthy judgment Judge Hunt described Alan Wilson as a 'regular participant' both in the journeys over to carry out reconnaissance on Hanley's home and in the discussions about how he would be murdered. Passing sentence, the judge said the bugged conversations in which Wilson had participated revealed he had 'played a serious role on a consistent basis in the preparations for this crime'. He pointed out that Wilson had issued instructions to both Joseph Kelly and Luke Wilson about how to get rid of the cars and how Hanley was to be killed.

The judge declared, 'The conspiracy in this case, as already noted, was directed to the commission of the most serious offence known to the law, that of murder. Moreover, this conspiracy involved intricate planning to kill at the behest of a serious criminal organization in the context of an ongoing feud.

'Preparations involved long-range planning, surveillance and the deployment of significant resources. Alan Wilson was intimately and frequently involved in the protracted course of essential planning and preparation. He only departed from the Caddy van shortly before the intended killing. He was apparently prepared to carry out his role in return for financial gain. He was ready, willing and able to participate in his designated role. His contribution to the conspiracy was essential, high-level and intentional.

'Only the fact he was not at the very top of the vertical chain of command of the criminal organization prevents us from starting at the top of the penalty scale of ten years. This is because the harm intended by the conspirators did not occur. The lack of death or serious injury was attributable to the excellent work of An Garda Síochána rather than to any restraint or lack of commitment on the part of the accused and his co-conspirators.

'Consequently, we have determined that the appropriate starting point in this case is a headline sentence of eight years' imprisonment consistent with the determination of this court in the related case of Luke Wilson.'

The judges now moved to the issue of mitigation, noting that 'a very limited number of these factors are present in this case'. Alan Wilson's guilty plea had 'resulted in the saving of time in terms of prosecution, court and police resources that may be better deployed elsewhere. Certainty is also a beneficial factor from the point of view of the prosecution. Furthermore, the plea was entered in this case at a reasonably early stage.'

The headline sentence had already been established by Luke Wilson's trial, but it was now that Alan Wilson's tireless efforts to have his conviction for the Blanchardstown attack overturned would bear fruit.

His success at the Court of Criminal Appeal – all funded by the taxpayer via free legal aid – meant Wilson had an 'effective absence' of previous convictions, the judges said. In a bid to win the court round further, Wilson also presented the judges with a letter of apology, which read, 'I apologise unreservedly for my actions and to all those that my actions have affected. I regret aiding the gang and should have known better. I was blinded at the time regarding the ramifications that a gang would have and truly regret the course of my actions.'

Herbert Kilcline would scarcely have recognized the man who used to order him to fill in forms on his behalf using the word 'ramifications', but in any case, the ploy worked. Two years were knocked off the eight-year headline and Wilson was ordered to serve six, also backdated to his arrest in November 2017.

It was a ridiculously short sentence for a man who had gone out on a near daily basis to examine how best to shoot another person dead, but the judges were hamstrung by the pathetic maximum sentence of ten years for a conspiracy-to-kill offence.

The final few paragraphs of the judgment made clear the court was aware Wilson had gotten off lightly. 'We once again compliment An Garda Síochána on their excellent work, which undoubtedly prevented yet another execution-type murder and saved a life,' it went on.

'To the accused, we confirmed the wisdom of his plea of guilty. Had he put the prosecution on proof of his guilt, which in our view was clearly established by the evidence, in the highly likely event of a conviction after trial there would have been no departure from a sentence of eight years.

'He is also arguably very fortunate that the limitations placed by statute on the sentencing powers of this court prevent the imposition of a sentence that might be regarded as truly reflective of his criminality as disclosed by the evidence in this case. Whether he makes good on his promise to desist on future association with criminals remains to be seen.'

Applying the standard 25 per cent remission for good behaviour – only ever revoked for the most serious misconduct – Wilson could expect to serve no more than four and a half years.

It was certainly a disappointment to Herbert Kilcline. 'He played a central role in trying to kill another human being and yet he only gets six years,' he said. 'People get longer sentences for burglary.

'He apologized to the court for his actions and I can only hope he's now reformed for my sake because I don't want to live in fear for the rest of my life. Wilson was working for the most dangerous criminal gang in the country and I think if he had succeeded in his plan he would have had the money to pay people to come after me.

'When he was around in the months before he was caught he didn't come near me but I still received an official warning from the gardaí that my life was under threat. It's good news for the people of Ireland that he's off the streets but he could quite easily have received the maximum sentence of ten years because he was directing two other men to murder a man at his home.

'I doubt any other criminal gang will employ him after he gets out because he was caught but I will still have anxiety and will be looking over my shoulder. He's just a nobody now because people in prison aren't afraid to attack him and this would never have happened a few years ago.'

*

The court now turned its attention to Howe and Brannigan. Having watched what happened to the other three, Howe – who had thirty-seven previous convictions – initially hedged his bets and did not enter a plea. But when his arraignment took place five days before Christmas, Howe threw in the towel and pleaded guilty. He was remanded in custody for sentence until the following March. Liam Brannigan, however, had not been captured on tape referring directly to the killing.

He decided to try and bluff his way out of it. His trial started with gardaí outlining how Brannigan had been observed in the Phoenix Park with Howe, handing over the tracking devices to the third man.

The prosecution said it intended to base its case on the incriminating statements made by the others and on the several trips Brannigan took over to Hanley's house, where he drove by the property.

Sean Gillane, for the DPP, said the court would hear evidence that the white Nissan Primastar van was used by Brannigan and his co-conspirators 'extensively as a spotter car' and for surveillance on Hanley and that the Renault Laguna was used for surveillance and for 'ferrying' co-conspirators in the plot.

He said the prosecution would use seized phones, vehicles, observations of movements and audio recordings obtained during a garda surveillance operation to prove Mr Brannigan was 'fully knowing of the plot' to kill Mr Hanley.

Gardaí had obtained over 3,500 hours of CCTV from business premises across the city. They included the Londis on Parkgate Street, Dublin 8; Southside Motors and the Topaz fuel station, both on Kylemore Road, Dublin 12; Applegreen on Parnell Road, Dublin 12; Leydens Wholesalers & Distributors on Richmond Road, Dublin 3; and C&F Motor Factors in Dolphin's Barn, Dublin 8.

The court heard that the only one who did not cooperate with authorities had been Hanley himself, who refused to hand over anything from the four security cameras he had placed around his home. Detective Sergeant Declan O'Connell told the court he had been forced to get a warrant and come back the next day to take the hard drive away with him.

Detective Sergeant O'Connell said he was later informed that it had been returned to factory settings, 'which effectively meant the drive was wiped clean'. Despite that, the footage was eventually retrieved: it showed both the white Nissan Primastar and the black Renault Laguna driving past Hanley's home and parking up across the street.

Images from other locations showed Brannigan, wearing a blue jacket, a white baseball cap, sunglasses, dark-coloured leggings and dark-coloured shorts, sitting in the passenger seat of the Laguna at both the Topaz fuel station on Kylemore Road and the Applegreen on Parnell Road in Dublin 12 on 3 October while the driver bought petrol in a canister. Separate footage from the same day showed the Laguna pull into the car park of Southside Motors, Kylemore Road, Dublin 12. Brannigan, wearing the same clothes, got out of the front passenger side of the car, entered the shop and bought an item.

On 6 November Brannigan was again wearing the same outfit as he got out of the car and filled a petrol canister at the same Applegreen just after 12.30 in the afternoon. Finally, there was the moment of Brannigan's arrest, when he could be seen – still dressed the same way – in the car park off Hanover Lane, Dublin 8, at 8.24 p.m.

In the footage he is seen talking on the phone before suddenly breaking into a run and launching what the court heard was 'an illuminated item' into the air. The CCTV was key to placing Brannigan in conspiracy with the others, so his defence decided to try and get this evidence thrown out.

His junior counsel John Berry complained that when detectives had requested the recordings from the companies that
provided them they had done so on 'an informal basis' and had
not referred to the Criminal Justice Act or the Data Protection
Act. Berry also claimed none of the firms could definitively say
if their CCTV systems were registered with the Data Protection Commissioner. 'You were directing the operation and you
didn't consider the data protection act or the data protection of
the public?' he asked Detective Sergeant Declan O'Connell.
'That's correct, yeah,' the garda replied.

Senior counsel Mr Ó Lideadha took things a step further
by claiming gardaí had unlawfully turned Dublin city's CCTV
infrastructure into a 'de facto surveillance operation'. The
barrister said the cameras were supposed to be registered,
but few of them actually were.

'Processing data, which is what those controllers did,
without registering is a criminal offence,' Mr Ó Lideadha
said. 'So what gardaí are doing is they are habitually using all
of the CCTV systems in operation in all of the homes and
businesses throughout the city of Dublin, knowing that
those systems are not functioning in compliance with the
law, knowing indeed that because they're not registered that
they're actually functioning in breach of criminal law.

'But it doesn't matter because it's so very useful. And
therefore what they do is they turn up and say, "Can you give
us access to all your video material?" to the people running
the systems (most of them commercial entities, of course)
and they say, "Come right in and do what you want."

'It's very convenient and very effective. The problem is it is
breaching not only the data protection law but criminal law
and gardaí know that. What they've done is they've turned the
city and all of the CCTV infrastructure into a de facto surveillance operation without any protections and in breach of law.'

But Sean Gillane countered that the argument was 'a contrivance, masquerading or hiding within the complexity of data protection, and the court should resist the temptation to disappear down a rabbit hole'. 'The Supreme Court has identified in the most explicit terms – the strongest possible terms – that when it comes to real evidence, and in particular CCTV evidence, there's a positive obligation on members of An Garda Síochána to seize it. It's an obligation from which they cannot escape.

'Far from acting illegally, I submit that An Garda Síochána are doing no more than what they are exhorted to do by the highest court in this land.' Gillane went on to say that if gardaí did not obtain such CCTV footage, courts would hear arguments from barristers to the effect that 'lazy guards' didn't do their job.

Next Ó Lideadha tried to have the audio evidence excluded. He pointed out that under the law a garda 'must form a bona fide belief' about a crime being committed 'in order for a constitutional invasion of privacy to take place'.

The head of the National Surveillance Unit, Detective Superintendent William Johnson, had given the go-ahead for the bugs to be put in following calls from two subordinates, but Ó Lideadha questioned why no notes had been taken of either of these calls.

He said the court had not heard any direct evidence or hearsay evidence about the state of mind of the officers making the request for the cars to be bugged. 'What we have in this is a missing link. We have no evidence from the relevant witnesses on that point,' Ó Lideadha insisted. 'The court is being asked to ignore the legislation, just like the gardaí did, and it is wrong. This cannot be dismissed. This is not a technicality – we're dealing with a huge power of a garda.'

The next day, on 30 October, the court gave its judgment

on both applications and found in favour of the state. All of the evidence had 'relevant and probative' value, Judge Paul Coffey said, also declaring the bugging audio as 'lawfully made' and 'valid'.

From that point onwards, Brannigan's goose was cooked, despite an attempt by the defence to claim that there had been excessive force during his arrest when a member of the Armed Support Unit had flattened Brannigan on the ground while he was on his hands and knees.

Ó Lideadha did his best to poke holes in the testimony of gardaí who said they could identify his client driving the Primastar and filling petrol canisters, leading to some tetchy exchanges in which one member of the National Surveillance Unit branded his assertions 'disgusting', 'very pedantic' and 'quite tedious'. There was further evidence heard of how the phone Brannigan had thrown away before his arrest had rung Alan Wilson's phone seven times that day and Joseph Kelly's eight times.

Finally, on 3 February 2020, the three judges delivered their verdict: guilty.

Judge Coffey said that 'such is the overwhelming weight of the consistency and cogency' of the evidence connecting Brannigan to the operation, the non-jury court was in no doubt that he was 'at the centre of the wheel' in the murder conspiracy.

Ó Lideadha pleaded for leniency, saying the majority of Brannigan's twenty-eight convictions were for traffic offences such as not displaying his car insurance or his licence. 'There are much more serious road-traffic offences,' he insisted.

The barrister said Brannigan had two sons in whose existence he played a 'very active role', giving them 'loving, positive engagement in various aspects of their lives'. Ó Lideadha also told the court that Brannigan had completed two-thirds of his studies in archaeology and history, which proved his 'potential'.

The eight-and-a-half-year sentence the court handed down did not come as a surprise. Like Luke Wilson, Brannigan had taken a gamble. Had he pleaded guilty, he would likely have walked away with six years like Dean Howe. By fighting the case, he landed himself more porridge, though Judge Coffey leniently suspended the last six months on condition that he complete his UCD degree behind bars or replace it with some other kind of vocational course if this was not possible.

Speaking outside the Criminal Courts of Justice later that day, Detective Superintendent David Gallagher said, 'The conviction today of Liam Brannigan and the earlier convictions of Dean Howe, Alan Wilson, Joseph Kelly and Luke Wilson before the Special Criminal Court on charges of conspiracy to murder are very significant successes against organized crime in Ireland.

'I want to pay tribute to the investigation team who showed great resilience in achieving these successes. This outcome impacts positively on the security and safety of our communities. Organized crime groups terrorizing our communities will not be accepted and An Garda Síochána will continue to prioritize those that engage in violence and threats to life.'

The last of Ireland's first-ever family of hitmen were finally off the streets.

Epilogue

It is difficult to know what knowledge can be acquired from the emergence of the Wilsons as hitmen for hire. Each of the five members of the family entered willingly into the business of murder for money, without a discernible breadcrumb trail that could have been spotted by law enforcement. In fact, when Eric Wilson's name first began to float around following the Reay and Coddington murders in Drogheda, there was shock among detectives who knew him at a young age.

Eric had been involved in dealing drugs, but there were no indications of what was coming. In the movies, his descent into contract killing would have been preceded by some life-changing event. In reality, Eric Wilson decided to get into the business for no other reason than he saw it as easy money to be made and he was 'good at it', as one individual who knows the family told the authors.

While gardaí have linked him to up to ten murders, it is possible he may have been responsible for even more. Likewise, while Alan Wilson was a virtual unknown to gardaí before the Marioara Rostas investigation, it is improbable he gained his 'Madman' and 'Soldier' nicknames from Brian Rattigan for nothing.

Gardaí have investigated Alan Wilson's potential involvement in the Roy Coddington murder. His remarks to the two gardaí in his candlelit bedroom, added to the bragging way he spoke to Joseph Kelly about 'going into three pubs to shoot people' also point to a man not unfamiliar with the art of murder. Keith and Luke Wilson were undoubtedly heading down the same road – only they were halted so early in their careers, while John Wilson ended up suffering the worst fate of all.

So what lessons can be learned from five members of the one family becoming contract killers? Criminologist and lecturer in forensic psychology John O'Keefe believes that once the older Wilsons got involved in crime, the younger generation coming after them were bound to follow. 'To have swathes of family members involved in any one familial job or profession is not unheard of,' he told the authors.

'Whether we are talking about top-end professionals, street traders or bus drivers, all can have an influence on offspring – and they on their siblings – as to whether they enter the same line of work. By the same token, if you have grown up in what I term the "Millwall philosophy" ("no one likes us we don't care"), you are every bit as likely to retreat into the dark web of serious and violent crime. It is after all your home – your base.

'The Wilson brothers, their cousin and their nephew learnt their behaviours growing up through interaction with others (including each other), learning their values, attitudes, techniques and their motives for criminal behaviour, which in turn make it much more socially easy to then adapt to criminal behaviours . . . serious ones. Their criminal behaviours were learnt, not invented or by imitation alone. The legal code is regarded as unfavourable to the Wilsons and so they rail against it: there is, after all, no advantage to going with it, from their perspective.

'Doubtless too, the family suffered from what is known as "strain" in criminology. In other words, the chaotic social structures they grew up in put pressure on them to commit crime, not just individually but also as a family grouping for security. Imagine having your own top-end criminal sub-gang in your own house you could always trust: this will have been like gold dust compared to other gangs, particularly the comparatively wobbly Kinahan sub-groupings.

'After all, who wants to work in Dunnes Stores when you can have all the bling in the world while being protected by your own family unit? Try being the middle brother in that group and suggest you have always had a hankering to do an undergrad in Harvard. Good luck.'

Ultimately, the five Wilson hitmen contributed to their own downfall through extraordinarily reckless behaviour, but investigators both here and in Spain still had to build watertight cases to ensure four of them were convicted.

Without the late Colm Fox's precautions around DNA evidence collection, Keith Wilson might yet be a free man. Then there was the pitch-perfect surveillance op, which eventually took down Alan and Luke Wilson. Those listening in were constantly on tenterhooks, having to make daily decisions on whether to intervene to prevent potential catastrophic loss of life or allow the plotters to incriminate themselves fully. Senior figures involved in that investigation say the importance of what was learned from that operation is incalculable, in terms of both experience gained by gardaí and the message it sent out.

For fellow investigator the now-promoted Detective Superintendent Dave Gallagher, the fact that key Kinahan lieutenants were also scooped up in the net was a major factor. 'Not only was the intended hit team intercepted and found in possession of the loaded firearm 500 metres from the address of the target convicted, but also those more senior criminal figures who had been involved in a higher capacity in the key planning and logistical support and who had distanced themselves in a perceived belief that they were removed from the consequences of their activity.'

Paradoxically, the success of the operation will act as a training manual for criminals on how to avoid being caught in future. No gangster worth his salt does business on the phone – encrypted or not – these days, and they are unlikely to talk freely in vehicles from now on either. This is something of a double-edged sword: it will be harder for police forces to record incriminating evidence but those involved in criminal acts will also find it much more difficult to carry out their business. Those engaging in surveillance on murder targets like Gary Hanley in future will either have to whisper into each other's ears or communicate through hand signals in case their car is bugged. That will be the reality from here on out.

Another unpleasant fact gardaí will have to face is that both Alan and Luke Wilson will be out of jail far sooner than they might otherwise be. The ludicrously light ten-year maximum sentence for conspiracy to murder – left unchanged by successive governments since 1861 – has since been amended to life in prison. It was too late to affect either of the killing cousins, but if they are caught again, they will almost certainly go away for the maximum. But another of the Wilson family's favourite tactics could work in their favour again unless steps are taken to prevent it.

A recurring feature of Alan Wilson's criminal escapades was witness intimidation. It was visibly present throughout the Marioara Rostas murder investigation and there were overt signs of it during his trial for the cleaver and shotgun attack in Blanchardstown. It also surfaced after Eric's monumental stupidity in Spain – when Irish-accented men called to The Lounge bar to issue threats – and during Keith Wilson's trial for the murder of Daniel Gaynor.

The Special Criminal Court was introduced precisely because of the problem of jury intimidation, but in recent years it has faced increasing calls for its abolition. The Irish Council for Civil Liberties (ICCL) has called it 'untenable in a democracy' and says it has the backing of the UN Human Rights Committee. The future of the court has probably been secured for a few years following the allegations of jury intimidation during the trial of cop killer Aaron Brady, but the questions will undoubtedly re-emerge down the line.

But gardaí involved in the Marioara Rostas case, such as former Detective Superintendent O'Gara, say abolishing it would be a huge mistake. 'Intimidation was a factor in the investigation and something we knew we had to deal with,' he said.

'There's a reason why Fergus O'Hanlon is in the witness protection programme. It was a very difficult time for everyone connected to the case, especially around when Fergus O'Hanlon had decided to cooperate with us. There was a real concern for the safety of people like O'Hanlon and others because of their decision and we took measures to protect people. People were genuinely in fear of their lives.

'It was of no surprise to us that there were threats issued on the street and specific notes on potential targets recovered, especially after Alan Wilson was charged with murder.'

How witness intimidation is dealt with in future will be down to future governments. But governments will listen to voters, who will have to make their voices heard too if institutions like the Special Criminal Court are to be retained.

One Fine Gael TD, Neale Richmond, said what happened during Aaron Brady's trial for the murder of Detective Garda Adrian Donohoe should never be forgotten. 'One only needs to look at the treatment of witnesses in the trial to see the importance of this feature of the court,' he said.

'Videos of a witness were circulated on social media, alongside comments calling the witness a "rat" or a "tout". It is certainly not a coincidence that five witnesses failed to appear before the court in this case and one described being "petrified" to do so.'

But if gardaí have one overriding regret from their years of dealing with the Wilsons, it is that nobody was ever convicted over the appalling death suffered by Marioara Rostas.

Senior investigators are unable to comment publicly on Alan Wilson's acquittal, but one figure centrally involved in the probe told the authors he regarded it as 'justice denied'. Another, Superintendent Joe Gannon from Pearse Street station, said the teenager's horrific end had left its mark on everyone involved in the inquiry. He said, 'The objective throughout was to recover her remains and return them to her family to enable a dignified burial. I will never forget the day she was found and arriving in the Dublin mountains and the eerie quietness of the whole search team as they stood around in solitude and silence just after she had been found. The forest [. . .] appeared like an apocalyptic scene, with trees felled and branches removed over the previous twelve days in the harshest of weather conditions.

'There was a great sense of relief and fulfilment that we had found her after four years. I will never forget the efforts of all the men and women who worked on the case from the outset right through to the finish. They never wavered or faltered in their determination to find her.

'There was some consolation Marioara was restored in death back to her family for a dignified burial enabled by the Department of Social Protection. The investigation was blessed with the presence of Detective Superintendent O'Gara and the then Detective Inspector Cryan and their teams. They were two of the most competent investigators I have ever had the pleasure of working with. We were afforded the full resources of the garda organization for this investigation and the subsequent trial.'

Sources close to the investigation say they do not expect anyone else to ever be charged over Marioara's death.

Gardaí may have lost that battle, but they did eventually win the war.

Acknowledgements

The authors would like to offer sincere thanks to everyone who shared their experiences and provided interviews about the Wilson clan, both on and off the record, especially those who can't be named.

Thanks to the retired garda members who shared their knowledge on Eric, John, Keith, Alan and Luke Wilson. Special thanks also to the team at the garda press office for facilitating an interview with Detective Superintendent Michael Cryan about the investigation into the murder of Marioara Rostas and for arranging other interviews relating to this project.

We are indebted to three people who took time to give advice on the book: a man who provided us with crucial information on Keith Wilson and the murder of Daniel Gaynor; a good friend who took time to read over the material; and a special note of thanks to 'The Jedi' for his support and continued friendship. We also received valuable guidance and advice from Barry Cummins and Paul Reynolds from RTÉ.

Praise is due to managing editor Patricia Deevy for all her hard work on the project. We would also like to thank our editor Djinn von Noorden for her enthusiasm and dedication and for improving our raw efforts. Thanks also to Michael McLoughlin, MD of Penguin Random House Ireland, for his continued support, and to libel expert Kieran Kelly for his direction.

We would like to thank *Irish Sun* editor Kieran McDaid,

Irish Sun picture editor Chris Doyle and our colleagues at the *Irish Sun* for their support. Special thanks also to Jon Lee at the *Irish Sun* picture desk who worked tirelessly to source the images for this book. Thanks also to photojournalist Padraig O'Reilly for permitting us to use one of his images and to *Irish Sun* photographer Crispin Rodwell for his hard work. Copyright as follows: 1c, 1d, 11b, 15a, 16a, 16b – Crispin Rodwell; 2b – Padraig O'Reilly; 5a, 11c, 15c – Garrett White; 5b – Mark Condren; 1a – *Irish Independent*; 1b – Juan Garcia; 15b – Courtpix; 16c – Collins Courts; 16d – Press Association; 6c – RTÉ News; 7ab, 13a, 14a – *Irish Sun*; 7b, 9d – *Irish Daily Star*, 9a – National Police Spain.

On a personal note, Stephen would like to thank his wife and sons for all their support during the writing process. Thanks also to his family and a special thanks to his parents-in-law, aka GoGo and Grandpa, for looking after his family in lockdown as the finishing touches were put to the book. Owen would also like to express his gratitude to his wife and family for their support.